Creation:

THE IMPACT OF AN IDEA

Creation:

THE IMPACT OF AN IDEA

EDITED BY

DANIEL O'CONNOR

AND

FRANCIS OAKLEY

CHARLES SCRIBNER'S SONS · NEW YORK

A–1.69[V]

Printed in the United States of America
Library of Congress Catalog Card Number 69-11958

We would like to acknowledge a two-fold indebtedness to the members of the Williams community. The first, to our students; discussion with them, formal and informal, has helped us over the last few years to focus and clarify the ideas reflected in this book. The second, to the President and Trustees of Williams College for a grant from the Class of 1900 Fund towards the cost of preparing the manuscript for the press.

D.O'C.
F.O.

Williamstown, Mass.
May, 1968

Scribner Source Books in Religion

FOR every topic worthy of consideration there are generally several alternative positions possible, each with its own conviction and its own ramifications. Through the examination of various views this series presents significant scholarship to engage the reader, inform him of the problem, and suggest various viewpoints by which he may come to a clearer understanding of his own position. The individual editors are authorities in their field. The topics are of importance not only to students of theology, but to those in other disciplines as well. Theological considerations are not isolated from the examination of the total man. Hopefully these books will be useful in the innumerable segments of man's intellectual endeavors.

The individual selections have not been altered for the sake of stylistic conformity such as in spelling or punctuation. This was prompted by a desire to maintain the feeling and style of the authors.

Contents

General Introduction

"What, indeed, has Athens to do with Jerusalem? What concord is there between the Academy and The Church?" [1]

Tertullian's question is merely rhetorical. The answer anticipated is in the negative. But the exchange involved is one that has continued over the centuries to generate harmonics in the minds of Christians of every church and sect. With this in view Étienne Gilson has used the expression "The Tertullian Family" to denote that tradition of Christian thinking distinguished by its contempt for the philosophical systems of the secular academy and by its conviction of the self-sufficiency of the Christian revelation. And having used the expression he goes on to insist that the Tertullian Family has not reigned unchallenged. Its members have always had to compete with those other Christian thinkers for whom religious commitment does not entail the rejection of philosophical wisdom but rather its extension and fulfilment.

The two attitudes involved have continued in tension throughout the history of Christianity. Few would want to question, however, that the second, more positive, position has been the dominant one. The very creedal formulations of the ancient and medieval church provide striking evidence for the openness even of *theologians* to the philosophical doctrines of the Hellenic and Hellenistic worlds, and

[1] Tertullian, *On the Prescription against Heretics,* Ch. 7; cited in Étienne Gilson, *Reason and Revelation in the Middle Ages* (New York: Charles Scribner's Sons, 1938), p. 9.

the historical investigations of the last century and more have indicated very clearly that the attitude of Christian thinkers confronted with Platonic, Neoplatonic, and Aristotelian modes of thought was, by and large, a strikingly receptive one.

It would be a redundancy, then, to belabor this point and we are not concerned to do so. The more interesting question, we would suggest, and the one much less frequently asked is this: What has Jerusalem to do with Athens? What impact, if any, has the dynamic of the Judaic and Christian message had upon those ancient patterns of philosophical thinking with which, in the course of history, it has so often and so intimately been brought into contact? The question is not an easy one to answer. The very receptivity of Christian thinkers to Greek philosophical ideas, their very willingness to formulate their positions in Neoplatonic or Aristotelian terms serve frequently to conceal the novelty of the conclusions at which they have arrived and the uniqueness of the perspective in which they have striven for an understanding of the universe, of man, and of society. But novel those conclusions often are and unique that perspective certainly is; and that novelty and that uniqueness spring ultimately, we would assert, from the peculiar conception of the nature of God that lies at the heart of Judaic and Christian belief, and, more particularly, from the doctrine of creation which that conception entails.

I

Creation: the doctrine is so familiar, so much a part of our day-to-day intellectual baggage that it takes an effort of the historical imagination to perceive its originality—the more so in that the central thrust of the idea is often wrongly conceived. It is not the notion of a *beginning* that forms the core of the idea of creation. If it did, there would be nothing unique about the Hebrew belief, for many peoples have adhered to the idea of a beginning of the world, and among these, civilizations existing prior to the Hebrews or unrelated to them.[2] The emphasis (and as we now know, the order of composition) [3] of the Book of Genesis bear out this point. The principal

[2] *Cf.* S. G. F. Brandon, *Creation Legends of the Ancient Near East* (London: Hodder and Stoughton, Ltd., 1963), p. 1.

[3] *Cf.* The discussion of "The Documentary Sources of Genesis" in E. A. Speiser, *Genesis, The Anchor Bible* (Garden City, N.Y.: Doubleday and Co., Inc.,

theme of Genesis in all three of its main documentary sources is not that of beginning, but that of the covenant, the faith in salvation and election. The promise given to Abraham and renewed for Isaac and Jacob is the book's overriding concern and also the chief object of the writers' faith. "They undergird this faith by the testimony that this Yahweh, who made a covenant with Abraham and at Sinai, is also the creator of the world." [4] It was at least partly under pressure from competing cosmogonies that the second, the so-called "Priestly," account of the creation (Gen. 1:1–2:4a), with its greater stress on the notion of beginning, was added.[5] Most probably the final redaction of this source was made in the post-exilic period when the Hebrews had been forced to clarify and formulate their faith in one God against the materially and culturally superior civilization of Babylon, with its complex polytheism.[6]

The account of the covenant recorded in Genesis is asserted to be a series of actual events which involved real persons, the patriarchal forefathers. Abram's divine call, his journey from Ur of the Chaldees, the birth of his son, and the sealing of the covenant—these are not conceived as archetypes "occurring" in mythical times, but as real events, moments in irreversible history. As Eliade has emphasized, the Hebrews were the first to put a value on historical events as such, thus breaking the traditional cycle of archetypal gestures which characterized all earlier archaic religions.[7] The importance of this discovery of history can scarcely be overemphasized. But the decisive events which give history a direction and a goal are events *in* history: the covenant, the testing of Abraham, the exodus from Egypt—these, and not the advent of history, though that is of course, presupposed.

To overemphasize the notion of beginning also raises insuperable problems of a philosophical nature.[8] We begin to imagine a time

1964), pp. XXII ff; and G. Von Rad, *Genesis, A Commentary* (Philadelphia: The Westminster Press, 1961), Part I.

[4] Von Rad, *op. cit.*, p. 44.

[5] *Cf.* Von Rad, *op. cit.*, pp. 43–65.

[6] *Cf.* Speiser, *op. cit.*, pp. XXV–XXVI. The materials incorporated in the final redaction are, of course, of great antiquity, going back to "the beginnings of ethnic consciousness in Israel." Speiser, p. XXVI.

[7] M. Eliade, *Cosmos and History* (New York: Harper & Brothers, 1959), pp. 102–112.

[8] We are indebted for several points in this paragraph to T. Mouiren, *The Creation* (New York: Hawthorne Books, Inc., 1962), Chapter I.

before the beginning, the state of things before the "day" of creation, the properties of the "nothing" from which the world was made. Our imaginations embark on a hopeless search for the link between the eternal and the temporal, the infinite and the finite. We run up against that impossibility, which Kant explained, of using the understanding—nourished as it is by sense and imagination—to grasp the idea of a radical beginning. Thus it is not surprising that some early Christian apologists, Origen, for example, maintained that the world though created was eternal, since no reason could be assigned why God should suddenly pass from not willing to create to the act of creation.[9] Obviously Origen is still thinking of a time before creation. Our imaginations seem unable to conceive of eternity without time (or time without space). These difficulties serve to remind us that the Biblical idea of creation is a mystery, an act not wholly penetrable precisely because it is by definition the act of an omnipotent God whose ways are never wholly scrutable to men. Furthermore, focussing on the aspect of beginning is likely to suggest that creative power was needed only to get the world underway. Thinking of this type has led, via Deism, to a mechanism totally alien to the Book of Genesis and incompatible with it.

What, then, is at the heart of the biblical idea of Creation? It is the belief that all beings are totally dependent on a transcendent, extratemporal and personal source. It involves the assertion of a radical transcendence, an "infinite qualitative difference" (Kierkegaard) between God and His creation. The world is not identical with the being of God, nor is it a part of His being, nor an effusion or emanation of His being. The world is brought into being without adding to or subtracting from the being of God. Looked at from the opposite side of the relation, the world lacks any intrinsic ground of being, it is not self-sufficient. Instead, the ground of its being is extrinsic to it. It is radically dependent, and dependent not only at its source but at every moment of its endurance. Without the sustaining power of God, the world would fall into nothingness. Creation and "conservation" have, therefore, the same meaning.

God created all things not from any necessity of His nature, but freely and without any struggle with other beings. Insofar as one can speak of motives, His motive is love, the free gift of existence. And the love that called the world into being is the same love that

[9] *Cf.* É. Gilson, *The History of Christian Philosophy in the Middle Ages* (New York: Random House, Inc., 1955), p. 40.

sustains it in time. In other words, the Creator is not some remote craftsman, but the providential Lord of history.

Finally, the faith of the Bible is a faith in one sovereign Lord, not in the confusing crowd of deities which populate all other Near-Eastern religions.[10] It is one God, Yahweh, who made heaven and earth, man and all life. "Hear, O Israel: The Lord our God is one God." (Deut. 6:4) Such was the conception of creation as it entered into the world of classical civilization.

II

But was this conception really unique to the Hebrew people? What of the Egyptians and Babylonians and the people who originally inhabited Palestine? There can be no doubt that these more ancient civilizations exerted great influence on the Hebrews. The Jews lived for centuries in Egypt, first as guests, later as slaves. Their captivity in Babylon, after the destruction of all the physical symbols of their religion, lasted for generations. Moreover, they had themselves assimilated the indigenous inhabitants of Canaan. It is no surprise then that they should be profoundly affected in customs, in language, and in literary traditions by all three civilizations.

Mythical elements are incorporated in the Old Testament; there are legends, for example, of a mighty battle between God and a great beast (Rahab, Leviathan, the crocodile), though they seem to be used as figures of speech applied to the nations inimical to Israel.[11] Moreover, the wisdom literature of Egypt circulated widely in Palestine, leaving its impress on the corresponding wisdom literature of the Old Testament.[12] Fragments of the older Canaanite mythology are also incorporated.[13] And in particular, the account of creation given by the Priestly source in Genesis is modelled on a Babylonian document called the *Enûma Elish.* There is considerable correspondence in details and, more striking, the

[10] The quasi-monotheism of Ikhnaton is a material conception of the divine which seems to have had no influence on the Hebrews in Egypt. *Cf.* E. Ehrlich, *A Concise History of Israel* (New York: Harper and Row, Publishers, 1965), p. 13.

[11] *E.g.* Isaiah, 51:9–10; Ps. 89:9–12; Job 26:12–13; and *cf.* Alexander Heidel, *The Babylonian Genesis,* 2nd ed. (Chicago: The University of Chicago Press, 1951), p. 108.

[12] *Cf.* Ehrlich, *op. cit.,* p. 90.

[13] *Cf.* Brandon, *op. cit.,* pp. 119 f.

sequence of events is roughly the same. According to some, even the syntax of the opening sentence of Genesis 1, a difficult and unusual sentence in Hebrew, is modelled on the opening sentence of the *Enûma Elish*.[14] But despite these borrowings, the two accounts are worlds apart in atmosphere and central import. In the *Enûma Elish* we witness first a confusing succession of gods and a violent struggle among them. After the father of all the gods, Apsû, has been slain, a hero god, the two-headed Marduk, leads a revolt against the mother of the gods, Tiâmat, who has meanwhile taken on the physiognomy of a sea monster and given birth to eleven kinds of monster serpents. Meeting her in single combat, Marduk kills her and hacks the body into two parts which supply the material out of which he then fashions heaven and earth. Finally, man is created out of the blood of an evil deity, Kingu, who had sided with Tiâmat. As a reward for his feat, Marduk is made supreme among the gods.[15] How different in tone and feeling the poetic imagery of the Genesis account! No doubt the Babylonian story must be read as an allegory. The symbolic imagination of the Babylonian story is rich, though the Hebrew writers certainly could employ such devices when they chose to. The true difference is in intent. The priestly writers of Genesis are not offering an allegory. "What is said here is intended to hold true entirely and exactly as it stands. Nowhere at all is the text only allusive, 'symbolic,' or figuratively poetic." [16] The content of the priestly account is theological doctrine, a doctrine that had been meditated for centuries; its verbal form was deliberately and carefully chosen.

But apart from questions of appropriate imagery it is obvious that the Babylonian account features a polytheism of good and evil deities whereas the Genesis story "is dominated by the monotheistic concept in the absolute sense of the term." [17] All commentators are agreed on this. Furthermore, the writers of the Old Testament adopt a critical and "demythologizing" attitude towards the borrowed materials. For example, the archetypal tale of the struggle between God and a fearful dragon of the deep, a story which recurs again and again in various Near-Eastern mythologies, is used in the Old Testament to refer to the victory which Yahweh has given to Israel

[14] *E.g.* Speiser, *op. cit.*, p. 12, disputed by Heidel, *op. cit.*, p. 90.
[15] For all of this, see Heidel, *op. cit.*
[16] Von Rad, *op. cit.*, p. 45.
[17] Speiser, *op. cit.*, p. 11.

over her archenemy Egypt.[18] Finally, the biblical writers frequently add a moralizing dimension to the borrowed motifs, a dimension not present in the original sources (*e.g.*, the stories of the flood[19] and the tower of Babel[20]). In contrast to all the other Near-Eastern conceptions, the God of Genesis acts alone and freely, without let or hindrance, to bring into being and sustain in being all that exists.

The question whether or not the opening lines of the Bible assert creation *ex nihilo* is disputed and we need not enter into the controversy.[21] The first explicit mention of the phrase which the Vulgate translates as *ex nihilo* is II Maccabees 7:28, dating from about the midsecond century before Christ. For our purposes it does not matter whether the Jews of earlier times conceived of a coexistent chaos. From the first century of the new era there is no longer any doubt. All orthodox Christian writers and all Jewish interpreters after Philo—though they may consider the world an eternal creation —nevertheless regard all being as created. When the idea of creation, as part of the Christian gospel, comes to exert an influence on non-Hebrew civilizations, it is understood to mean a total dependence of all things on the divine *fiat*.

III

The idea of creation brings in its wake a whole chain of implications. Not that they were all perceived at once. Centuries were required before some of them—for example, those affecting conceptions of personality or of the nature of political life—were clearly understood. This book is designed to isolate and identify a variety of such implications. But at this point it may be well to describe three quite general implications which cut across most of the others, and which will serve to reveal more distinctly the inner dynamic of the doctrine of creation itself.

It follows immediately from the idea of creation that the created

[18] *Cf.* A. T. van Leeuwen, *Christianity in World History*, trans. by H. H. Hoskins (New York: Charles Scribner's Sons, 1965), Chapter II.
[19] Speiser, *op. cit.*, p. 55.
[20] Speiser, *op. cit.*, p. 76.
[21] *Cf.* Heidel, *op. cit.*, pp. 90 ff. and Von Rad, *op. cit.*, pp. 47 ff. for affirmative answers; Brandon, *op. cit.*, p. 156 and Speiser, *op. cit.*, pp. 12 f. for negative answers.

world, this world opened up to our seeing, hearing, and touching, is *real.* To describe the sensible world as illusory would be inconsistent with a creationist metaphysics. It is true that the material domain is thought to be encompassed by a spiritual or supersensible domain. But both domains are real in some sense—because both are created. Of course, the doctrine of creation does not prescribe any particular philosophical account of the reality of matter. Various philosophical accounts will be compatible with it. Even Berkeley, for example, could claim with justice that his doctrine of matter was eminently in accord with revelation, since it insists above all on the reality of what is perceived by the senses. A creationist philosophy can never be consistently "spiritualist," if that term is meant to deny reality to matter, including therein, of course, the human body and all its functions.

It is also true that created nature must be conceived of as essentially related to mind, primarily to Creative Mind, yet also to created mind. It is the very essence of things to be creatively thought.[22] Or, to put it most emphatically, "real things *are* something thought. . . . They are real precisely because they are thought." [23] This essential (and enduring) relation to Creative Thought is the reason why things are intelligible. Their intelligibility and clarity, their power to reveal themselves flow from the fact that their very being is a relation to Mind. The created thing is made to be known. But, on the other hand, it must also be admitted that nothing is wholly intelligible—by reason of that same relation to Creative Thought. For the finite mind is not capable of exhausting the meaning of that dependent relation which constitutes every created thing. The human mind can no more exhaust the being of a fly, as Aquinas somewhere remarks, than the secrets of the cosmos.

The intelligibility of the created world in some sense is thus a corollary of the idea of creation, but Christian theologians have differed widely on the interpretation of that intelligibility. Their differences are central to the theme of this book for they can be laid out in a spectrum which has, at one end, the Greek view of intelligibility through participation in archetypal forms and, at the other,

[22] For the idea of this paragraph we are indebted to two books of Joseph Pieper: *Wahrheit der Dinge* (München: Kösel, 1947) and *The Silence of St. Thomas,* trans. D. O'Connor (London: Faber and Faber, Ltd., 1957).
[23] Pieper, *Silence,* p. 51.

such an emphasis on the inscrutable omnipotence of God as to eliminate all intelligibility. The Greek view, as presented for example, in Plato's *Timaeus,* is not as it stands, compatible with the Christian doctrine of creation. In Plato's version, the divine artisan is provided with a rational and orderly plan, not of his choosing, which he attempts to realize in a recalcitrant and chaotic matter. Augustine, following the Neoplatonists, assimilated this doctrine by construing the rational plan as creative ideas in the mind of God and by eliminating any pre-existent matter. Many theologians followed this solution, even though it is obviously closer to Greek than to biblical modes of thought. The solution presents an optimistic intellectualism since it is hard to see what limit in principle, other than time, there could be to human knowledge. (And indeed, given eternity, the corresponding conception of the "beatific vision" is just such a limitless knowledge.)

A more biblical interpretation begins by stressing the omnipotent creative power of God (which absolutely speaking knows no real limitations) and accounts for intelligibility as the result of the ordained power of God, that is, as the order and pattern we in fact discover in nature. This view rejects an *a priori* deduction of rational and necessary order. Instead it refers us to the empirical investigation of such regularities as in fact occur in nature or in human activity. This view claims less than the one inspired by Greek philosophy, it claims only a *de facto* intelligibility directly dependent on the Divine Will. But its location of intelligibility primarily in observed regularities is an idea with momentous consequences, perhaps the most important of the novel conceptions introduced into Western thought by Christian theology. These crucial differences and their attendant consequences will be elaborated more carefully below. Here we wish only to remark that a created reality is in principle accessible to the human mind but never exhaustively grasped by it.

Finally, it is clear that the idea of creation directly implies that everything created is *good.* The priestly account in Genesis repeats this as a kind of liturgical refrain. "And God saw all that he had made, and found it very good." (Gen. 1:31) The early Christian church found itself repeatedly required to defend this implication of the doctrine of creation against a variety of forms of Gnosticism. The Gnostic religion, as Hans Jonas points out, has died out so completely that we tend to forget what a formidable rival it presented to Christianity in the first centuries.[24] Arising at about the same time, the two doctrines moved into the spiritual vacuum left by the increasing skepticism surrounding the official paganism of the Roman Empire. Perhaps the greatest attraction of Gnosticism in all its forms was its apparent success in explaining evil by equating it with material reality and attributing the creation of matter to a malevolent demiurge (often identified with Yahweh). We know for example, from the poignant accounts Augustine wrote of his long adherence (nine years) to Manichaeanism, what an attraction such a doctrine could have for an idealistic youth.[25]

Within each man, the doctrine claims, there is a spark of divinity which was somehow separated from God and lodged in the compound prison of world and body.[26] The Creator-God of Genesis is "a blind and arrogant Creator believing Himself the Most High and lording it over the creation, the product, like Himself, of fault and ignorance." [27] God himself is not responsible for the world; He knows and cares nothing for it. "To the divine realm of light, self-contained and remote, the cosmos is opposed as the realm of darkness." [28] The moral law, being but the expression of a malevolent creator's will whose aim it is to ensnare forever the lost sparks of divinity, may be ignored as a ruse. Indeed it may be openly defied as a form of resistance to cosmic tyranny.[29] Contempt for all things earthly and material may issue in a fierce asceticism in order to avoid as much contamination as possible. Thus, the Gnostics were capable of prodigious fasts, of following austere modes of life, of refusal to marry, and the like. But that contempt may just as well issue in a nihilistic libertinism for which "everything is permitted." As Jonas shows, both inferences were drawn and acted upon by extremists.

The early defenders of Christianity were thus hard pressed to uphold the goodness of the created world. We find, for example, Athenagoras in the early second century having to insist that it is not just the spirit (divine spark) with which Christianity is con-

[24] *Cf. The Gnostic Religion*, Revised Edition (Boston: Beacon Press, 1963), Introduction. We follow Jonas' reduction of *one* essential Gnostic faith despite the great variety of sects.
[25] *Confessions*, Book IV.
[26] Jonas, *op. cit.*, pp. 42–47.
[27] Jonas, *op. cit.*, p. XIII.
[28] Jonas, *op. cit.*, p. 42.
[29] Jonas, *op. cit.*, p. 46.

cerned but the whole person, body and soul and spirit. And he argues at length for the doctrine of the resurrection of the body after judgement, precisely to counter the Gnostic devaluation of it.[30] Under the pressure of the Gnostic attack, a Christian writer, Theophilus of Antioch, gives the first unambiguously clear expression about the year 181 to the notion and the formula of creation *ex nihilo*.[31] And Irenaeus, perhaps the most forceful critic of the Gnostics, hammers away at the theme that human nature is indivisible: soul—spirit—and—body.[32] Finally about the year 230, in a long polemical work by Hippolytus, a Roman bishop, we find a definitive statement of the faith of the early church in the doctrine of creation. After a detailed résumé of the main doctrines of all the Greek philosophers from Thales, through Plato and Aristotle, down to the Epicureans and Stoics, and of the use made of them by various Gnostic writers, Hippolytus formulates in the last pages his own belief:

> The one God, the first and only Deity, both Creator and Lord of all, had nothing coeval with Himself, not infinite chaos, nor measureless water or solid earth, nor dense air, not warm fire, nor refined spirit, nor the azure canopy of the stupendous firmament. But He was One, alone in Himself. By an exercise of His will He created things that are, which antecedently had no existence, except that He willed to make them.[33]

Such was the character of the belief which triumphed over Gnosticism and outshone even the splendor of Greek speculation on the cosmos. Its influence on European modes of thought and life has been profound. It has been a perennial source of novelty. The essays collected in this volume are attempts to draw out some of the novel implications of this belief for the understanding and use of nature (Part I), for the understanding of the human condition and its potentialities (Part II), and for the structure and dynamics of human society (Part III). It will be readily apparent that the essays selected for inclusion are concerned only with the most striking of these implications. It will be equally apparent that we ourselves cannot claim even an approximate completeness for the introduc-

[30] Gilson, *op. cit.*, p. 19.
[31] Gilson, *op. cit.*, p. 20 and corresponding notes.
[32] Gilson, *op. cit.*, p. 23.
[33] Hippolytus, *The Refutation of All Heresies,* Vol. VI in the *Ante-Nicene Christian Library* (Edinburgh: T. & T. Clark, Publishers, 1868), pp. 393 f.

tory statements which preface each of the three parts of the book. Their purpose is a modest one and they will have fulfilled it if they signal clearly the main thrust of the argument and if they succeed in conveying to the reader something of the background against which the idea of creation must be seen in order to grasp its historic significance. For the benefit, however, of those who may wish to pursue the several topics in a somewhat more systematic fashion, we have concluded the book with a select, annotated bibliography.

PART I

Nature

CHAPTER 1

Introduction: Two Philosophies of Nature

DANIEL O'CONNOR

The empirical science of Europe finds its remote origins in the ancient Near East. Among the Egyptians and Mesopotamians of the third millennium we find, for instance, the first efforts at a quantitative astronomy and considerable refinement in such skills as surgery and engineering.[1] But it is to Greek civilization from the sixth century onwards that we must look for the first unambiguous prototype of Western science. The achievements of Greek science are many and varied. They range from patient observation and classification of natural data to bold speculative hypotheses, such as heliocentrism and atomism, which required many centuries to bear fruit. Two of the most important ingredients of the modern scientific revolution: the mathematization of physical reality and the practice of systematic observation, were already anticipated by the Greeks. The Pythagoreans and, in particular, Plato in his *Timaeus*,[2] developed the conception that nature is intelligible because it exhibits mathematical form. And, on the empirical side, Aristotle invented scientific zoology by introducing a systematic classification of animal life, in terms of behavior, ecology, and pathology.[3]

[1] *Cf.* René Taton (ed.), *History of Science: Ancient and Medieval Science* (New York: Basic Books, Inc., 1963), Chs. 1 and 2.

[2] *Timaeus,* 31b and seq.

[3] *Cf. Historia Animalium, De Partibus Animalium, De Generatione Animalium.*

And yet the science of antiquity differs radically from modern science.[4] Plato regarded the natural elements as incorporating the regular geometrical solids, but he also thought of them as possessing souls and as behaving according to intrinsic purposes. Aristotle made many detailed observations with a fine eye for accuracy, but his observations served only to illustrate, never to establish, a scientific conclusion. For him, scientific knowledge (which, in contrast to modern views, he identifies with the attainment of certitudes) is based on the essential natures of things, on their forms. Behavior too, whether it be the falling of heavy bodies towards their "natural place" or the growth of animal flesh, is a necessary attribute of changeable things, part of their natures. Aristotle's physics is thus an inquiry into the natures of things, which are not realities of the sensible order. Form, essence, definition, these are the preoccupations of the Aristotelian scientist, not the observation of particular phenomena under controlled conditions and the search for "the exact form of observed regularities."[5] We are therefore forced to conclude: no development along the same lines would have led to modern science. It was, on the contrary, an essential requirement for the emergence of modern science that the main conceptions of Aristotle's physics should be rejected rather than developed, and it is customary to evaluate earlier anticipations of the seventeenth century revolution by the extent to which they overcame Aristotle and the Greeks generally. The science of modern times differs from the science of antiquity not merely in degree but in kind.

The basic differences between ancient and modern science grow out of their differing philosophies of nature, their basic presuppositions about nature which, in turn, affect the questions they put to her. It is often said that the ancients asked: what and why? and the moderns: how? Though perhaps overly neat, this claim points toward genuine differences. Ancient thinkers sought to penetrate to

[4] Following the practice of the authors here introduced, I use the term "modern science" to refer to the system of ideas which culminated in Newton's *Principia:* a celestial and terrestrial mechanics. And although this science presupposed the rejection of teleology in Aristotle's sense, it is explicitly *not* contended here that *other* sciences then (in the seventeenth century) or *all* sciences now can do without the idea of *telos* in every form. Much mischief is done by equating the term "science" with a) physics, or b) a particular philosophy of nature, e.g., mechanism or animism.

[5] I borrow the idea and the phrase from Chap. III of S. Toulmin, *The Philosophy of Science* (New York: Harper and Row, Publishers, 1960).

the reality underlying appearances, a reality they usually conceived as cognate with reason, consciously intending or at least subservient to rational purpose, and hence, open to rational understanding. Even the materialists regarded true reality as inaccessible to the senses. Modern science of nature, on the other hand, is preoccupied with sensory phenomena and seeks to find formulae which will express orderly sequences and patterns in them. All conceptual tools and abstract models serve the same purpose: to make sense out of the phenomena. Greek philosophy of nature precluded the use of sensory information as the foundation or the evidence for science, modern philosophy of nature precludes anything but sensory information.

Differences in presuppositions entail, as F. M. Cornford has pointed out, differences in method, objective, and underlying impulse between the two sciences.[6] The speculations of the pre-Socratics, for example, are expressed in the form of cosmogonic myths. They are wholly concerned with matters beyond the reach of direct observation, with such matters as the ultimate "stuff" of the cosmos, and the transition from chaos to cosmos. It does not occur to them to test their assertions experimentally. Anaximenes held that the primitive air or mist passed from the gaseous state to the liquid and thence to the solid, growing steadily colder and denser. But there is no record of his setting out a jar of water on a frosty night to see if its volume would decrease.[7] The neglect of experiment, which this example illustrates, is the most striking difference from modern science.

> Modern science describes natural substances instead of defining them, it discovers their properties by observation and experiment instead of by "intuitive induction" and demonstration, it classifies their species instead of dividing their genera, it establishes between them the relation of cause and effect instead of the relation of ground and consequent.[8]

Yet, as Foster goes on to point out, it is incorrect to say that sensory experience played no part in ancient science. Sensory experience played a different part: it illustrated the conclusions reached by

[6] F. M. Cornford, "Greek Natural Philosophy and Modern Science" in *Background to Modern Science* (New York: The Macmillan Co., 1938).

[7] Cornford, *op. cit.*, p. 9.

[8] M. B. Foster, "The Christian Doctrine of Creation and the Rise of Modern Natural Science" in *Mind*, XLIII, N.S. (1934), p. 454.

rational inference. And again, this follows from the major assumption of Greek philosophy of nature. "All the peculiarities of Greek natural science are derived from the assumption that the essence of a natural object is definable, as the essence of a geometrical object is." [9] If the natural object is definable its properties can be deduced from its essence, its specific and generic place in the natural order inferred rationally. It follows then "that empirical evidence must be inadmissable in the same degree and for the same reason in establishing the conclusions of natural science as it obviously is in establishing the conclusions of Euclidean geometry." [10]

Evidently then ancient and modern science will differ as to their objectives. The Greeks want to find out what things really are. Both Plato and Aristotle found this real nature not in the matter of things but in their form. That was because "they looked on the world as a product of craftmanship; and the essence of such products lies in their form." [11] The notion of craft (*techne*) and its attendant idea of preconceived form is one of the strongest motifs in both Plato and Aristotle, coloring their philosophies of art and politics as well as their philosophy of nature. One fully understands a manufactured object only when one comprehends the purpose its maker envisioned for it. Thus a knife may be made of stone or metal, the material is not essential. What is essential is its purpose or function: it is made to cut. If it ceases to cut, it ceases to be a knife, though of course it continues to be stone or metal. This function is its form or essence. And form is not to be equated with sensible shape, though shape may give a clue to form. Form is intelligible, shape is sensible. A table may be round or square, high or low, three-legged or four-legged, etc., so long as it fulfills its function. In Aristotle's view of the sublunary world, all natural objects imperfectly realize the essential forms which define their natures. They are thus engaged in a ceaseless activity of realizing the properties natural to them. In Aristotle's technical language, the formal cause (essence) also serves as a final cause (purpose) when considered as the nature which each thing is striving to realize more perfectly. Stones fall to their natural place, men strive to realize the maximum excellence of all their natural faculties. Unless hindered, things follow a natural bent towards their goals. Only man deliberates about the means to reach

[9] *Ibid.*
[10] *Ibid.*
[11] Cornford, *op. cit.*, p. 10.

his natural goal; all other beings follow the bent of their natures without inner hesitation or resistance, though of course they interfere with one another. And this is what principally distinguishes the sublunary sphere from all the spheres surrounding it, the conflict and disorder of the one, the perfect harmony and order of the others. The objective of Greek science is thus to find out *what* things are, which will in turn yield an answer to the question *why* they behave as they do. In modern science the objective is to understand *how* things behave by formulating rules which accurately describe regularities of behavior.

Let us consider, finally, the third of Cornford's *differentiae*, the underlying motive or impulse for science in the two cultures. The world offers a great variety of aspects for scientific study. The selection which the scientist makes among them depends in great part, as we have seen, on his philosophy of nature, that is, on his conception of the kinds of rationality he can discover: what principles and what causes. But his selection also depends on his underlying motive, what needs and desires he feels, what value he sets upon this or that end in life.[12] As Cornford points out, "natural philosophy as pursued in the classical period had no bearing whatsoever on mechanical inventions." [13] But the aim of modern science, since the Renaissance at least, has been "to multiply the conveniences of life and to extend the empire of man over the material world—in a word, the increase of wealth and power." [14] And he goes on to cite the fact that the great civilization of Greece rested on a large slave class who performed the menial tasks and secured the necessities of life so that the ruling class could have leisure for politics and theoretical pursuits. This fact tended to remove any pressure that might otherwise have been felt towards the invention of labor-saving devices and therefore played an important role in shaping the underlying impulse of Greek science toward pure theory. One should also recall in this connection the aristocratic Greek contempt for manual labor and even for the crafts, as being subject to necessity and hence servile or nonliberal.[15] The leaders of the seventeenth-century scientific revolution, on the other hand, were all interested in practical

[12] Cornford, *op. cit.*, p. 16.

[13] *Ibid.*

[14] Cornford, *op. cit.*, p. 18.

[15] For a thorough discussion of this theme see Chapters 3 and 4 of Hannah Arendt, *The Human Condition* (New York: Doubleday and Co., Inc., 1959).

inventions and machinery, even if they did not all wholly subscribe to the spirit of Francis Bacon's motto, "knowledge is power."

How can we account for the differences in method, objective, and underlying impulse which separate ancient and modern science? What non-Greek element could be the source of the transformation? Non-Greek it must be, since the Greek philosophy of nature does not permit the modern view. It is Michael Foster's thesis in the article presented here that the non-Greek source is Judeao-Christian revelation and, in particular, its conception of God as Creator. Greek philosophy of nature, Foster shows, flows from Greek theology. The modern philosophy of nature, he asserts, flows from Christian theology. And, in turn, the methods, objectives, and underlying impulse of modern science are determined by that philosophy of nature. The argument which Foster develops in his long and closely reasoned article has been succinctly formulated by E. L. Mascall:

> A world which is created by the Christian God will be both contingent and orderly. It will embody regularities and patterns, since its Maker is rational, but the particular regularities and patterns which it will embody cannot be predicted *a priori*, since he is free; they can be discovered only by examination. The world, as Christian theism conceives it, is thus an ideal field for the application of the scientific method, with its twin techniques of observation and experiment.[16]

Foster's argument is primarily philosophical rather than historical. He is arguing about the relations between systems of ideas and the impact which novel ideas must have when their implications have been fully explored and assimilated. Documentation is supplied and the main line of the historical development is sketched, but the strategy of the argument follows the logic rather than the history of ideas. Francis Oakley's article, however, pursues historically one aspect of the complex relations between Christian theology and natural science, the idea of "laws of nature." He traces the idea from the thirteenth to the seventeenth centuries in the writings of theologians and scientists, establishing that the dissemination by the voluntarist or nominalist theologians of the notion of laws of nature as divinely imposed upon the universe was a principal factor in the overthrow of Aristotelian physics. It was a factor which also shaped an alternative philosophy of nature for the empirical science

[16] E. L. Mascall, *Christian Theology and Natural Science* (New York: The Ronald Press Co., 1956), p. 132.

already emerging in the fourteenth and fifteenth centuries, but, because of a recession during which humanist literary and ethical interests dominated, it was definitively established only in the seventeenth century. To these two complementary studies of the origins of theoretical science we add a provocative discussion by Lynn White of the reasons for the rapid technological progress in Western Europe. White lays heavy emphasis on attitudes toward *praxis,* labor and the uses of nature, which were foreign to the classical world but fostered by Christianity.

Christianity's reevaluation of labor and work, epitomized in the fact that Jesus Christ worked as a carpenter and St. Paul earned his living as a tentmaker, is of great importance in explaining the relation between Christianity and modern science. For, as White points out, this directly stimulated the search for labor-saving machines and techniques, especially for those occupations which seemed unworthy of a child of God. In an interesting essay on the "Motives and Incentives for Science in Antiquity," Ludwig Edelstein has also assigned a theological motive as part-cause for the relative disinterest of the Greeks in technology. The Greeks, he says,

> . . . did not feel that it was their business to make the world over altogether. Men no more claimed than did their gods to be creators out of nothing, to act with a free will that imposes its law on things that have no nature of their own. Rather did they feel called upon to shape matter that was given and, here below at any rate, refractory to reason. . . . On the other hand, it would seem to be true that the increase in practical inventions noticeable since the Renaissance is in part due to the fact that man wished to participate "in the creative passion" of his God.[17]

But the interest in technology also influenced the direction in which theoretical science would move. It is thus no accident that the keystone of the scientific revolution is rational mechanics, a science whose concepts are derivative from the experience of work and labor. Jean Abelé has strongly insisted on this point in contrast to Greek attitudes. "The very notion of a rational mechanics was, I repeat, entirely foreign to Greek thought." [18] The biblical injunction to make the earth fruitful was thus given fresh impetus by the

[17] In A. C. Crombie (ed.), *Scientific Change* (New York: Basic Books, Inc., 1963), p. 26.

[18] Jean Abelé, *Christianity and Science* (New York: Hawthorne Books, Inc., 1961), p. 67.

Christian doctrine of the Incarnation of the Son of God in human, bodily form. And, although there have been tendencies towards spiritualism and other-worldliness in Christianity from the beginning, the content of Christian theology has impelled a reverence for material creation including the body and all its functions. With the use of material things: water, salt, oil, bread, and wine, as vehicles for the grace of salvation, Christianity may be said to have developed a special kind of "worldliness" which had an important role in preparing a psychological climate favorable to science. It is, then, no surprise to find that the leaders of the seventeenth century revolution, Galileo, Kepler, Descartes, and Newton considered that they were following a Christian imperative when they explored the order of nature.[19]

The general conclusion towards which all these essays tend is to assign a decisive role to Christian theology in the inception of an empirical science of nature—the role of necessary condition. That conclusion is given strong external support, as Oakley points out, by Needham's monumental *Science and Civilization in China.* The absence in Chinese thought of the idea of creation was one of the factors preventing a development of Chinese science in the direction of the Newtonian synthesis.[20] The path which Chinese science in fact followed was set out by the pantheistic naturalism of Taoist theology. It is no doubt superfluous to add that though our authors insist upon Christian theology as a *sine qua non* for the development of modern science, they do not regard it as the only one. Other conditions are also requisite. To mention only the most obvious: sufficient mathematical development, stability and leisure, freedom of inquiry, and the presence of creative imagination and human genius.

Since Foster's essays first appeared in the thirties, much light has been shed on the history of science in the period from late antiquity

[19] The dedication of Descartes' *Meditations* and the General Scholium of Newton's *Principia* are well known. Less known but typical of the spirit of most of the seventeenth century pioneers is Kepler's prayer at the end of his *Harmonices Mundi,* part of which says: "Now I have finished the work of my calling and have used all the powers of the talent Thou hast given me. I have manifested the glory of Thy works to the men who will read these demonstrations. . . ." Quoted in Abelé, *op. cit.*, p. 77.

[20] J. Needham, *Science and Civilization in China* (New York: Cambridge U. Press, 1956), pp. 161–164, 580–583.

to the seventeenth century. Oakley draws upon the research done on the period subsequent to the condemnations of 1277 for his own argument. But what about the earlier period? Why, we may wonder, if Foster's thesis be granted, did it take so long for the Christian ideas to transform Greek modes of thinking? And what about the history of science in Byzantium and Islam, both civilizations with a strong belief in creation by a transcendent, personal God? In order to round off the argument of this first Part, I will attempt some very general answers to these questions, drawing upon the wealth of recent publications in this field.

Let us take the latter question first and begin with the older civilization, Byzantium. Beginning with the founding of the imperial city, Constantinople, in 330, the Eastern half of the Roman Empire was favorably situated to perform an indispensable service in the transmission of Greek civilization, including Greek science. Byzantine scholars were the first link in the long chain of transmitters of that priceless heritage; it progressed from Byzantium to Syria, then to the Arabs, to the Jewish translators of Moorish Spain and finally, beginning in the twelveth century, into the Latin West. Spared until 518 from harassment by the barbarians who were destroying much of the Latin West, the scholars of the East, at centers like Alexandria and Athens as well as at the capital, recopied and commented on the Greek classics. The fifth and sixth centuries in the East thus present a small prototype of the great flowering of Latin commentaries in the thirteenth and fourteenth centuries. After that early period, owing partly to the constant pressure from Islam and the West, scientific activity slacked off and, in spite of revivals in the eleventh and fourteenth centuries (the one in the eleventh featuring a Renaissance of Platonism four centuries before the West), never equalled the promising beginnings. The net result of scientific activity in the eleven hundred year history of the Empire seems disappointing. Though there are still great gaps in our knowledge of Byzantine history, the judgement of J. Théodorides seems likely to stand. After a survey of Byzantine scientific accomplishments he concludes: "No one could maintain that Byzantine scientific texts were of outstanding scientific value, or that most of them were more than poor compilations of earlier Greek or Hellenistic works or commentaries." [21] And he goes on to speculate about

[21] Cf. Theodorides in Taton, *History,* for the information of the preceding paragraph. The quotation is from p. 451.

the reasons for this failure: "One of the main reasons for this deficiency was the total subordination of science to the Church and the concentration on Platonic and Neoplatonic doctrines, and thus on abstract speculations." [22]

The Byzantine love for theory and abstract speculation—inherited from their Greek ancestors—seems to have been conservative in impulse, a loving contemplation of past acquisitions rather than bold theorizing.[23] In large measure this attitude may be ascribed to the fact that for roughly two-thirds of their history, the Byzantines lived under constant siege in a defensive posture vitiated by a sense of pessimism.[24] They thought of themselves not as a dynamic center for new learning but as a last bastion of culture, civilization, and beauty, destined to fall one day to the barbarian or the infidel.[25] M. Le Guillou, summing up the dominant traits of Byzantium after the defeat of the Iconoclast Movement in 843, writes: "That meant the leaving of the world of progress, of the quest for truth, of activity, for a world of contemplation (*theoria*), settling down into a false eternity and rejecting history in favour of eschatology." [26] The Byzantine failure to advance Greek science, much less to transform it into an empirical science, may then be set down to a lack of that underlying attitude of "worldliness" which, as we saw above, is a possible consequence of a creationist theology and an incarnational religion, as well as a necessary condition for science as we know it.

The scientific activity of Arabic civilization was much more considerable than that of Byzantium, and much more is known of its details. In spite of splendid early achievements, however, Arabic science declined in the latter half of the thirteenth century and soon faded out. The Arabs did not participate in the scientific revolution of later centuries and its results had to be imported from the West. It seems a fair generalization to say that, "In their search for truth, Arabian scientists were primarily interested in gathering knowledge which had stood the test of time, possibly on the assumption that nothing new could be discovered. But this very search gave them a taste for methodical investigation and opened up unsuspected

[22] *Ibid.*

[23] *Cf.* Steven Runciman, *Byzantine Civilization* (New York: Meridian Books 1956), in particular p. 190.

[24] Runciman, Chap. VIII.

[25] *Ibid.*

[26] M. L. Le Guillou, *The Spirit of Eastern Orthodoxy* (New York: Hawthorne Books, Inc., 1962), p. 107.

avenues."[27] Nevertheless, among those avenues opened up was a greater sense of the variety of methods useful in the study of nature, including an appreciation of experimental methods, at least in medicine.[28] Aristotle's physics was attacked from various quarters and for various reasons; as in the West, there were distinct gropings towards the key idea of inertia.[29] There were also a few attempts to mathematicize aspects of Aristotle's theory of motion.[30] But no wholesale attack was made on Aristotelian physics, nor did the non-Aristotelian ideas coalesce into a consistent alternative. Again, as in the case of Byzantium, one can only speculate about the reasons for this. External historical factors may once again be adduced for this decline: the defeats in Spain and the devastating Mongol invasions.[31] In the light of the main argument of this part, however, one feature of Arabic intellectual life stands out very prominently: those interested in science lacked any solid support from Islamic philosophy and theology, and lacking this, they could not achieve a coherent philosophy of nature. The Arab philosophers, such men as Alkindi, Alfarabi, Avicenna and Averroës, were, like all medieval philosophers, commentators of Aristotle. But their version of Aristotle was a strongly Neoplatonic one, partly because they regarded him as the author of the so-called "Theology of Aristotle," a determinist and pantheist tract culled from the writings of Plotinus and Proclus. All of these thinkers and particularly Averroës, the most influential Arab philosopher in the West, tended to follow the authority of Aristotle unswervingly, even in matters which contradicted the faith of Islam. To take the most crucial point, when these commentators "introduced from the Mohammedan religion into the Aristotelian system the idea of creation, they interpreted this in such a way as to deny free will not only to man but even to God himself."[32] With respect to the needs of an experimental science Arabic philosophy, especially the dominant Averroism, remained a conservative, even a reactionary force, wholly committed to Aristotle's physics.

Muslim theology offered little support to experimental science. It

[27] R. Arnaldez and L. Massignon in Taton, *History*, p. 387.

[28] S. Pines, "What Was Original in Arabic Science?" in A. C. Crombie (ed.), *Scientific Change* (New York: Basic Books, Inc., 1963), p. 191.

[29] Pines, *op. cit.*, pp. 203 ff.

[30] Pines, *op. cit.*, pp. 200 f.

[31] Pines, *op. cit.*, p. 203.

[32] A. C. Crombie, *Medieval and Early Modern Science* (New York: Doubleday Anchor, 1959), Vol. I, p. 57.

is true that the Koran was read as inviting the faithful to observe nature and to seek rational knowledge.[33] But many of the doctrines of the leading Arabic philosophers were clearly heretical from the standpoint of Islam and thus even Aristotelian science came to be regarded with suspicion. Moreover, the long and complex struggle, amid sectarian controversy, to define Muslim orthodoxy drained off intellectual energies and issued in an orthodoxy unfavorable to science. The theology of al-Ash'ari which became dominant in the prevailing Sunni tradition of Islam, stressed the absolute omnipotence of God to such lengths as to deny any efficacy to secondary causes. God alone causes all.[34] With respect to nature, this view resulted in a temporal as well as spatial atomism; event succeeds event according to the inscrutable Divine Will and there is thus no basis in reality for the causal principle.[35]

We turn now to the second question posed above: why the long delay in the efficacy of Christian theology for the study of nature? Our answer is considerably facilitated by the brief discussions of Byzantium and Islam. For most of the "delay" was spent in the same task of assimilating and then overcoming the philosophical heritage of Greece. It is important to remember that the havoc wrought by the barbarians had nearly extinguished the light of learning in the West. An essential continuity with Hellenic and Hellenistic civilization was never lost in the East. In the slow painful recovery of the West from the late tenth century onwards, the recovery of Greek learning, beginning in the twelfth century, had a staggering effect: a powerful new world of ideas had suddenly emerged, a superior culture, a threat or at least a challenge to Christian thought. The impact of this can be seen most dramatically perhaps in the great success of Averroism, a doctrine incompatible with Christianity, in the medieval universities. It is not surprising that the confrontation with the ancients, and preeminently Aristotle, should have taken a long time. What is surprising is that Christian thinkers early manifested a critical and independent attitude towards the ancient learn-

[33] R. Arnaldez and L. Massignon in Taton, *History*, p. 386.

[34] *Cf.* H. A. R. Gibb, *Mohammedanism* (New York: Oxford U. Press, Inc., 1962), Chapter 7 and esp. p. 118.

[35] *Cf.* B. Lewis, *The Arabs in History* (New York: Harper & Row, Publishers 1960), Chapter 8, and esp. pp. 141–143; and W. Watt, *Islamic Philosophy and Theology* (Edinburgh: Edinburgh University Press, 1962), Chapter 9. It is interesting to note that Hume's attack on the causal principle is thus anticipated by al-Ash'ari in the tenth century and Nicholas of Autrecourt in the fourteenth.

ing. Although many members of the arts faculties became advocates of the Averroistic interpretation of Aristotle, all the prominent Christian theologians, in contrast to their Muslim and Jewish counterparts, refused to surrender any of the major articles of their creed. As the articles of Foster and Oakley show, the key to the overthrow of Aristotle's physics comes in the Christian rejection of the idea of nature as a necessary emanation from God. In his comprehensive history of the science of the medieval period, A. C. Crombie makes a similar judgement:

> The Aristotelian system came into circulation accompanied by the Averroistic doctrines that the universe was a necessarily determined emanation from God's reason, instead of a free creation of His will as Christian theology taught; that the ultimate rational causes of things in God's mind could be discovered by the human reason; and that Aristotle had in fact discovered those causes, so that the universe must necessarily be constituted as he had described it, and could not be otherwise. By means of the Christian doctrines of the inscrutability and absolute omnipotence of God, the thirteenth-century theologians and philosophers liberated rational and empirical inquiry into the laws that nature in fact exhibits from this absolute subjection to a metaphysical system.[36]

The impetus provided by Christian theology thus led Western thinkers from the early thirteenth century on to embark on that "conception of natural science as in principle inductive and experimental as well as mathematical, and . . . to develop the logical procedures of experimental inquiry, which chiefly characterize the difference between modern and ancient science."[37] In addition to theology, a consistent philosophy was available to these investigators from the early fourteenth century and most of them share it: the schools of Nominalism in England and France which rejected the substantial forms and final causality of Aristotle's physics, emphasizing instead the direct intuition of particular phenomena. This philosophy, as Oakley demonstrates, gave direct added impetus to scientific observation and experiment.

Why then did experimental science rise and come to fruition in the Christian West? Not because of the discovery of separate aspects of that science, such as the crucial role of experiment or the quantifying of observables. These aspects were discovered earlier in

[36] Crombie, *op. cit.*, Vol. II, p. 315.
[37] Crombie, *op. cit.*, Vol. II, pp. 7 f.

other cultures, in some cases in a more refined form. What distinguishes the West and makes it the natural breeding place of experimental science is the *constellation* of necessary factors: a philosophy of nature based on a coherent theology, an attitude favorable to research, discovery and experiment, access to the learning of the Greeks and especially Greek mathematics as further developed by Indian, Byzantine, and Arabic thinkers, and finally, external conditions of relative peace and leisure. Of these factors the most decisive was the new philosophy of nature, if we measure it against the most formidable and difficult of the obstacles: Greek natural philosophy.

CHAPTER 2

The Christian Doctrine of Creation and the Rise of Modern Natural Science

M. B. FOSTER

For the convenience of this article I shall use the term "modern science" in a restricted sense, so as to exclude from consideration its most recent developments. Thus by "modern physics" I mean what is now sometimes called "the classical physics". I do this not because I wish to imply that what I say of it is not true also of the most recent developments of science, but because I do not wish to raise the question here whether it is or not.

I approach my subject by way of a consideration of modern philosophy, and I apply the term "modern" to philosophy with a similar restriction, meaning by "modern philosophy" the philosophy which arose at the end of the Middle Ages and developed along the two main lines of Empiricism and Rationalism from Hobbes to Hume and from Descartes to Leibniz. About this philosophy as a whole I shall make two assumptions which I think will not be disputed. The first is that it was devoted (in so far as it was concerned with a theory of nature) mainly to establishing the possibility or justifying the presuppositions of the modern science of nature. It is necessary to use these two alternative descriptions because the relation of philosophy to science varied according to the degree of develop-

From *Mind,* Vol. XLIII, 1934. Reprinted by permission of publishers.

ment which the latter had achieved at the time. By the later centuries of the modern era the sciences of nature had become so firmly established that they formed a datum from which philosophical speculation could start. This does not of course mean that the philosopher dogmatically accepted the truth of any scientific hypothesis. He assumed only that a science of nature was possible (because it was actual), enquired into the presuppositions of its possibility, and tested his conclusions by their compatibility with it. This procedure is what Kant first named the Critical Method, but it was to some extent unconsciously anticipated by his predecessors in the later portion of the period which we are considering. But the assertions made about nature by the earlier philosophers of this period, while the sciences of nature were still in the founding, could not be grounded by such a method. Obviously the argument that nature must be such and such because otherwise the science of nature would not be possible, is cogent only when it is granted that the science of nature is actual. What I wish admitted is simply that these pioneers of modern philosophy, writing before the modern science of nature was fully established and not grounding their conclusions on its existence, did yet ascribe to the world of nature those very characteristics which the modern science of nature must presuppose in it as the condition of its own possibility. Thus Descartes, for example, denied that final causes are operative in nature; and modern physics was based upon the presupposition that final causes are not operative in nature. Locke declared that the Real Essence of natural objects was unknowable; and the modern empirical sciences of nature presupposed that the real essence of their objects was unknowable.[1] In a word: the early modern philosophers ascribed to nature the character which constituted it a possible object of modern natural science in advance of the actual establishment of that science.

I wish it admitted, secondly, that, these modern doctrines of nature being, as they were felt by their authors to be, incompatible with the Aristotelian doctrine of nature maintained in the Scholastic philosophy, precisely the element in them which is alien to Aristotle is the ground of the peculiar characteristics by which modern natural science is distinguished from the science of the Greeks or the Scholastics. Thus, to take the same two examples, when Locke

[1] Because if it were knowable, properties of the object would be deducible from it, not established by the evidence of experience.

asserts that the real essence of natural objects is unknowable, he is both contradicting Aristotle and by the same assertion ascribing to nature the characteristic which necessitates in the science of it that empirical quality by which the modern inductive sciences are distinguished from any science which had preceded them. When Descartes declares that only efficient causes operate in nature, he is substituting for the Aristotelian conception of nature another incompatible with it; and the difference between the Cartesian and the Aristotelian conceptions of nature is the ground of the difference between the modern science of physics and its ancient counterpart.

The general question arises: What is the source of the un-Greek elements which were imported into philosophy by the post-Reformation philosophers, and which constitute the modernity of modern philosophy? And the particular question—which is merely part of the general question repeated: What is the source of those un-Greek elements in the modern theory of nature by which the peculiar character of the modern science of nature was to be determined? The answer to the first question is: The Christian revelation, and the answer to the second: The Christian doctrine of creation. The main object of this article is limited to establishing the answer to the particular question, but I will preface the attempt by a few remarks upon the general one.

Opposition to Greek philosophy in general, and to that of Aristotle in particular, was not raised for the first time in history when the post-Reformation philosophers rejected Scholasticism. On the contrary, the opposition between Christian revelation and Greek philosophy was as old as Christianity itself, and the endeavour to overcome it through the progressive assimilation of Christian dogmas by the philosophical understanding was the spring of the whole development of medieval philosophy.[2] Scholasticism itself is much more than a re-edition of Aristotle. If we ask from what source this *plus* is derived, there can be only one answer: it is clearly and obviously derived from the Christian revelation. My contention is that the conflict waged against Aristotle after the Reformation was only

[2] This is brought out with fine lucidity in É. Gilson's *L'esprit de la philosophie médiévale*. But my whole article is a protest against Gilson's further assumption, that we must look to a resurrection of Scholasticism for a continuation of this great task, and against his implied judgment that the work of the classical modern philosophers represents a declension from the path upon which medieval philosophy set out.

a continuation of the conflict waged against him before it; that as the one party in this opposition (Greek philosophy) remained the same after as before the Reformation, so also the other remained the same; and that the un-Greek element in modern has the same source as the un-Greek element in medieval philosophy: namely the Christian revelation. There is hardly a stronger argument for the truth of this contention than to draw the consequences of denying it. If we deny it we must suppose both that the un-Greek (*i.e.*, specifically modern) element in modern philosophy was without a source, and that the un-Greek (*i.e.*, specifically medieval) element in medieval philosophy was without an issue. This supposition can hardly even be entertained by one who has not been hardened in the belief that the history of philosophy begins again *de novo* with Descartes.

To say this is by no means to deny that there was a crisis in the history of thought at the time of the Reformation or that modern differs from medieval philosophy in vitally important respects. The effect of the Reformation in the sphere of thought was analogous in two ways to its effects in the sphere of conduct. In the latter sphere it had the effect, first, of extending the Christian order of conduct from the religious (*i.e.*, monastic) to the secular life. This involved, of course, the disappearance of the 'religious' life as such, but by no means therefore of the principles by which it had been governed. They continued to be applied, with a rigour only intensified by their diffusion, in the Puritan asceticism of the economic life.[3] The Reformation had the consequence, secondly, of transferring the direction of conduct from the external authority of the priest to the internal authority of conscience. But conscience only imposed from within the same laws of conduct which the priest had imposed from without. The Reformation marks a term in the education of the Christian peoples analogous to that which Aristotle proposes as the end of the ethical training of the individual. The first stage in the acquisition of virtue by the individual is his submission to certain principles of conduct prescribed by another, but the end of this submission is his acquirement of a disposition to act in accordance with these principles. When this is achieved, he is emancipated from his tutelage, and his actions are determined henceforth from within himself. But this does not in the least imply that his actions are now liberated from the control of the principles to which they were formerly sub-

[3] I refer especially to Max Weber's great work, *Die protestantische Ethik und der Geist des Kapitalismus.*

mitted. It means simply that they are now animated by these principles whereas previously they were conformed to them. Similarly, at the Reformation conduct was emancipated not from direction by Christian principles, but only from their external prescription. Conscience itself was an 'acquired disposition', informed by submission to that very prescription, and if its possessors could mistake it for a 'natural' faculty, that was only because it had been acquired so thoroughly.[4]

In the sphere of thought the Reformation had effects analogous to both of these. In the first place (I am reversing the order), philosophers claimed for reason emancipation from the authority of faith, to which it had been so long submitted. They did not realise that the reason for which they claimed autonomy was a reason itself informed by this very submission, and that what they called 'common sense' or 'the natural light' was only an internal revelation of what had previously been revealed externally to faith. If the reason upon which they relied had been in fact what they took it for, a 'natural' faculty bereft of the enlightenment of the Christian revelation, it could have discovered no truths not discovered by reason to the Greeks, and could not therefore have laid down the foundations upon which modern science was raised.

The delusion of the early modern philosophers that their philosophy was based wholly on the evidence of reason[5] (if they were Rationalists) or of experience (if they were Empiricists) prevented them from looking further for the source of their doctrines, or from so much as entertaining the supposition that they were indebted to

[4] "Der gesunde Menschenverstand und das natürliche Gefühl roher Türken zum Mass-stab genommen, gibt abscheuliche Grundsätze. Wenn *wir* aber von gesundem Menschenverstand sprechen, von natürlichem Gefühl, so hat man dabei immer im Sinn einen gebildeten Geist; und die, welche die gesunde Menschenvernunft, das natürliche Wissen, die unmittelbaren Gefühle und Offenbarungen in ihnen zur Regel und Mass-stab machen, wissen nicht, dass, wenn Religion, das Sittliche, Rechtliche sich als Inhalt in der Menschenbrust findet, dies der Bildung und Erziehung verdankt wurde, die nur erst solche Grundsätze zu natürlichen Gefühlen gemacht haben." Hegel, *Geschichte der Philosophie,* III, ii., 2; *Werke,* 2nd ed., vol. XV, p. 439.

[5] When Raymond de Sebonde declares in the prologue to his *Theologia Naturalis sive Liber Creaturarum,* that the exercise of the natural reason upon the Book of Nature suffices a man to know without difficulty "whatever is contained in Holy Scripture" (C. C. J. Webb, *Studies in the History of Natural Theology,* pp. 292 ff.), that is only an extreme form of the delusion shared in some degree by all the modern Rationalist philosophies.

Christian revelation. But it has been open to no succeeding philosopher to share the delusion. The work of criticism very speedily showed that neither the Rationalist nor the Empiricist philosophy was really based upon the evidence upon which it pretended to rely. No experience, to take one example, could serve as evidence to Locke of the existence of material substances, nor any reasoning demonstrate to Descartes the existence of a material world. No doubt, the assurance of 'common sense' might suffice for the one, and of the 'natural light' for the other. But then it must be admitted that "common sense" is something other than sense and the "natural light" something other than reason; and the way is open for the enquiry: What is the source of that certainty which is derived neither from reason nor from sense? [6]

It will not be enough to show that this certainty had its source in the Christian revelation; it has to be shown also that it had its issue in the establishment of the presuppositions of modern natural science. That these presuppositions are not themselves established by the evidence either of reason or of sense, any acquaintance with the "problem of induction" or with Hume's difficulties about causation is sufficient to show. And in fact the criticism to which the Rationalist and Empiricist philosophies were subjected, in divesting them of all those conclusions to which they were not *upon their own premises* entitled, did divest them of every certainty which the procedure of modern natural science requires for its justification. If these philosophies have never laid themselves open to that criticism; if they had begun by resigning themselves to the scepticism to which they were ultimately reduced; or if, having laid themselves

[6] Mr. A. K. Stout ("Descartes' Proof of the Existence of Matter", MIND, April, 1932) has argued that Descartes' own doctrine is not that the existence of the material world is assured directly by the 'natural light', but that it is assured directly by something which Descartes distinguishes from the 'natural light' as the 'teaching of nature', and by the 'natural light' only indirectly, inasmuch as it is competent to establish the general veracity of the 'teaching of nature' (though not the truth of any particular one of its dictates).

Acceptance of Mr. Stout's conclusions (which I am by no means disposed to question) would necessitate a certain revision of my terminology, but not any essential modification of my argument. However significant it may be that Descartes should have admitted the existence of a source of certainty other than reason, the admission is practically nullified by the proviso that the general veracity of the 'teaching of nature' must be demonstrable by reason. The proviso makes the certainty of the existence of matter to depend ultimately, if not immediately, upon the 'natural light'.

open to it, they had succumbed to it too soon—they would not have performed the function which in fact they performed in the establishment of modern science. What prevented them from succumbing sooner was their reliance upon the revelation which had raised them above scepticism in the first place. Regius and Malebranche, for example, being unable to defend against criticism Descartes' demonstration of the existence of the material world, do not therefore surrender the doctrine; they only recur overtly to the authority of revelation to establish a truth which Descartes had referred to the deliverance of the natural light. The very ease with which this transition is made is sufficient to indicate that Descartes' 'natural light' was informed by the same revelation.

The time came much later when the appeal to revelation lost the power of directing thought. Kant, who was perhaps the first to perceive quite clearly that the *whole* of the ontological doctrines of modern Rationalism were covertly dependent upon the authority of revelation, regarded this as a sufficient ground for dismissing them, and not as a confirmation of their truth. But by this time the 'dogmatic' philosophies had done their work. A body of natural sciences had arisen upon the presuppositions which they had laid down, and it was possible *now* for the philosopher to establish the presuppositions by the 'critical' method of working back to them from the sciences which were based upon them. During the whole period in which the modern natural sciences were in an early stage of growth the influence of religious authority upon philosophical thought was consistently exerted to preserve it from conclusions, whether sceptical or otherwise, which would have been incompatible with the possibility of these sciences; and religion surrendered this control only when the sciences were established firmly enough to serve in their turn as a datum for philosophical speculation. I will give an illustration at the risk of anticipating what belongs later. Descartes and Kant both reject final causation in nature, but their arguments differ significantly. Kant argues in effect from the absence of final reasoning in science to the absence of final causation in nature; nature must be without final causes because it is presupposed to be so by the science of mathematical physics. But Descartes proceeds in the reverse direction. The avoidance of final explanations by the physicist is not cited as a fact, but prescribed as a rule. The scientist, he says, *ought* to abjure the search for final explanations *because the purposes of God are inscrutable*. This argument is an enthymeme of which the premises to be supplied are that nature is *created* by God, and that the activity of creation is not directed by an intelligible purpose. So that Descartes' prescription to the physicist is based upon the metaphysical implications of Christian dogma.[7]

In the second place, as the Reformation in the practical sphere had the effect of extending the application of Christian principles of conduct beyond the religious to the secular life, so in the theoretical sphere it carried out the implications of Christian doctrines beyond the sacred into the profane sciences. The medieval philosopher had of course believed the Christian doctrine that nature is created. But the belief had been efficacious only in his theology. In his science of nature he had continued to seek for final causes, to define essences and to deduce properties: in a word—he had continued to employ the methods of Aristotelian science, entirely oblivious of the fact that Aristotle's science was based upon the presupposition that nature is not created. The modern investigators of nature were the first to take seriously *in their science* the Christian doctrine that nature is created, and the main differences between the methods of ancient and the methods of modern natural science may be reduced to this: that these are and those are not methods proper to the investigation of a created nature.

With this we may turn to a closer examination of the particular question. We have to determine, first, what the differences are which distinguish the methods of modern from those of Greek natural science; we have to show that these differences depend upon differences between the modern and the Greek philosophy of nature, and that these in their turn are derived from the differences between the Christian and the Greek conception of God and of God's relation to the world.

I have said what I shall mean by the term 'modern science of

[7] The same connection may be illustrated by another example. Of Aquinas's presentation of the doctrine of the 'star-moving Intelligences' Prof. Webb remarks that "the chief interest to us of these speculations . . . lies in the fact that Thomas Aquinas is so thoroughly alive to the danger involved *to the religious principles of Christianity* in the acknowledgement of the divinity of the heavenly bodies" (*Studies in the History of Natural Theology,* p. 274. My italics). Acknowledgement of their divinity was the basis of the distinction between Celestial and Terrestrial physics, with the abolition of which modern physical science may almost be said to have begun. There could hardly be more striking evidence of the truth of my thesis than the fact that this criticism was first undertaken in the interest of the religious principles of Christianity.

nature', but it might appear a difficulty to determine what is to be meant by the contrasted term 'Greek science of nature'. Greek science of nature was in most of its branches an attempt rather than an achievement, and an enquiry into its character might seem to be surrounded by all the difficulties which attend an investigation of the rudimentary and the embryonic. Even to determine what its methods were might seem to require an antiquarian learning which I am far from possessing and which could in any event hardly promise to yield results of philosophical importance.

I shall not embark on such an investigation and my purpose does not require that I should do so. We need not elicit the principles of Greek science from the vestiges of Greek sciences, because we possess a classical formulation of the principles in the Aristotelian Logic. By Greek science I shall mean such science, or attempted science, of nature as conformed to the canons of Aristotelian Logic; and I shall not be disturbed by the fact, if it be one, that the Greeks developed some sciences not so conformable; or that the systematic attempt to apply Aristotelian methods to the investigation of nature was characteristic rather of the medieval scholastics than of the Greek philosophers. The peculiar characteristics by which modern is to be distinguished from Greek natural science may consequently be determined simply as those which render the former unconformable to the canons of this logic.[8]

Judged by this criterion one of the most important and striking differences, though no doubt it is not the only difference, between the methods of modern and those of ancient natural science is the presence in the former of an empirical element lacking in the latter. Modern science describes natural substances instead of defining them, it discovers their properties by observation and experiment instead of by 'intuitive induction' and demonstration, it classifies their species instead of dividing their genera, it establishes between them the relation of cause and effect instead of the relation of ground and consequent. In each case the modern procedure will be found to differ from its ancient counterpart by the part which sensuous experience plays in it. This is not to say that sensuous experience played no part in ancient science, but that it played a different part: it supplied the illustration but not the evidence of the conclusions of science.[9]

[8] *Cf.* in this connection C. R. Morris, *Idealistic Logic,* chap. iv.

[9] This is not, of course, the point at issue between Aristotle and Plato. They

All the peculiarities of Greek natural science are derived from the assumption that the essence of a natural object is definable, as the essence of a geometrical object is. Once let this be granted, and it follows that the properties must be deducible by reason from the essence, the species derivable by reasoning from the concept of the genus, the necessary connections between it and other objects such as can be perceived by reason to be involved in the essence; it follows, in a word, that empirical evidence must be inadmissible in the same degree and for the same reason in establishing the conclusions of natural science as it obviously is in establishing the conclusions of Euclidean geometry.

The methods of Greek natural science thus depend upon the assumption that the essences of natural objects are definable. What does this scientific assumption presuppose about the nature of the physical world?

Definition is an act of reason containing no element of sense, however necessary it may be that sensuous perception should precede it. No doubt I must have seen lines, or touched them, before I can define the line. But when I have reached a definition, then 'the line' which I have defined is intelligible only, neither visible nor tangible. That in objects which is intelligible as distinct from sensible is what the Greeks called their form as distinct from their matter. That the form of things is intelligible, and therefore definable, does not of itself constitute the whole of the assumption required to justify the procedure of Greek science, namely that the *essence* of things is intelligible, and therefore definable. It needs the complementary assumption, which the Greeks also made, that the form of things is their essence, *i.e.*, that of the two elements, formal and material, of which every actual thing is composed, the form alone makes the thing to be what it is, whereas the matter contributes no positive element to its being. Matter is the correlative, in the object, of sense in the subject, as form is the correlative of reason; and thus the Greek assumption about science, that there can be no empirical evidence for scientific conclusions, depends upon the Greek assumption about nature which may be loosely designated the assumption of the 'unreality of matter'. The designation is loose, because it is not meant simply that matter is not actual except in union with form; for it is true equally, at least according to

differ only in estimating differently the importance to be assigned to the sensible *as illustration.*

Aristotle, to say that form is not actual except in union with matter. What is meant is that the σύνολον of matter and form, which alone is actual, is determined to be what it is wholly by the one element of form. The object is *nothing more than* a realisation of form; its matter is the source of no being in it over and above that which it derives from its form, it is the source only of the imperfection with which the latter is realised. The method of Greek natural science thus involves a theory of nature according to which the actual world is distinguishable into the two elements of form and matter, the former intelligible, the latter sensible. Because the 'intelligible nature' is the ground both of all being and of all action in the actual world, whereas matter accounts only for diminution of being and impediment of action, it follows that intelligent comprehension of form is sufficient for the understanding both of what is and of what happens in the actual world, so far as this is capable of being understood, whereas sensuous experience represents no addition to, but only defect of, such understanding.

We have to ask finally what theory of God is presupposed in this theory of nature, and here I shall invert the natural order of investigation by stating my conclusion first. The theory of nature presupposes that neither of the two elements of which nature is composed is dependent for its being upon a power outside nature, *i.e.*, that neither of them is created. If matter were created it would possess a positive being, if form were created it would not be intelligible. The twin Greek doctrines of the 'unreality' of matter and the intelligibility of form imply that matter and form are alike eternal. We may say in advance, then, that any development of Greek theology, if it is to remain consistent with the presuppositions of Greek natural science, must stop short of the attribution to God of an omnipotent power over nature. Nature may be conceived as dependent upon a supernatural power for the activity by which its two elements are conjoined, but not for the being of either element. I shall endeavour to show, in the briefest possible outline, how Greek theology observes this limitation even in its highest developments, and I shall make some remarks upon each in turn of the three following Greek theological conceptions: (i) the conception of God as identical with nature, or of nature as itself divine, (ii) the conception of God as subject of a purely theoretical activity, (iii) the conception of God as artificer or Demiurge of nature.

(i) The identification of God with Nature finds its earliest expression in the deification of natural powers which is characteristic of the Greek polytheistic religion. So long as this identification is both naïve and complete, so long, *e.g.*, as the god is simply not distinguished at all from the natural object, it does not seem, indeed, that the religion founded upon it can give rise either to a theology or to a science of nature. But Greek [10] religion, though it may have begun with such a naïve identification, did not end with it. The withdrawal of the Gods to Olympus implies the recognition of *some* distinction between the natural and the divine. This is no absolute distinction; if it had been, Greek religion would have cast off at a stroke the character which distinguishes it as pagan from either the Jewish or the Christian; but it was sufficient to entail that the sensible object should be regarded henceforth not simply as the god, but as the *appearance* of the god, and its growth or motion rather as the *manifestation* of a divine activity, than as being itself divine.

This partial distinction between God and nature supplied the foundations of Greek science, for the Greek did not free himself from the teachings of his religion when he became a philosopher. The attitude of belief, no doubt, gave way in him to that of understanding, but what he now understood was only what he had previously believed. The great philosophical distinction which Socrates initiated and Plato worked out between the idea and the sensible object was only the explication of the distinction which had been already made in Greek religion between the God and the sensible object.

It will hardly be denied that this philosophical distinction was the

[10] I am using the term 'Greek' with an arbitrary limitation of meaning. By 'Greek religion' I mean the Greek Olympian religion, by 'Greek philosophy' the tradition of philosophy which began with Socrates and culminated in Aristotle, by 'Greek natural science' the science of nature based upon that philosophy, the actual pursuit of which was perhaps rather characteristic of Medieval Scholasticism than of the Greeks themselves. I need hardly say that I do not intend to deny the existence of what I ignore. There was, of course, a Greek religion other than the Olympian, a Greek philosophy before Socrates (there seems to have been a close connection between pre-Socratic philosophy and extra-Olympian religion), and there were at least the rudiments of a Greek natural science which was not a science of formal causes. Reaction against Aristotle in the early-modern philosophers was often enough accompanied by a renaissance of the theories of pre-Socratic philosophers. It remains none the less true that the reaction derived its force from Christian dogma, and only its watchwords from the pre-Socratics. These doctrines were revived and others discarded because these were more readily conformable to the doctrine of Creation.

foundation of the Greek science of nature, and if it be granted that the possibility of Greek natural science depended ultimately upon the distinction between God and nature achieved even by Greek religion, there may be a readier acceptance of the thesis that the far higher development of modern natural science depends upon the far deeper distinction between God and nature achieved by the Christian religion. The limitations of the pagan distinction are reflected in the peculiarities of Greek scientific procedure. If the gods are to be distinguished from nature, and yet not completely distinguished from it, they must be conceived as *appearing* in nature and as natural objects. The same difficulty concerning the relation of the sensible to the supersensible arises within the Platonic philosophy, and the solution of it is the same: the sensible is related to the idea as appearance to that which appears. The application of these categories to nature implies that the sensible (which is the material) is, *quâ* sensible and material, merely apparent, and this implication justifies the *a priori* methods of Greek natural science. But the doctrine of Creation implies that the material is real *quâ* material.

It is true that the doctrine of nature implicit in Greek polytheism is not of itself sufficient to supply the presuppositions even of Greek natural science. That the forms should be isolable in thought from the accidents of their material embodiment, is not sufficient to constitute them proper objects of a science. A scientific understanding (as distinct from a still quasi-æsthetic contemplation) demands that its objects be perceived to be interrelated one with another as members of a single system,[11] and this involves a view of the universe different from that involved in any mere polytheism. On the other hand, it does not involve any form of Theism, or belief in a God transcending nature. Nature must be conceived as a unity, but the principle which constitutes it one need not, for any of the considerations yet advanced, be held to possess an existence apart from nature, or to be related to the multiplicity of natural objects in any other wise than that, *e.g.*, in which the principle of life in an organism is related to its bodily members. Though this principle of unity may be termed 'God', it is God only in the sense in which that term is compatible with Pantheism, or a God still imperfectly distinguished from nature. The Greek, in other words, in becoming a monotheist did not necessarily thereby cease to be a pagan; and

[11] The possibility of syllogistic inference in especial depends upon the systematic interrelation of species.

Pantheism is no less incompatible than polytheism with the attribution of reality to sensible particulars.

(ii) There are Greek theological doctrines which transcend the limitations of Paganism. I shall content myself here with considering two of these, with pointing out in what respects they differ from the doctrine of God as Creator, and with trying to show that it is precisely in virtue of these points of difference that they are enabled to remain compatible with the Greek theory of nature, especially in the two crucial regards which I have mentioned.

The first of these is Aristotle's conception of God as First Mover. It is not without significance for my thesis that Aristotle's proof of the existence of a transcendent God is based upon the necessity of accounting for the communication of motion by efficient causes in nature; in other words, that he approaches most nearly to the Christian doctrine of God at the very point at which his conception of nature approximates most closely to that of modern physics. But Aristotle's God, though admitted to be transcendent, is bereft of any power over nature except the single power of originating motion. Neither the matter nor the form of natural objects depends on him; and even of motion in nature he is not himself the efficient but only the final cause. He is not the source of energy in nature; that must be held to arise within nature from the active potency of the form to realise itself; but is only the end upon which all energy in nature is directed. The only activity of which God is the source is his own theoretical activity; and this activity terminates not upon the world but upon himself.

It may well be questioned whether Aristotle's restriction of God's operation upon the world is really consistent with his argument for God's transcendence; whether, in other words, that argument does not demand the conclusion that motion in nature has a source as well as an end outside nature. However this may be, it is certainly that restriction which enables Aristotle to retain essentially unmodified the conception of nature already outlined. Nature owes God nothing except that harmony of its operations one with another which they derive from their direction upon a single end; and which might in fact be as well accounted for by the Pantheistic hypothesis, that nature is animated by a single soul.

The attribution to God of an activity of will sweeps away this restriction, and with it the possibility of maintaining the Pagan conception of nature as self-dependent.

(iii) There is one Greek doctrine of God which ascribes to him a power of efficient causation in the constitution of the actual world. This is Plato's doctrine of the Demiurge or Artificer, and because this, of all Greek theological doctrines, bears the closest superficial resemblance to the Christian doctrine of Creation it will serve best to throw into relief the essential contrast which still persists between the conception of God as Creator and any conception of the divine activity which is consistent with the presuppositions of Greek natural science. The doctrine that God is a Demiurge is perfectly consistent with them, because the activity of a Demiurge (the activity which the Greeks called Techne) is essentially both (i) *informative* and (ii) *purposive,* that is to say, it is (i) confined to the information of a given matter, and (ii) directed by the antecedent conception of an end. The activity consists in the realisation in matter of the end, which becomes by realisation the form or essence of the object produced, but since the form must be conceived by the workman *before* he starts his work it cannot derive its being, but only its embodiment, from his activity. The form must be "given" to the Demiurge no less than the matter of his work; thus, if God is Demiurge of the actual world, his work is confined to the uniting of its two elements, form and matter, but cannot extend to the bringing into being of either element.

The ascription to God of the activity of a Demiurge is thus compatible with the fundamental assumption of Greek natural science, that form and matter are eternal. We may, indeed, see more vividly what is involved in this assumption if we reflect that to make it is to attribute to natural objects *a constitution identical with that of the products of a Techne.* Plato in the Timæus may be unique in asserting that the natural world is the product of a Demiurge; but Aristotle asserts,[12] and all the methods of Aristotelian science presuppose, that natural objects *are as though they were* the work of a Demiurge.

We may illustrate the connection between this presupposition and those methods by an analogy. Any product of one of the useful arts is clearly and indisputably the work of an artificer. If we

[12] *Cf. Physics,* II, 8, 199*a,* 12. *εἰ οἰκία τῶν φύσει γιγνομένων ἦν, οὕτως ἄν ἐγίνετο ὡς νῦν ἀπὸ τέχνης · εἰ δε τὰ φύσει μὴ μόνον φύσει ἀλλὰ καὶ τέχνῃ γίγνοιτο, ὡσαύτως ἂν γίνοιτο ᾗ πέφυκεν,* and *ib.* 6, 30. Natural objects differ from products of art according to Aristotle only in the one respect, not relevant to the present issue, that they have their principle of action within them.

imagine an investigator (say an archæologist who has uncovered the remains of an unknown civilisation) confronted with a collection of unfamiliar artefacts, it will be possible for him, provided only that he knows them to be artefacts, to institute an enquiry into them by an application of the very methods which Aristotle thought proper to a study of nature.

His first task will be to determine what the different objects are, or to define them; the initial assumption that they are products of an artificer involves the consequence that they are capable of definition. His method of determination will be that of intuitive, not of empirical induction, and what he determines will be the real, not the nominal essence of the objects. He will collect the greatest possible variety of examples of each kind, and will observe their sensible qualities, but his procedure will not be that of the empirical scientist as Locke, *e.g.*, describes it in his doctrine of Abstraction. He will not tabulate the sensible qualities which all his examples have in common, assign a general name to such a complex of qualities, and determine to call by that name in future every object which shall be found to possess all of them. On the contrary, he will use his variety of sensible examples as the geometrician may use a variety of drawn figures, strictly as illustrations, and to facilitate his passage by an act of intuitive reason to a comprehension of something which is not itself sensible at all, but is the reason (λόγος) of the object.[13] What is comprehended will be at once the end which governed the design of the artificer, and at the same time the form of the product (since it is clearly that in the product which the artificer added to his materials, *i.e.*, is that element in it which is to be distinguished from the material). It will be the real essence, because the end conceived by the artificer will in fact have caused the product to possess the qualities (its peculiar spatial configuration, *e.g.*), which it is found to have; and hence discovery of the essence will enable the investigator to understand the reason of what he had previously only observed to be a fact.[14]

13 "We found cuttings in the rocks which puzzled us for a long time, till I, who had seen the same in Syria, discovered that they were winepresses" (*Letters of Gertrude Bell*, I, p. 240). This discovery was not a detection by any of the senses of a sensible quality which had hitherto eluded them; what is discovered could not have been rendered *visible* by any microscope.

14 Of a jug, *e.g.*, the experience of his senses can inform him that it has a flat base and a projecting lip; but only a discovery of its purpose can enable him to understand why it has.

The essence once defined can serve as the ground of demonstration of essential properties; if an object is to serve a given purpose, it must possess such properties as are evidently indispensable to its fulfilment.

Definition of the essence makes possible its subsumption under a genus and its differentiation into subordinate species by the method of Division: a method differing from that of empirical classification in that it proceeds *a priori* by an insight into the essential nature of a thing, not *a posteriori* by comparison of similar sensible qualities.[15]

That properties should be demonstrable *a priori* of the essence and that species should be subsumable *a priori* under genera, these are the two conditions necessary for the possibility of a Syllogistic inference which should be free from the fallacy of *Petitio Principii.* The investigator we have imagined could make a fruitful use of the syllogism in constructing a science of his manufactured articles.

In a word: their susceptibility of definition makes it possible to apply to manufactured articles all the other Aristotelian methods. The science of nature would conform similarly to the canons of Aristotelian Logic *if nature were the work of a Demiurge.*

For an object to be definable, two conditions must be satisfied: (i) its form must be intelligible, and (ii) its form must be its real essence. Both conditions are satisfied by the products of a Techne, and the possibility of an Aristotelian science of nature depends upon the assumption that both conditions are fulfilled by natural objects.

But the doctrine that nature is created involves the denial that natural objects can satisfy either condition.

(i) That the form of an object is intelligible, means that it is distinguishable in conception from the sensible material of its embodiment. The form of an artefact is thus distinguishable, because the activity of the Demiurge who made it was purposive, that is to say, was directed by conception of an end. What he conceived as

[15] Thus the unknown artefacts of our illustration could be classified empirically in any of a variety of ways according to similarity of sensible characteristics (colour, *e.g.*, texture or surface or size) by one who did not know their purpose; or even if they had had none. But the discovery of the one true system of genera and species, according to which a given object is to be classed, *e.g.*, as a kind of lamp, and not as a species co-ordinate with the sauce-dishes which it resembles in appearance: this presupposes knowledge of the purpose of the objects and is achieved by methods different from those of empirical classification.

end, we distinguish as form; and we are enabled to conceive in distinction from sensible accidents precisely so much as he conceived in advance of his execution.

But the work of creation is not purposive; and as there is no end distinctly conceived by the creator in advance of his execution, so there is no form distinguishable by us from the accidents of its embodiment. This may be most easily seen in the contrast of fine or creative art with the activity of a Demiurge or artificer. It is notorious that the creative artist, *e.g.*, the painter, has no clear knowledge of what he is going to achieve before he has achieved it; and the critic on his side, when confronted with a work of creative art, is indeed aware that there is 'something more' in it than the sensible material—a great painting is more than a certain complexity of coloured surfaces—but this 'something more' (we may call it loosely 'the meaning') is *not* capable of being conceived in distinction from the sensible material in which it is expressed. The meaning of a painting is not intelligible in the sense in which the purpose of a wheelbarrow is.

The form of natural objects would be distinguishable (and the objects therefore definable) only if the activity of God were purposive, *i.e.*, directed upon an end which is not itself the product of his activity. But if God is a Creator, natural objects can have no form distinguishable as the object of the intellect.

(ii) The doctrine of Creation attributes to God an autonomous activity of will. No doubt it is also implied in the conception of God as a Demiurge that he is the subject of some practical action. His work is not exhausted according to this doctrine in the theoretical contemplation of the forms, but he engages beyond that contemplation in the non-theoretical activity of embodying them. But it is characteristic of the work of a Demiurge that in it the practical is wholly subordinated to the theoretical activity. The entire activity of the craftsman, in so far as he is a craftsman, is dictated by the end or plan which is the object of his theoretical conception. No doubt the will of any human artificer may escape from this dictation by his reason; he may add details to his work which are not necessitated by the dictates of his craft (if he is a bad workman) or are even contrary to them (if he is a corrupt one). But this insubordination of will is a mere defect and simple failure to achieve the perfection of an artificer.

That in an artificial object which is not necessitated by its idea is the *contingent*, and just as the insubordination of will is nothing but an imperfection in the artificer, so the presence of the contingent is nothing but a defect in the artefact.

Bad workmanship is not the only cause of contingency in the product. This may arise also from recalcitrance of the material; and since bad workmanship cannot be argued in the divine Demiurge, contingency in the natural world must be attributed to this source. Natural objects are contingent, *i.e.*, they fail to conform to their idea, precisely in so far as they are material.

Now if natural objects either are artefacts (according to the theory of the divine Demiurge) or are (according to the Aristotelian theory) in this respect analogous to artefacts that they *are* nothing but an embodiment of form, then the unavoidable element of contingency which they derive from their matter is nothing but a defect of their being. It does not make them something more than an embodiment of form, but makes them only a bad embodiment of form; just as two inches more on one leg of a table does not make it more than an artefact, but only a bad artefact.

Objects are intelligible in so far as they are informed, sensible in so far as they are material. The contingent, therefore, or that in them which is not derived from their form, is sensible only, without being intelligible. But since the contingent has been found to represent only a defect of being, it will follow that natural objects are sensible only in so far as they fail to achieve their being. That in them which constitutes them objects of sensation is no increment, but only a defect of their intelligible nature; and therefore sensation can contribute no evidence concerning the nature of the thing which should be additional to what is perceived by reason. As the being material is a defect and not an increment of being, sensation is an imperfection of knowledge,[16] not a way of knowing.

The absence of an empirical element in Greek natural science follows from this.

But the will of the maker can be subordinated to his reason, as the will of the Demiurge is, only so long as "making" is identified with formation, because form alone can be the object of reason. In the creative act the will must exceed any regulations which reason can prescribe. That is to say, the 'insubordination' of will to reason, which could be only a defect in God so long as God is conceived as Demiurge, becomes essential to his activity so soon as he is thought

[16] It is at the very most the *occasion* of knowledge.

of as Creator. It is what constitutes him, not a bad Demiurge, but something altogether more than a Demiurge.

The *voluntary* activity of the Creator (*i.e.*, that in his activity which exceeds determination by reason) terminates on the *contingent* being of the creature (*i.e.*, on that element of its being which eludes determination by form, namely its matter and the characteristics which it possesses *quâ* material). If such voluntary activity is essential to God, it follows that the element of contingency is essential to what he creates. So soon as nature is conceived to be created by God, the contingent becomes more than an imperfection in the embodiment of form; it is precisely what constitutes a natural object more than an embodiment, namely a creature.[17]

But the contingent is knowable only by sensuous experience. If, therefore, the contingent is essential to nature, experience must be indispensable to the science of nature; and *not* indispensable merely as a stage through which the human scientist must pass on his way to attaining adequate knowledge by reason, but indispensable because knowledge by reason cannot be adequate to a nature which is essentially something more than an embodiment of form. This 'something more', the element in nature which depends upon the *voluntary* activity of God, is incapable of becoming an object to reason, and science therefore must depend, in regard to this element, upon the *evidence* of sensation. The reliance upon the senses for evidence, not merely for illustration, is what constitutes the empirical character peculiar to modern natural science; and the conclusion follows that only a created nature is proper object of an empirical science.

[17] I suggest that we use the term "real" to attribute to a thing the being which is proper to a created object. Its meaning differs from that of the Greek ὄν precisely as created from uncreated being. That is why, for instance, reality is incapable of degrees, whereas οὐσία was capable of an indefinite number of them. What is created *ex nihilo* must be entirely present so soon as it has ceased to be wholly absent; but an object of which it is the whole being to be an embodiment of form, achieves a greater or less degree of being according to the degree of perfection with which form is realised in it. It is not without significance that the term 'real' in its modern sense passed into secular language only after the Reformation (see *O.E.D.*), *i.e.*, at the period at which the concepts of Christianity began to revolutionise the sciences of nature.

Again, the terms 'nature' and 'natural' bear a different meaning from the Greek terms φύσις and φύσει. The difference is simply that we mean by nature '*created* nature', and call 'natural' what is proper to a created nature. We are generally conscious of the difference, but oblivious of its source.

What we have attempted to show is that the method of natural science depends upon the presuppositions which are held about nature, and the presuppositions about nature in turn upon the doctrine of God. Modern natural science could begin only when the modern presuppositions about nature displaced the Greek (this was, of course, a gradual process, but its crisis occurred at the date of the Reformation); but this displacement itself was possible only when the Christian [18] conception of God had displaced the Pagan, as the object (not merely of unreasoning belief, but) of systematic understanding. To achieve this primary displacement was the work of Medieval Theology, which thus laid the foundations both of much else in the modern world which is specifically modern, and of modern natural science.

Creative activity in God, material substance in nature, empirical methods in natural science—how closely each of these three involves the other is made clear by an examination of almost any of the great philosophies of the early modern period. A defect in the philosophical conception of God is reflected in corresponding defects both in the doctrine of nature and in the theory of natural science. Thus it is a mark of the philosophy of the Rationalist tradition that it is unable wholly [19] to digest that un-Greek element in

[18] I mean Christian, not Jewish. The Christian doctrine of God derived much from the Greek and thus included within itself, besides much from Jewish sources, much also from the very doctrine which it displaced. *Cf.* p. 468 *inf.*

[19] The qualification is to be emphasised. Modern Rationalism differs markedly from Greek Rationalism in its theories of God, nature and science, and the differences are due, as I have illustrated above, by the example of Final Causation, to its absorption of the truth of Christian doctrine. What I am maintaining here is that this absorption was still incomplete.

I must stress the fact that the limitation of the scope of this essay precludes me from doing justice to the philosophy of modern Rationalism. I have confined myself in the main to a single characteristic (the presence of an empirical element) by which modern differs from ancient natural science, and I have endeavoured to show its connection with a single Christian doctrine (that of the Creation). It is the essence of the *Empiricist* philosophy of nature to stress that element of natural objects which exceeds the grasp of the intellect, and it is easy therefore to give the impression that Empiricism alone is adequate either to exhaust the truth of Christian doctrine, or to supply the pre-suppositions of modern natural science; while modern Rationalism succeeds in doing either, if at all, only in so far as it has absorbed some of the truth of Empiricism. But modern differs from ancient natural science in other respects besides the part played in it by experience, and Christianity has other doctrines relevant to a philosophy of nature, besides that of Creation. My argument does not exclude the Christian theology according to which God is endowed with a *voluntary* activity in the creation of the world. Descartes' 'clear and distinct idea' of God is the idea of an infinite *thinking* substance, and although the influence of Christian dogma is strong enough in many places to modify his language, so that, having proved the existence of God, he proceeds to attribute to him activities other than theoretical, what constitutes him Rationalist is precisely that this attribution is not more than verbal. Christian dogma works in him strongly enough to modify his language, but not strongly enough to transform his thought. The God of which he has *demonstrated* the existence is a God whose whole essence is to think. His Rationalist doctrine of nature corresponds with his Rationalist doctrine of God: as he cannot conceive a voluntary activity in God, so he cannot conceive the reality of a contingent element in nature,[20] and his identification of matter with extension is the inevitable consequence of his identification of the divine activity with thought. Spinoza carried the Rationalism of Descartes to its logical conclusion. He explicitly denied those elements both in the activity of God and in the being of nature, which Descartes had failed to conceive clearly, but which [21] the influence of Christian dogma had been powerful enough to prevent him from denying. It is obvious that the Rationalist doctrine of nature is incompatible in its turn with the presuppositions of empirical science. If the contingent in nature is condemned to the status of appearance, sensation can make no positive contribution to knowledge; and the only natural science possible upon the presuppositions of Spinoza's philosophy would be a science which should be, like Spinoza's 'Ethics', *more geometrico demonstrata.*

The Rationalist philosophy of nature had to be corrected if it was to be rendered consistent with the possibility of an empirical natural science. From what source could the correction come? The time had not yet arrived when it was possible to argue back from the existence of a body of natural science to the nature which it presupposed as its object. Neither could direct inspection of the natural

either the possibility that modern Rationalism does justice to some features of modern natural science which Empiricism ignores or even that it has absorbed the truth of some Christian doctrines which Empiricism has neglected.

[20] *Cf. e.g., Princ.*, II, viii: "That quantity and number differ only in thought (*ratione*) from that which has quantity and is numbered."

[21] At least the former of which.

world afford evidence either to support or to disprove any theory of its metaphysical constitution. There was no standard by which the Rationalist doctrine of nature could be corrected, there was a standard only for the correction of the Rationalist doctrine of God. That had to be remoulded so as to conform to the Christian doctrine that God is Creator, and this remoulding carried with it as an implicit consequence such a modification of the theory of nature as would have rendered it consistent with the presuppositions of empirical science.[22]

It may serve to obviate a misunderstanding, to which I have perhaps laid myself open, if I conclude with a remark on the philosophies of modern Empiricism. Berkeley, to take the example most apt to my purpose, stresses the share of sense in knowledge even to the denial of any share to reason, and he stresses the practical activity of God to such an extent that he would be forced, if he were consistent with himself, to deny to God any but a practical activity.[23] Must it

[22] The essential connection which subsists between the doctrine that God has will on the one hand, and that a science of nature must be empirical on the other, may be illustrated clearly by a reference to the Leibnizian distinction between the possible and the actual. Possible is whatever is object of God's understanding and of our 'clear and distinct' (*i.e.*, intellectual, non-empirical) perception. The addition of existence to the possible Leibniz attributes to an activity distinguished from God's understanding as God's will. Existence is not intelligible; and since it is involved in the doctrine of God's will that existence is an addition to, not a diminution of, the being which belongs to the possible, the consequence cannot be avoided that intelligence is *inadequate* by itself to the knowledge of existent nature, and requires to be supplemented by sensation: *i.e.*, that an empirical element is necessary to natural science.

Conversely the rationalist doctrine that sense is only defect of understanding may be seen to be incompatible with the attribution of will to God. According to this doctrine the sensible *is* the intelligible imperfectly known; *i.e.*, it derives its sensible character from the imperfection of human perception, and therefore not from an activity of God.

Leibniz maintains a rationalist epistemology side by side with a voluntarist theology, in spite of their mutual incompatibility. Nothing short of the authority of Christianity could have prevailed upon him to admit the latter doctrine into his philosophy in the teeth of the opposition of the former. If he had but attached yet more weight to this authority, it would have led him to reform his rationalist presuppositions into consistency with his theology, and *thereby* into consistency with the procedure of empirical science.

[23] This implication of Berkeley's philosophy is clearly brought out in Mr. J. D. Mabbott's admirable article "The Place of God in Berkeley's Philosophy", in the *Journal of Philosophical Studies*, January, 1931.

not then be admitted, I imagine the objection, that Berkeley's philosophy has *wholly* assimilated the truth of the doctrine of Creation? And yet Berkeley's philosophy is incompatible with the belief in a material substance, and signally fails to justify the presuppositions of the modern science of nature. How is this to be reconciled with the thesis of an intimate connection between the doctrine of creation and the presuppositions of empirical science?

This supposed objection rests upon the mistaken identification of the Christian doctrine of Creation with the un-Greek element in the Christian doctrine. The failure of modern Rationalism was its failure to do justice to this un-Greek element, the failure of modern Empiricism was its failure to do justice to anything else. The Christian doctrine on this, as on all other subjects, itself includes an element derived from Greek philosophy, and any doctrine from which all Greek elements are excluded is less than Christian. It is Christian to ascribe to God an activity of will, but it is not Christian to deny to God a theoretical activity or to ascribe to him a *blind* activity of will. It is a consequence of the Christian doctrine of Creation that the created world must contain an element of contingency, not that it must be nothing but contingent. It was because he drew this latter consequence, and was unable to attribute to matter the possession of any intelligible (as opposed to sensible) qualities that Berkeley was led to his denial of material substance, and to the conclusion, implicit in his philosophy if not admitted by himself, that a science of nature is not possible. Thus Berkeley falls short equally with Spinoza of expressing in his philosophy the whole of what is contained in the Christian doctrine of God. Spinoza had denied voluntary activity to God, Berkeley denies everything but voluntary activity. Similarly in their doctrines of nature, whereas Spinoza had denied contingency, Berkeley denies everything else; Spinoza's world is a nature, but is not created, Berkeley's is created but is not a nature, and so both are compelled, though for opposite reasons, to deny material substances, which can exist only in a

It is significant that Berkeley, like Descartes, is preserved from a consistency of error principally by the necessity of conforming to Christian doctrine in his theory of God. He does not shrink from the consequence that the science of mathematical physics is impossible, nor from outraging Common Sense by his denial of material substance, but he cannot allow himself to rest in the conclusion that the divine activity is one of blind will.

created nature. This denial necessitates finally that both fail equally, again in opposite respects, of consistency with the presuppositions of modern natural science. Of Spinoza's world no science could be empirical, of Berkeley's no experience scientific.

CHAPTER 3

Christian Theology and the Newtonian Science: The Rise of the Concept of the Laws of Nature

FRANCIS OAKLEY

R. G. Collingwood has suggested that the basic contrast between the Greek view of nature and what he calls the *Renaissance* view, springs from the difference between their respective analogical approaches to nature.[1] Whereas, he argues, the Greek view of nature as an intelligent organism was based on an analogy between the world of nature and the individual human being, the *Renaissance* view conceived the world analogically as a machine. Instead of being regarded as capable of ordering its own movements in a rational manner, and, it might be added, according to its immanent laws, the world, to such a view, is devoid both of intelligence and life, the movements which it exhibits are imposed from without, and "their regularity . . . due to 'laws of nature' likewise imposed from without."[2] Collingwood concludes, therefore, that this view presupposed both the human experience of designing and constructing

From *Church History,* Vol. XXX, 4, December, 1961. Reprinted by permission of the publishers.

[1] *Idea of Nature* (Oxford, 1945), pp. 3–9. As Collingwood himself admits (p. 4), "the name is not a good one, because the word 'Renaissance' is applied to an earlier phase in the history of thought. . . . The cosmology I have now to describe . . . might, perhaps, be more accurately called post-Renaissance."

[2] *Ibid.*, p. 5.

machines, and the Christian idea of a creative and omnipotent God.

This is, I believe, a good way of characterizing the change in philosophical approach which made possible the development of the classical or Newtonian physical science. It is, no doubt, an historical commonplace that this change in approach entailed the rejection of the Aristotelian qualitative physics, with its apparatus of final causes and ultimate explanations of nature, and its replacement by a natural science preoccupied with quantity, efficient causes, and power over nature. But Collingwood does well to remind us of the intimate relationship between this change in approach and the rise to prominence of the concept of imposed laws of nature. For if it is difficult to locate precisely the ultimate source of this important concept (as also of the cognate juridical concept of the natural law, for both of them have their roots deep in classical and Semitic antiquity),[3] historians are generally agreed that in the course of the seventeenth century the idea of the laws of nature sprang from comparative obscurity into a lasting prominence. The crucial figures in the establishment of this prominence seem to have been Descartes—perhaps the first of the important scientific thinkers to have been quite explicit on the matter,[4] Robert Boyle (1627–91), who has been described as "the most influential publicist of the mechanical philosophy in England," [5] and Newton, whose writings assured it a prominent place in the scientific language and thought of the West. The question has been raised, therefore, as to why, after centuries of theological currency, this concept attained during the course of the seventeenth century a position of such importance in the physical sciences. Only two monographs have, in the past, been addressed to this problem. The first of these was written in 1942 by

[3] Scrutiny of the *Oxford English Dictionary* s.v. *Law* reveals two primary current meanings for the expression *natural law*. It is defined, on the one hand, as that law, prescribed by no enactment or formal compact, which is implanted by nature in the human mind, or is capable of being demonstrated by reason. On the other it is defined as referring, in "the sciences of observation," to the theoretical principles deduced from particular facts, applicable to defined groups or classes of phenomena, and expressible by the statement that particular phenomena always occur if certain conditions are present. For purposes of clarity I propose to use the term *natural law* to refer to the juristic concept, and the term *laws of nature* to indicate the scientific usage.

[4] See *Discours de la Méthode, Cinquième Partie.—Oeuvres de Descartes,* ed. Jules Simon (Paris, 1841), pp. 26–27.

[5] Richard S. Westfall, *Science and Religion in Seventeenth Century England* (New Haven, 1958), p. 73.

Edgar Zilsel[6] (who was also the first, to my knowledge, to formulate the problem), and the second, in 1950, by Joseph Needham,[7] who was, however, primarily concerned with explaining the absence of a parallel concept in Chinese thought. Both Zilsel and Needham suggest a solution based on arguments drawn from historical changes in the structure of society, but neither of them can fully resolve the manifest difficulties which such arguments themselves entail. In the pages which follow, therefore, it will be my purpose, in the first place, to take a look at this solution and at its attendant difficulties; secondly, to propose a very different but, I believe, less unsatisfactory solution to the problem; and, finally, briefly to assess the significance of this new solution.

I

Zilsel is careful to insist that our problem cannot be regarded as being identical with the whole vast problem of the rise of the modern experimental science, for, as he correctly points out (p. 276), it did not necessarily follow that the mechanical regularities detected in nature should eventually be interpreted as divine laws. The fact that they were so interpreted was, in his opinion, the outcome of concomitant social developments.

He starts out with the assumption that the idea of the reign of God over the world resulted from "a comparison of nature and state," from a transfer into the divine realm of men's conceptions of earthly kings and their reigns, and to this he adds the related assumption that the Stoic doctrine of the universal natural law is correlated with the rise of the great monarchies after Alexander the Great. This being granted, it seems equally reasonable to relate the rise of the concept of the laws of nature in the sixteenth and seventeenth centuries to the decline of feudalism, the beginnings of capitalism, and the appearance of royal absolutism. Thus "it is no mere

[6] "The Genesis of the Concept of Physical Law" *The Philosophical Review,* LI (1942), pp. 245–79.

[7] The L. T. Hobhouse Memorial Trust Lecture, No. 20, delivered on 23 May, 1950 at Bedford College, London, and published under the title: *Human Law and the Laws of Nature in China and the West* (London, 1951). An expanded version bearing the same title is to be found in the *Journal of the History of Ideas,* XII (1951), pp. 3 ff., and 194 ff., and also as Section 18 of Joseph Needham and Wang Ling, *Science and Civilization in China,* II (Cambridge, 1956), pp. 518–583—to which book my references will be given.

chance that the Cartesian idea of God as the legislator of the universe developed only forty years after Jean Bodin's theory of sovereignty." [8]

This explanation—which Needham believes "must surely be in principle the right one" [9]—entails, however, manifest difficulties. Even if the dubious verifiability of the initial assumption is allowed to go unquestioned (and it should not), two formidable objections may be raised. In the first place, such an hypothesis, as Needham perforce admits, "brings us face to face with the paradox that in China, where 'imperial absolutism' covered an even longer period" than in the West, we hardly meet at all with the idea of the laws of nature.[10] And, in the second place, it is predicated upon a failure to distinguish between the disparate metaphysical assumptions underlying the Stoic and related views of the natural law on the one hand, and the seventeenth century concept of the laws of nature on the other, assumptions basic to the philosophic traditions from which these sprang. The distinction in question may be said to be vital to the solution of our problem and it merits close attention. It was most clearly drawn by A. N. Whitehead who, in his *Adventures of Ideas*,[11] pointed out the crucial contrast between laws of nature conceived as imposed upon the universe and natural law perceived as immanent in the structure of reality itself. Whitehead was, it is true, concerned with analyzing cosmological assumptions, but the doctrine is as valid and relevant in the juridical and ethical sphere as it is in the scientific.[12]

The theory of law as immanent, he argues, involves the assumption that things are interdependent in such a way that when we know the nature of things we also know their mutual relations with one another. "Some partial identity of pattern in the various characters of natural things issues in some partial identity of pattern in the mutual relations of these things." [13] The laws of nature are the formulation of these identities of pattern. Thus it could be adduced as a law of nature that animals unite to produce offspring, or that

[8] "The Genesis of the Concept of Physical Law," pp. 277–279.
[9] *Science and Civilization*, II, p. 542.
[10] *Ibid.*, p. 543.
[11] *Adventures of Ideas* (New York, 1937), pp. 142–147.
[12] For an interesting attempt to apply the distinction to the juridical sphere see M. Ginsberg, "The Concept of Juridical and Scientific Law," *Politica*, IV, No. 15 (March, 1939), pp. 1 ff.
[13] *Adventures of Ideas*, p. 142.

stones released in mid-air strive to reach the ground. This view of the laws of nature involves, he concludes, "some doctrine of Internal Relations," some notion that the characters of things are the outcome of their interconnections, and the interconnections of things the outcome of their characters.[14]

The doctrine of imposed law, on the other hand, adopts the alternative metaphysical theory of external relations. Individual existents are regarded as the ultimate constituents of nature, and these ultimate constituents are conceived to possess no inherent connections one with another, but to be comprehensible each in complete isolation from the rest. The relations into which they enter are imposed on them from without, and these imposed behavior patterns are the laws of nature. It follows, therefore, that these laws cannot be discovered by a scrutiny of the characters of the related things, nor, conversely, can the nature of the related things be deduced from the laws governing their relations.

With this distinction clearly in mind it would be revealing to glance back at the ideas of natural law and laws of nature current in the long centuries before the Scientific Revolution. Immanent law would be found to be typified by Stoic—perhaps even generally by Greek views. These conceived the material world to be impregnated with reason, and regarded natural law as universally valid and inherent in the very structure of things—so much so, indeed, that the Stoics could regard it as including not only the universal practice of men, in all times and in every country, but also the movements of the heavenly bodies and the habits of animals.[15] Imposed law, on the other hand, would find its best illustration in Semitic, and, in particular, in Jewish monotheism. For the God of the Old Testament gave to Moses the Ten Commandments and "to the sea his law, that the waters should not pass his commandment." [16] And the two views would be found united in the Christian view, which was, according to Whitehead, "a compromise between the immanence of law and imposed law due to the Platonism of Christianity" [17]—a statement which is certainly true, to a very considerable degree, of

[14] *Ibid.*, p. 144.
[15] This pantheistic Stoic view is fundamental to the statements about natural law which are to be found in the *Corpus Juris Civilis*—see *Inst.*, I, 2, 11; *Dig.*, I, 1, 1, § 3; I, 1, 2.
[16] Prov. viii, 29.
[17] *Adventures of Ideas,* p. 133.

medieval thought. In this, as in so many other matters, it reflects an amalgamation of Semitic and Hellenic elements. This somewhat uneasy compromise is evident in Aquinas. His God is, admittedly, a Christian God, omnipotent and transcendent, but his eternal law, which orders to their appointed ends all created things, irrational as well as rational, is undoubtedly immanent in the universe.[18] Thus although God is not thought of as being wholly immanent in the world, it should be noted that the eternal law finds its ultimate foundation in the intellect, and, therefore, in the very Being of God, so that Aquinas can at one point say that the eternal law is nothing other than God.[19]

This quasi-immanent view of natural law continued to flourish in the seventeenth century, finding clear if modified expression in the mature position of Grotius,[20] but it did not recommend itself to the scientific *virtuosi*. Collingwood, it may be remembered, was careful to describe the "laws of nature" to which the *virtuosi* attributed the regularity of the movements of the universe, as having been "imposed" upon the universe "from without" by an omnipotent Creator —God.[21] Thus Descartes could speak not of a natural law immanent in the structure of the universe, but of "the laws which God . . . put into nature," [22] and if Newton himself was not quite as explicit, it was, no doubt, because he felt it too obvious a point to mention.[23] In the very first sentence of his Preface to the *Mathematical Principles of Natural Philosophy* he tells us that the modern

[18] And in so far as it concerns man and is apprehended by his reason, the eternal law is called the *natural law*—*Summa Theologia*, Ia 2ae, qu. 94, art. 2 *Resp.*
[19] *S.T.*, Ia 2ae, qu. 91, art. 1 *ad tertium.*
[20] Thus he can argue that God himself "cannot make that which is intrinsically bad, not be bad." For "as the essence of things . . . by which they exist, does not depend on anything else, so also it is with the properties which necessarily follow that essence; and such a property is the evil of certain acts, when compared with the nature of a reasonable being. And therefore God himself allows himself to be judged according to this norm."—*De Jure Belli et Pacis*, Bk. I, ch. 1, §X, 5; ed. William Whewell (Cambridge, 1853), p. 12. It should be noted, however, that in his earlier *De Jure Praedae, Commentarius*—ed. H. G. Hamaker (The Hague, 1868)—he had taken as his point of departure the principle that the divine *will* is the basis of natural law (see ch. 2, pp. 7–9). This work was written in the winter of 1604–5 but rediscovered only in 1864 and first published in 1868.
[21] *Idea of Nature*, p. 5.
[22] *Cf. supra*, n. 4.
[23] He definitely believed, as Whitehead puts it, "that the correlated modes of behaviour of the bodies forming the solar system required God for the imposi-

investigators of nature, "omitting the substantial forms and the occult qualities [of the ancients], have undertaken to explain the phenomena of nature by mathematical laws." [24] And there can be no question of these laws being intrinsic to the nature of things. No amount of study of bodies at rest will tell us anything about their possible motion, for motion is not the outcome of some "occult quality," or the realizing of some hidden potentiality, but merely the effect of "forces impressed." [25] Newton himself, therefore, can tell us in the *Optics* that God could "*vary the laws of nature,* and make worlds of several sorts in several parts of the universe," [26] and Roger Cotes in his Preface to the second edition of the *Principles* (which he wrote presumably with Newton's approval) is quite clear about the imposed character of the laws of nature. "The true business of natural philosophy," he tells us,

> is . . . to inquire after those laws on which the Great Creator actually chose to found this most beautiful Frame of the World, not those by which he might have done the same, had he pleased. . . . Without all doubt this world . . . could arise from nothing but the perfectly free Will of God directing and presiding over all. From this Fountain it is that those laws, which we call the laws of Nature, have flowed, in which there appear many traces indeed of the most wise contrivance but not the least shadow of necessity.[27]

There is clearly, then, a sharp dichotomy between Stoic and related views of the natural law as immanent in the world, and the view, characteristic of the seventeenth century *virtuosi,* that the laws of nature were imposed upon the world from the outside by the decree of the omnipotent God who created it. And the failure both of Zilsel and of Needham to perceive this cleavage does much to vitiate the solution which they give to the problem they raise. For,

tion of the principles upon which all depended."—*Adventures of Ideas,* p. 144. And thus, in his first letter to Bentley, Newton could write that "the motions which the planets now have, could not spring from any natural cause alone, but were impressed by an intelligent agent."—*Opera quae exstant omnia,* ed. Samuel Horsley, IV (London, 1782), p. 431.

[24] *Philosophiae Naturalis Principia Mathematica,* Praefatio; *Opera Omnia,* II, p. ix.

[25] See *Principia,* Axiomata, Lex I; *Opera Omnia,* II, p. 13; *Principia,* Bk. 3, Schol. Gen.; *Opera Omnia,* III, p. 174.

[26] *Opera Omnia,* IV, p. 263.

[27] *Opera Omnia,* II, pp. xx and xxiii; the translation cited is that of Andrew Motte, revised by Florian Cajori (Berkeley, 1946), pp. xxvii and xxxii.

once this distinction is made, Zilsel's ascription of the rise of Stoic ideas of natural law to the pervasive influence of a growing royal absolutism ceases to be obvious.[28] Similarly, it becomes necessary for him to offer some explanation for the fact that Grotius, living in an age of growing royal absolutism, rejected the complementary view of natural law as imposed by a divine sovereign, in order to embrace the more traditional but less easily reconcilable theory. But what is in fact required is a redefinition of the very problem itself. Needham asked "why, after so many centuries as a theological commonplace in European civilization, the idea of the laws of nature attained a position of such importance in the sixteenth and seventeenth centuries?" [29] But this question reveals a misunderstanding of the problem and one which, in effect, closes the way to its solution. For, as we have seen, it is important to realize that it was one particular theory—the theory of the *imposed* laws of nature which has "so much in common with Old Testament ideas"—which the works of the *virtuosi* (and especially of Newton) made a commonplace of scientific and popular thinking. In the light, therefore, of considerations such as these, I would suggest that the real problem is this: why, after so many centuries of almost total submersion in Greek ideas of immanent law, did the Semitic [30] concept of imposed laws of nature burst into prominence in seventeenth century scientific thought? It is this question that I propose to answer.

II

Even if it were possible to ignore the damaging imprecision with which Zilsel and Needham formulate the question, there would still be one simple but telling argument against the sociological approach which they adopt—that such an approach is unnecessary. For when Descartes spoke of God as putting laws into nature, it would seem more probable *a priori* that he was drawing on a theological rather than a political tradition. This probability is heightened by the fact that he was, after all, a devout Christian whose religion was so closely connected with his scientific thinking that

[28] As the Stoics conceived of natural law as immanent in the universe the idea of command could play no part in such a conception.

[29] *Science and Civilization in China*, II, p. 542.

[30] 'Semitic' rather than 'Judaic' because as Needham points out (p. 533) the idea was probably of Babylonian origin.

Robert Boyle could comment to the effect that atheism "would subvert the very foundation of those tenets of mechanical philosophy that are particularly his." [31]

In order, however, to identify this tradition, it is necessary, first of all, to resist the temptation which still endures among historians to speak of "*the* medieval view of things" or "*the* medieval view of the world." [32] Even if we forget about the uncertainties and ambiguities which persisted in the natural law thinking of the canon and civil lawyers of the Middle Ages and concentrate upon the theologians alone, we will find that their views about natural law were by no means uniform. Side by side with that *realist* view of quasi-immanent natural law so well expressed by Aquinas, there had developed, from the late thirteenth century onwards, a tradition which conceived law as imposed upon the world by the divine will.[33] This was the beginning of that fruitful stream of *voluntarist* natural law thinking, which, although it made its way with profound effect into the ethical, political and scientific thought of the modern world, has attracted less than its due share of attention from the historians of these subjects. The history of this tradition of thought remains, therefore, to be written, and the following outline is proffered as nothing more than a rough sketch.

The year 1277 may be suggested as the overt starting point of the new tradition. It was in that year that Etienne Tempier, Bishop of Paris, and Robert Kilwardby, Archbishop of Canterbury, formally condemned, as contrary to the Christian faith, a host of philosophical propositions, including some put forward by Aquinas.[34] Behind these condemnations lay the fear, widespread also among the more orthodox Arab and Jewish thinkers, that the metaphysical necessitarianism of Aristotle and his Arabic commentators, Avicenna

[31] *A Disquisition about the Final Causes of Natural Things. The Works of the Honourable Robert Boyle,* ed. Thomas Birch, V (London, 1772), p. 401.

[32] For an example see S. F. Mason, "Science and Religion in 17th Century England," *Past and Present,* No. 3 (1953), esp. pp. 28–30.

[33] For a comparison between the views of Aquinas and those of the followers of the voluntarist tradition, and for a discussion of the importance of this tradition in the *juridical* sphere, see Francis Oakley, "Medieval Theories of Natural Law: William of Ockham and the Significance of the Voluntarist Tradition," *Natural Law Forum,* VI (1961), pp. 65–83.

[34] See Étienne Gilson, *History of Christian Philosophy in the Middle Ages* (New York, 1955), pp. 405 ff.

(980–1037) and Averroës (1128–1198), endangered the freedom and omnipotence of the Semitic and Christian God. The honeymoon of philosophy and theology, as Gilson puts it, was over. The condemnations marked the formal beginning of the theological reaction that was to vindicate the freedom and omnipotence of God at the expense of the ultimate intelligibility of the world.[35] The compromise which had united a transcendent Semitic Creator-God with an intelligible Hellenistic world was abrogated, and with it any idea of natural law as immanent. For the quasi-immanentism characteristic of Aquinas' doctrine of natural law—a compromise position which, it will be remembered, Whitehead had ascribed to "the Platonism of Christianity"—did, in fact, involve the attempt to Christianize the Platonic doctrine of Eternal Forms or Ideas by locating them in the divine mind as exemplars in accordance with which God created the world and ruled it. And thus Aquinas could define the Eternal law as "nothing other than the idea of the divine wisdom in so far as it directs all acts and movements."[36]

This quasi-immanentism was hedged around with cautious qualifications, but the condemnations of 1277 made it clear that these qualifications had not been cautious enough. Subsequent theologians had to do their thinking in the full glare of this persuasive clarification, and it is not surprising that many of them tended to set God over against the world which he had created, and to regard the order of this world as deriving, not from the realization of the divine ideas, but rather from the peremptory mandate of an autonomous divine will. This reaction was already manifest in the primacy over

[35] This amounted to an abandonment of any attempt to reconcile the Greek conception of a necessarily existing universe, ruled by strict necessity, with the Biblical notion of a freely created world ruled by a free and omnipotent divine will. Arab thinkers had already faced the same problem and had adopted a comparable solution. Al Ash'ari (d. 936) and his followers vindicated the Semitic notion of God by adopting an atomistic view of the world as constituted of disjointed moments of time and points of space, connected together only by the will of God and possessing, therefore, no natural necessity. They held to this position so strictly that they were driven into a thorough-going occasionalism—see L. Gardet and M-M. Anawati, *Introduction à la théologie musilmane*, Etudes de phil. méd., XXXVII (Paris, 1948), pp. 52–66. This viewpoint was also adopted by early Jewish thinkers—see Ernest Renan, *Averroës et l'Averroisme* (Paris, 1861), p. 106, and Isaac Husik, *A History of Medieval Jewish Philosophy* (New York, 1958), p. xli.

[36] *S.T.*, Ia 2ae, qu. 93, art. 1 *Resp.*

the divine intellect which Duns Scotus (ca. 1270–1308) accorded to the divine will,[37] and it attained full stature in the ethical voluntarism of William of Ockham.

What Ockham did was to ground natural law, and, indeed, all ethical values, on the will of God. Natural law, therefore, ceased to be "a dictate of reason as to what is right grounded in the being of God but unalterable even by him," and became "a divine command . . . right and binding merely because God was the lawgiver."[38] Thus "evil is nothing other than the doing of something opposite to that which one is obliged to do."[39] Hate of God, adultery, robbery—all such vices—could be stripped of their evil and rendered meritorious "if they were to agree with the divine precept."[40] For "God is obliged to the causing of no act."[41] It is true that, of his ordained power (*potentia ordinata*), God condescends to work within the framework of the moral law which he has already established, and to which right reason is the infallible guide,[42] but of his absolute power (*potentia absoluta*), by which he can do anything that does not involve a manifest contradiction, he could abrogate that order entirely.[43] The dictates of natural law, the infallibility of right reason, the very fact that it is virtuous to act in accordance with right reason—all of these amount to nothing more than inscrutable manifestations of divine omnipotence.[44]

Such a theory of natural law falls, clearly enough, into Whitehead's category of *imposed law*. And this was the theory that was propagated by the followers of the *via moderna*, the nominalist philosophers who became so strong in the later Middle Ages, especially at Oxford and Paris. Notable among these were Pierre d'Ailly (1350–1420) and Jean Gerson (1363–1429), the renowned ecclesi-

[37] See C. R. S. Harris, *Duns Scotus*, II (Oxford, 1927), pp. 214–217.

[38] Otto von Gierke, *Political Theories of the Middle Ages*, trans. Maitland (Cambridge, 1927), p. 173, n. 256.

[39] *Super Quatuor Libros Sententiarum* (Lyons: Jean Trechsel, 1495), II, 5 H.

[40] *Sent.* II, 19 O.

[41] *Sent.* II, 19 P.

[42] *Sent.* I, dist. xli, qu. 1 K.

[43] *Opus Nonaginta Dierum* (Lyons: Jean Trechsel, 1495), ch. 95 (no foliation); see esp. § *Nota de duplici potentia dei.* Cf. *Quodlibeta Septem una cum tractatu de sacramento altaris* (Strasbourg, 1491), Quodl. VI, qu. 6; English translation of this question in Richard McKeon, *Selections from Medieval Philosophers*, II (New York, 1930), pp. 372–375.

[44] *Sent.* I, dist. xli, qu. I K. For a more complete analysis of Ockham's position see Oakley, "Medieval Theories of Natural Law," pp. 68–72.

astical statesmen and Chancellors of the University of Paris whose works were widely read in the fifteenth and sixteenth centuries.[45] And to their names may be added, among others, that of Robert Holcot (d. 1349),[46] as well as those of Gabriel Biel (d. 1495), Jacob Almain (d. 1515), John Major (d. 1540), and Alphonse de Castro (d. 1558). The Jesuit philosopher Suarez (1548–1617) cited all of them as supporters of the voluntarist theory and it should be noted that his own natural law thinking bore the strong impress of their point of view.[47]

This way of thinking was by no means limited to the scholastic philosophers. Luther was well acquainted with the works of d'Ailly and Biel and through him the theory of imposed natural law seems to have made its way into Protestant thought.[48] De Lagarde, indeed, sees in the thought of the reformers in general a reiteration of the nominalist idea of law.[49] More recent researches have shown that this is certainly true of Zwingli,[50] while in the case of Calvin, though it would be rash to ascribe the voluntarism of his ethic to nominalist influence, it remains true to say that he, too, viewed the moral law as completely dependent on the will of God, which law he equated with the testimony of the natural law implanted by God in the souls of men.[51]

Suarez's *Treatise on Laws*[52] stands as evidence for the persistence into the seventeenth century of this way of thinking, as also does the *Apologia* for Jean Gerson written by the Sorbonne theo-

[45] For d'Ailly's views see, e.g., *Quaestiones super libros Sententiarum* (Lyons, 1500), I, qu. 9, art. 2 S, fol. 122 r; and for Gerson, L. Vereeke, "Droit et morale chez Jean Gerson," *Revue historique de droit français et étranger,* XXXII (1954), pp. 413–427.

[46] See W. Kölmel, "Von Ockham zu Gabriel Biel: Zur Naturrechtslehre des 14 und 15 Jahrhunderts," *Franziskanische Studien,* 37 (1955), pp. 218–259.

[47] *De Legibus ac Deo Legislatore,* Bk. I, ch. 5, 8–9; *Selections from Three Works of Francisco Suarez S. J.*, I (Oxford, 1944), p. 26.

[48] *D. Martin Luthers Werke,* 43 (Weimar, 1912), p. 71—"Vorlesungen über 1 Mose," ch. 19, 14; cf. also ch. 19, 17–20 and ch. 20, 2.

[49] Georges de Lagarde, *Recherches sur l'esprit politique de la Reforme* (Douai, 1926), pp. 147–187.

[50] John T. McNeill, "Natural Law in the Teaching of the Reformers," *The Journal of Religion,* XXVI (1946), pp. 177–178.

[51] *Institutio Christianae Religionis.* Bk. IV, ch. 20, § 16; (Berlin, 1846), p. 486. Cf. the voluntarism of the Protestant scholastic Zacharius Ursinus (1534–84) *Opera Theologia,* I (Heidelberg, 1612), p. 483.

[52] Bk. II, ch. 6, 20–23; pp. 126–128.

logian Edmond Richer (1559–1631).[53] Earlier in the same century, as we have seen, Grotius had adopted a similar position in his *Commentary concerning the Law of Booty*. And a few years later, Pufendorf (1632–94)[54] and Hobbes[55] were to conceive of natural law in similar terms—Hobbes, indeed, being in a poor position, because of his mechanistic view of the universe, to adopt any view of natural law other than as imposed by God. The growing lack of interest in the divine origin of the natural law and the characteristic imprecision of eighteenth-century thinking on the subject do much to obscure the ultimate fate of the tradition, though at the turn of the century the Puritan divine Samuel Willard (1640–1707) was teaching in his New England congregation that the equity of God's law "is founded on the good will and pleasure of God," and that that law is revealed to man not only by the Scriptures but also by "the light of nature . . . so that men are said to do by nature the things contained in the law."[56] And, even towards the end of the century, Blackstone was still speaking of the natural law which governs man as "the will of his maker."[57]

It is already clear that the doctrine was by no means the monopoly of the professional theologians, or even of the thinkers of any one creed or of any one country. And if we were to extend our list of those who subscribed to this theory of imposed natural law, we would have to include (among others) not only the English Puritan divines John Preston (1587–1628) and William Ames (1576–1633), or their New England colleague John Norton (1606–1663),[58] not only the Anglican theologian Robert Sanderson (1587–1663) and the early Cambridge Platonist, Nathaniel Culver-

[53] *Apologia pro Joanne Gersonio* (Lyons, 1676), pp. 4–7.

[54] *De Jure Naturae et Gentium* (London, 1672), Bk. II, ch. 3, § XX.

[55] *Leviathan,* Part II, chs. 30–31; ed. Michael Oakeshott (Oxford, 1946), pp. 219–235.

[56] *A Compleat Body of Divinity* (Boston, 1726), Qu. XIV, Sermon LIV, p. 188. It should be noted that Willard was less extreme on this matter than were many of his predecessors among the New England divines—cf. Qu. IV, Sermon XXIV, p. 76.

[57] *Commentaries on the Law of England,* Sect. II, 40; (New York, 1830), p. 26.

[58] Preston, *Life Eternall or A Treatise of the Knowledge of the Divine Essence and Attributes,* 2nd ed. (London, 1631), Part I, p. 143; Ames, *The Marrow of Sacred Divinity* (London, 1642), Bk. 2, ch. 3, § 14, p. 210; Bk. 1, ch. 5, pp. 44–45; Norton, *The Orthodox Evangelist* (London, 1654), ch. 4, pp. 91–95.

well (*ca.* 1615–*ca.* 1651) [59] but also John Locke, and at least one other Fellow of the Royal Society—the botanist Nehemiah Grew (1641–1712).[60]

When Descartes spoke of God's having imposed laws upon nature, all he really had to do, therefore, was to transfer from the moral order into the realm of natural philosophy the well-established theological doctrine of an omnipotent Legislator-God, whose sovereign will lies at the very heart, not only of the divine laws revealed in the Scriptures, but also of that natural law to which right reason is man's unswerving guide. There can be little doubt that he was familiar with this tradition—the less so, indeed, in that Ralph Cudworth (1617–88), one of the Cambridge Platonists and an indefatigable opponent of the voluntarist ethic, could identify Descartes as one of the principal advocates of this pernicious doctrine, which, he complained, was dear to those who "think nothing so essential to the Deity as uncontrollable power and arbitrary will." [61] But Cudworth's perceptive remarks can be more profitably employed in exposing the redundancy even of speculations as

[59] Sanderson, *De obligatione conscientiae Praelationes Decem* (London, 1710), Praelectio Quarta, pp. 97–101. This work was first published in 1660 at the request of Robert Boyle, to whom it is dedicated. Culverwell—*An Elegant and Learned Discourse of the Light of Nature* (London, 1652), chs. VI and IX, pp. 78, 98–99—professes a modified form of voluntarism.

[60] *Essays on the Law of Nature,* ed. W. van Leyden (Oxford, 1954), Essays I and VI, pp. 110–113, 187–189; cf. the editor's introduction (pp. 37–43), where he points out the extent to which Locke was influenced by Culverwell and Sanderson. [On Locke's voluntarism see Francis Oakley and Elliot W. Urdang, "Locke, Natural Law, and God," *Natural Law Forum,* XI (1966), pp. 92–109.] Grew, *Cosmologia Sacra* (London, 1701), Bk. 3, ch. 5, § 4, p. 121 Cf. also John Wilkins (1614–1672), also a Fellow of the Royal Society, who is, however, more ambiguous on this point—*Of the Principles and Duties of Natural Religion* (London, 1675), Bk. II, ch. 9, pp. 395–396.

[61] *Treatise concerning immutable morality,* Bk. I, ch. 3, 1 (New York, 1838), p. 18. It is worth noting that Cudworth, along with other Cambridge Platonists who attacked ethical voluntarism, did so in terms of a theory of immanent or quasi-immanent natural law—see Cudworth, *Treatise,* Bk. I, ch. 2, § 2, p. 14; Bk. IV, ch. 6, § 3, p. 130. Cf. Edward Fowler (1632–1714), *The Principles and Practices of Certain Moderate Divines of the Church of England abusively called Latitudinarians* (London, 1671), pp. 12–13, and J. Tulloch, *Rational Theology and Christian Philosophy in the Seventeenth Century,* II (London, 1872), pp. 172–173, 435–436, where he discusses the views of George Rust (d. 1670) and John Smith (1618–1652).

cautious as these. For he linked the renewed popularity of the voluntarist theory with the revival of "the physiological hypotheses of Democritus and Epicurus," and with their successful application "to the solving of some of the phenomena of the visible world." [62] And this suggestion, however debatable, may serve to remind us that natural law theories are by no means insulated from the main body of philosophy, but reflect or presuppose congruent concepts of nature.[63] It is to be expected, therefore, that changes in natural law theories will entail, or be entailed by, concomitant changes in concepts of nature, and this expectation will be fulfilled, if keeping the point in mind, we glance back at the contrasting views of Aquinas and Ockham.

The natural law, according to Aquinas, is nothing other than the Eternal Law in so far as it concerns man and is apprehended by him, and the Eternal Law itself is the divine reason in which all things, irrational as well as rational, participate—in that "they derive from it certain inclinations to those actions and aims which are proper to them." [64] This law is certainly conceived as being in some sense immanent in the world, and it is hardly surprising, therefore, that this concept of nature, impregnated as it is with those "substantial forms and occult qualities" which were to be anathema to the scientists of the seventeenth century, is at least cognate to that organic view which Collingwood spoke of as "the Greek idea of nature." Nor is it surprising that Ockham's abandonment of the theory of natural law as immanent went hand in hand with something of a revision of this idea of nature.

Gilson has spoken of Ockham's thought as being a post-1277 theology "in a more than chronological sense," and as being dominated "by the first words of the Christian creed: I believe in one God, the Father Almighty." These claims are by no means exaggerated.[65] Ockham regarded the divine liberty as compromised not only by the *realist* connection of the natural moral law with the doctrine of the divine ideas but also by the very doctrine of the divine ideas itself—which he further condemned, at least in its tra-

[62] *Treatise*, Bk. I, ch. 1, § 4, p. 9.

[63] Cf. A. P. d'Entrèves, *Natural Law; An Introduction to Legal Philosophy* (London, 1951), p. 11.

[64] *S.T.*, Ia 2ae, qu. 91, art. 2 *Resp.*

[65] *History of Christian Philosophy*, pp. 410, 498. Cf. *Quodl.* VI, qu. 6; McKeon, II, p. 373; L. Baudry (ed.), *Le Tractatus de Principiis Theologiae attribué à G. d'Occam* (Paris, 1936), p. 45 and n. 1.

ditional form, as dissolving into an un-Christian multiplicity the perfect unity of God. Not only the moral law but the whole of Creation, he insisted, must be radically contingent upon the undetermined decisions of the divine will. And, believing this, he had little choice but to abandon the traditional doctrine of the divine ideas, and to dismiss with it the whole realist metaphysic of essences upon which it depended.

Such a basic shift in philosophical perspective could not but determine the lineaments of his philosophy of nature. Ockham's universe can hardly be regarded as in any sense organic. It is one in which there are no necessary intermediaries between, on the one hand, an infinitely free and omnipotent God, and, on the other, the things which he has created and which are utterly contingent upon him. Hence the dismissal of any necessary connections in nature between distinct things, even between cause and effect.[66] Hence, too, the belief that we can in no way deduce the order of the world by any *a priori* reasoning, for, being completely dependent upon the divine choice, it corresponds to no necessity and can be discovered only by an examination of what is *de facto*.[67] Thus, from Ockham's fundamental insistence upon the omnipotence and freedom of God follows, not only his ethical and legal voluntarism, but also his empiricism.

Because he held to these views it has often been concluded that there is no point in looking for any plan or system in an Ockhamist universe, just as in the realm of his ethical teaching, historians have been apt to argue that there is no place for any true concept of natural law.[68] But to draw either of these conclusions is to suppose that Ockham conceived of God as a wholly capricious Being, and to overlook a distinction which he drew concerning the modes of the divine activity—a crucial distinction, the very existence of which invalidates such a supposition. For Ockham reasoned that although God could, of his *absolute* power, order the opposites of the acts which he has in fact forbidden, nevertheless, by his *ordained* power, he has actually established a moral order, within the framework of

[66] Thus God can produce in us intuitions of non-existent objects—*Quodl.* VI, qu. 6; McKeon, II, pp. 372–380.

[67] Baudry, p. 23.

[68] See e.g. Perry Miller, *The New England Mind* (New York, 1939), pp. 157–158, and H. A. Rommen, "The Natural Law of the Renaissance Period," *University of Notre Dame Natural Law Proceedings* (Notre Dame, 1949), pp. 94–95.

which the natural law is absolute and immutable. This was no mere *ad hoc* argument relevant only to the realm of ethics, for Ockham regarded the distinction as applicable to all operations of the divine will and it occupies, indeed, a fundamental position in his thought. He believed that although God's absolute power can suffer no limitation, it normally expresses itself in accordance with the order which has actually been ordained—whether it be the order of grace or of nature. God has made certain promises to us in the Scriptures, and, as Christians, we must believe that he will fulfill them. Similarly, whether we are Christians or not, we can perceive in the regularities of nature certain constant rules and we can safely assume that God will *normally* operate within the limits they impose. But one big reservation is assumed in all this, and Ockham draws attention to it by the use of such qualifications as *given the divine order* and *in the present order.*[69] It is true that God will normally act in accordance with the supernatural or natural order which he has ordained but it must not be forgotten that, of his absolute power, he could always abrogate the present moral and natural economy, or momentarily transcend it, as he does in the case of miracles. It is, for example, a matter of everyday experience that water dampens and fire burns, but by the absolute power of God these effects need not necessarily proceed from their causes—and to illustrate the point, Ockham cites the fate of Daniel's three companions, Shadrach, Mishach and Abednego, whom King Nebuchadnezzar threw into the fiery furnace but who emerged unscathed.[70]

It would be incorrect to assume, therefore, that the philosophical revolution resulting from the Ockhamist preoccupation with the omnipotence of God necessarily entailed an incoherent universe arbitrarily peopled with unpredictable events. It is true that Ockham's rejection of any necessary connections in nature, coupled, as it was, with his denial of the reality of final causes and his concentration upon efficient causality,[71] eliminated the possibility of any organic view of nature comparable with that of Aquinas, but his alternative is not, as is often suggested, a systemless chaos, but rather something that looks not unlike the universe pictured by the

[69] *Sent.* III, 12 CCC.

[70] *Opus Nonaginta Dierum,* ch. 95, § *Hereticum est dicere omnia de necessitate evenire.*

[71] See A. C. Crombie, *Medieval and Early Modern Science,* II (New York: Anchor Books, 1959), pp. 32–33.

scientists of the seventeenth century. Crombie, indeed, has pointed out that Ockham's position was cognate to that of the seventeenth century *occasionalists,* the most famous of whom was Malebranche, —thinkers who believed that "in his activities God usually followed fixed rules, so it was possible for natural philosophers to formulate general scientific laws." [72] And although I know of no instances in which Ockham himself uses with a clearly scientific connotation the precise expressions *laws of nature* or *natural law,* nevertheless, in common with other nominalists, he does make use of the legal metaphor to indicate the fixed order according to which God, of his ordained power, acts. Thus, he himself uses the expression *by the common law* as synonymous with *in the present order* or *given the divine order,*[73] while, in the same way, Pierre d'Ailly, later on in the fourteenth century, employs among others such revealing phrases as *by the common course of nature, by the common laws and naturally,* and *naturally or by the ordained law.*[74] And it is, perhaps, hardly surprising that d'Ailly goes a little further, and not only speaks of God as having ordained "a natural law" in the things of this world, but even admits the relevance to the universe of that very clock analogy which was to be vulgarised in the seventeenth century by Robert Boyle and which was to become a cliché of eighteenth-century Deist theology.[75]

What we are seeing here is something which—given a realization of the existence of internal connections between theories of natural law and views of nature—was only to be expected. It is the emergence of the conception of divinely imposed laws of nature in the writings of those very thinkers who had adopted and popularized the cognate view of a juridical natural law as grounded, not in the

[72] *Ibid.,* p. 313.

[73] *Sent.* Prol., qu. VII; *Sent.* II, qu. 19 O. Again, discussing the distinction between the absolute and ordained powers of God, Ockam can say: ". . . est sic intelligenda quod posse aliquid aliquando accipitur *secundum leges ordinatas et institutas a Deo,* et illa Deus dicitur posse facere de potentia ordinata; aliter . . ." etc. (Italics mine).—Quodl. VI, qu. 1.

[74] *De libertate creaturae rationalis,* in J. Gerson, *Opera Omnia,* ed. Ellies du Pin, I (Antwerp, 1706), col. 632; *De Trinitate,* in Gers., I, col. 619; *Quaestiones super I, III et IV Sententiarum* (Lyons, 1500), I, art. 2 JJ, fol. 96r. He also uses the expression *by the natural or naturally ordained power* in contrast with *supernaturally . . . or by the absolute power*—*Sent.* IV, qu. 1, art. 2 J, fol. 188r.

[75] *Sent.* IV, qu. 1, art. 2 N, fol. 188r; *Tractatus de Legibus et Sectis,* in Gers., I, col. 793.

nature of things, but in the will of a sovereign Deity. It is no doubt possible to exaggerate the extent to which the views of these late medieval thinkers coincide on this point with those held later on by the scientists of the seventeenth century, but it is not easy to do so. To establish this contention, it is requisite only to recall to mind those ideas of Newton which we have already examined [76]—indeed Newton was by no means of the most explicit of the *virtuosi* on the subject. We do not even have to go beyond the circle of his colleagues in the Royal Society to hear Walter Charleton (1619–1707) speaking of God as the "Rector General of President Paramount" of the universe, "by whose sovereign dictates all subordinate ministers are set on work, in order to the execution of his pleasure, and in their operations vary not a hairsbredth from the rules prescribed by his will"—which rules he describes elsewhere as "the severe laws of Nature" with which God has "bound up the hands of his Creatures, limited their activities, and punctually consigned them their several provinces." [77] Nor should we fail to note, in the same treatise, his rejection of the "Platonic" and "Stoic" idea of Fate in so far as it

> blasphemously invades the Cardinal Praerogative of Divinity, Omnipotence, by denying him [God] a reserved power, of infringing, or altering any one of those laws which he himself ordained and enacted, and chaining up his armes with adamantine fetters of Destiny.[78]

An onslaught which would have been worthy of the most positively "post-1277" theologian!

And if we turn to Robert Boyle, who, as a philosopher of science, was perhaps the most influential of all the English *virtuosi* before Newton, we will not only find him speaking of God as "the supreme and absolute lord" of creation who "established those rules of motion, and that order among things corporeal which we are wont to

[76] The *General Scholium* which Newton appended to the second edition of the *Principles* contains the clearest statement of his physico-theological principles. In it he was careful to affirm, not only that "this most beautiful system of the sun, planets and comets could only proceed from the counsel and dominion of an intelligent and powerful Being," but also that this Being is to be considered as an omnipotent cosmic sovereign who "governs all things, not as the soul of the world, but as Lord over all"—*Opera Omnia*, III, pp. 171–173.

[77] *The Darkness of Atheism dispelled by the Light of Nature: a physico-theological Treatise* (London, 1652), ch. 4; Sect. 5, pp. 125, 136; cf, Nehemiah Grew, *Cosmologia Sacra*, Bk. 4, ch. 5, pp. 194–195.

[78] *Darkness of Atheism*, ch. 10, Sect. 1, p. 329.

call the laws of nature,"[79] not only pointing out that "the laws of motion, without which *the present state and course of things* could not be maintained, did not necessarily spring from the nature of matter, but depended upon the will of the divine author of things,"[80] but also insisting that this "present state and course of things" —which he also refers to as *the ordinary course of things* and as *the instituted order*[81]—can be abrogated by God, who, being omnipotent, can "do whatever involves no contradiction."[82] Thus he can conclude that "though some modern philosophers have made ingenious attempts to explain the nature of things corporeal, yet their explications generally suppose the present fabric of the world, and the laws of motion that are settled in it."[83]

This remarkable coincidence between the views of fourteenth-century theologians and seventeenth-century scientists can only serve to confirm what we have already suggested—that they were linked by an enduring theological tradition. In so far as this tradition manifested itself in the *voluntarist* conception of the natural law, it had, as we have seen, a continuous history at least from the late thirteenth century onwards. If it is less easy to establish a similar explicit continuity in the case of the scientific conception of divinely imposed laws of nature, it is by no means impossible, for the two ideas went hand in hand. Thus, among the ranks of the early Reformers we find Zwingli (1484–1531) speaking of God as having brought the world under "law and order," or defining "naturally" as "in accordance with the order constituted at the beginning," and Melanchthon saying that though "the whole machine of the world" serves "perpetual laws," and though philosophers speak of the heavenly bodies as being moved "necessarily," nevertheless, this physical necessity is to be understood only "of the order now instituted," for God is "a most free agent, not, as the Stoics used to teach, bound by secondary causes."[84] Similarly, among the English

[79] *A Free Inquiry into the Vulgarly received notion of Nature, Works,* V, p. 197; *On the Excellency and Grounds of the corpuscular or mechanical philosophy, Works,* IV, p. 68.

[80] *The Christian Virtuoso, Works,* V, p. 521.

[81] *A Free Inquiry, Works,* V, p. 216.

[82] *Some considerations about the Reconcileableness of Reason and Religion, Works,* IV, p. 159.

[83] *Of the High Veneration Man's Intellect owes to God, Works,* V, p. 149.

[84] Ulrich Zwingli, *Ad illustrissimum Cattorem Principem Philippum sermonis de providentia dei anamnema* (Zurich, 1530), fols. 20r, 63r; Philip Melanchthon,

Puritans, as early as 1585, we find Dudley Fenner (1558?–87) speaking of God's *ordinary* government of things as being that which is in accordance with "the common law" which he has imposed upon nature,[85] while the Federal theologians, from William Ames in England at the beginning of the seventeenth century to Samuel Willard in Boston at the end, speak with striking uniformity of God's ordinary providence as being that mode of government "whereby God observeth that order in things which was appointed from the beginning," and of "that order in natural things" as being "the law of nature common to all things."[86] Nor do they fail to point out that God is "a great Monarch, who . . . holds the creature in full subordination to His absolute pleasure," and is by no means bound to observe the "constituted order of nature," but by his extraordinary providence (as in the case of miracles) can produce effects which "outdo the laws of nature, or do invert the common order and course of things."[87]

As is only to be expected, the continuity is (if possible) even more explicit in the works of Suarez who, though he regarded as merely metaphorical the application of the expression "law" to the non-human world, frequently speaks, nevertheless, of laws of nature in the scientific sense.[88] This involves no contradiction, for although, as he has said, "things lacking reason are, properly speaking, capable neither of law nor of obedience," he regards this law, however, as that which *God binds himself* to follow in all those actions which he does according to his ordinary or ordained power. Thus he can define the ordinary power of God as that power by which "he operates in accordance with the common laws which he has established in the universe," and can add that when we say that

Initia doctrinae physicae, Opera Omnia, ed. C. G. Bretschneider, XIII (Halis Saxonum, 1846), pp. 206–207. Cf. Ursinus, *Opera Theologica,* I, col. 573.

[85] *Sacra Theologia* (Geneva, 1589), Bk. 2, ch. 10, fol. 18r; cf. William Perkins (1558–1602), *An Exposition of the Symbole of the Creed of the Apostles, Workes,* I (Cambridge, 1612), p. 160.

[86] Ames, *Marrow,* Bk. 1, ch. 9, p. 40; cf. Increase Mather, *The Doctrine of Divine Providence Opened and Applyed* (Boston, 1684), Sermon 2, p. 45; Samuel Willard, *Compleat Body,* Qu. XI, Sermon XLVII, p. 146.

[87] Willard, *Compleat Body,* Qu. IV, Sermon XII, p. 38, Qu. XI, Sermon XLVII, p. 146; Increase Mather, *Doctrine of Divine Providence,* Sermon 2, p. 47; cf. Norton, *Orthodox Evangelist,* ch. 5, pp. 103–104.

[88] *Metaphysicarum Disputationum,* I (Moguntiae, 1600), Disp. XXII, § 4, pp. 568, 569; II, Disp. XXX, § 17, p. 150; *De Legibus,* Bk. 2, ch. 2; *Selections,* I, p. 104.

God cannot do something by his ordained power, we mean that he cannot do something "according to the ordinary law which he has imposed upon himself." [89] And Suarez points in the general direction of at least one Fellow of the Royal Society—John Locke, who, in common with Sanderson, not only speaks of God as having imposed his will upon nature in the form of constant laws, but also assumes this to be an idea so widely accepted that he uses it as a justification for suggesting that man, in his moral life too, is subject to a natural law.[90]

Thus the idea of laws of nature imposed by God upon the world was undoubtedly common coinage in the sixteenth and seventeenth centuries, even before Descartes, Boyle and Newton made it a commonplace of scientific thinking, and what we are suggesting here is simply that it was so widespread precisely because it was the expression of a tradition in natural theology which dated back well beyond the late thirteenth century but which had been prominent since that time and which was little affected and perhaps even strengthened by the upheaval of the Reformation. It is true that the innovations of the Reformers, though they were concentrated upon other areas of theology, have served nevertheless to obscure the lack of change in natural theology, and some scepticism may no doubt remain about the exact nature of this alleged continuity. In theology as in philosophy the number of possible positions is, after all, a strictly limited one. The occurrence in the course of history of parallel but totally unrelated doctrinal positions should, therefore, be the occasion of little surprise. Nor, from the point of view of the history of science should we forget Crombie's warning that "the problem of the relation of seventeenth century science to medieval science still remains a *questio disputata.*" [91]

The evidence is not lacking, however, to eliminate any lingering doubts about the real continuity of this tradition. We should not allow ourselves to be misled by the constant attacks on medieval

[89] *De Legibus,* Bk. 1, ch. 1, Bk. 2, ch. 2; *Selections,* I, pp. 8 and 104; *Met. Disp.,* II, Disp. XXX, § 17, p. 150. Robert Boyle himself came very close to the same position—see *The Christian Virtuoso, Works,* V, p. 521.

[90] *Essays on the Law of Nature,* Essay I, pp. 108–110; Sanderson, *De oblig. consc.,* Prael. Quarta, p. 101. Locke's editor suggests that the position of Locke as well as that of Culverwell was influenced by that of Suarez (pp. 36–37).

[91] "The Significance of Medieval Discussions of Scientific Method for the Scientific Revolution," in *Critical Problems in the History of Science,* ed. Marshall Clagett (Madison, 1959), p. 80.

scholastic thinking that are to be found in the writings both of the theologians and of the scientists of the seventeenth century. Such attacks seem to have been very much a matter of convention and should not be taken as proof that their authors regarded the works of the scholastics as worthless. Among the ranks of the scientists, Charleton was not unwilling publicly to acknowledge his dependence upon scholastic theological ideas, and the feeling of familiarity which a student of nominalist theology experiences upon reading, for example, William Ames's *Marrow of Sacred Divinity* is by no means misleading.[92] Moreover, John Norton, the New England Puritan divine, could comment, in 1654, that the scholastic thinkers, because of their pre-eminence in rational disputation

> of late years have crept (for a time) into more credit among schools, than the most judicious and orthodox of our best new writers (Luther, Calvin, Martyr, Bucer and the rest), and their books were much more vendible and at a far greater price.[93]

More precisely, in the specific area which is our present concern, the nominalist origin of the voluntarist tradition of natural law thinking was not unknown, even in the seventeenth century, for Ralph Cudworth, the most learned of those who were opposed to this view, while he directs his barbs against Hobbes and the Calvinist theologians, can tell us, nevertheless, that:

> though the ancient fathers of the Christian Church were very abhorrent from this doctrine, . . . yet it crept up afterward in the scholastic age, Ockham being among the first that maintained: ". . . That there is no act evil but as it was prohibited by God, and which cannot be made good if it be commanded by God." . . . Herein Petrus Alliacus [Pierre d'Ailly] and Andreas de Novo Castro, with others quickly followed him.[94]

But in the last analysis, it is unnecessary even to rely upon indirect evidence of this type. For conclusive evidence of the explicit continuity of the tradition in question appears in the remarkable

[92] Charleton, *Darkness of Atheism,* fols. a2v, b4v. Scrutiny of the catalogue of Ames's library reveals that he possessed a rich collection of scholastic material ranging from Aquinas to the Spanish scholastics of the sixteenth century, and including among others works of Scotus, Buridan and Gabriel Biel—see *Catalogus variorum et insignium librorum clariss. et celeberrimi viri D. Guilielmi Amesii* (Amsterdam, 1634).

[93] *Orthodox Evangelist,* fols. 1v–2r.

[94] *Immutable Morality,* Bk. 1, ch. 1, § 5, p. 11.

endurance of that characteristic distinction between the *absolute* and *ordained* or *ordinary* powers of God which we have already had occasion to examine. This distinction crops up in the works of nearly all of those writers whom we have cited as holding either to a voluntarist theory of natural law, or to a conception of divinely imposed laws of nature, or—as in many cases—to both.[95] And this is hardly surprising, for in order to realize the extent to which this distinction is bound up with the idea of divinely imposed laws of nature, it is sufficient merely to recall Suarez's definition of the ordained or ordinary power of God as that power by which "he operates in accordance with the common law which he has established in the universe"—a law which, in fact, reflects a self-imposed commitment on the part of God to rule the universe along the lines of the natural order which he himself has established in it. The history of this distinction, which played a crucial role in the thought of Ockham, and of such late medieval theologians as d'Ailly, Major,[96] Durandus of St. Pourcain (d. 1332), Robert Holcot, Thomas Buckingham (d. 1351), and Adam of Woodham (d. 1358),[97] can be traced down at least as far as the sermons delivered at Boston by Samuel Willard at the end of the seventeenth century and the beginning of the eighteenth.[98]

Perry Miller has stressed the importance of the idea in Puritan

[95] Although it is unimportant in the present context, it should perhaps be noted that this distinction underwent slight fluctuations in meaning in the course of the three centuries during which it was current.

[96] D'Ailly, *Sent.* I, qu. 13, art. 1 D, fol. 159r; Major, *In primum Sent.*, dist. 44, qu. 3.

[97] See Gordon Leff, *Bradwardine and the Pelagians* (Cambridge, 1957), pp. 165–254.

[98] It is cited explicitly, to my knowledge, by Luther, *Vorlesungen über I Mose*, ch. 19, 14–20, ch. 20, 2; *Werke*, 43, pp. 71–72, 82; the Anabaptist Balthasar Hubmaier, *Das ander Biechlen von der Freywilligkait der menschens . . .* (Nicolsburg, 1527)—English translation in G. H. Williams (ed.), *Spiritual and Anabaptist Writers* (Philadelphia, 1957), pp. 132–133; William Perkins, *A Godly and learned Exposition, Works*, III, pp. 233–234; Suarez, *Met. Disp.*, II, Disp. XXX, Sectio 17, p. 150; Ames, *Marrow*, Bk. 1, ch. 6, §§ 16–20, p. 21; Norton, *Orthodox Evangelist*, ch. 1, p. 19, and Willard, *Compleat Body*, Q. 4, Sermon 22, p. 70. And it is at least implied in some of the arguments of Melanchthon, *Initia Doctrinae Physicae, Opera Omnia*, XIII, p. 207, and Robert Boyle himself—*Some Considerations about the Reconcileableness of Reason and Religion, Works*, IV, pp. 161–163. Cf. Malebranche's distinction between the 'general' and 'particular' will of God which is very similar in its import—see Ginette Dreyfus, *La Volonté selon Malebranche* (Paris, 1958), pp. 101–109.

theology,[99] where, indeed, it generated another but closely related distinction between the *ordinary* and *extraordinary* Providence of God. This distinction, prominent in the thought of Ames, Thomas Shepard (1605–49), John Morton and Increase Mather,[100] also figures significantly in the writings of John Wilkins, Charleton and Boyle—all three of them luminaries of the Royal Society.[101] Thus Boyle can note that miracles involve departures from God's "ordinary and general concourse," and can describe them as "extraordinary and supernatural interpositions of divine providence," by which God may be seen "to over-rule or controul the established course of things in the world by his own omnipotent hand." [102] Similarly, he can argue that:

> if we consider God as the author of the universe, and the free establisher of the laws of motion, whose general concourse is necessary to the conservation and efficacy of every particular physical agent, we cannot but acknowledge, that, by withholding his concourse, or changing these laws of motion which depend perfectly upon his will, he may invalidate most, if not all the axioms and theorems of natural philosophy: *these supposing the course of nature*. . . . It is a rule in natural philosophy that causae necessariae semper agunt quantum possunt: but it will not follow from thence, that the fire must necessarily burn Daniel's three companions or their clothes that were cast by the Babylonian King's command into the midst of a burning fiery furnace, when the author of nature was pleased to withdraw his concourse to the operation of the flames, or supernaturally to defend against them the bodies that were exposed to them. . . . Agreeably to this let me observe to you that, though it be unreasonable to believe a miraculous effect when attributed only to a mere physical agent, yet the same thing may reasonably be believed when, ascribed to God, or to agents assisted with his absolute or supernatural power.[103]

[99] *The New England Mind,* pp. 33–34.

[100] Ames, *Marrow,* Bk. 1, ch. 9, p. 41; Shepard, *The First Principle of the Oracles of God,* in *Three Valuable Pieces* (Boston, 1747), pp. 9–10; Norton, *Orthodox Evangelist,* ch. 5, pp. 103–104; Mather, *Doctrine of Divine Providence,* Serm. 2, qu. 2, pp. 45–47.

[101] Wilkins, *Principles and Duties of Natural Religion,* Bk. 1, ch. 7, pp. 85–87; Charleton, *Darkness of Atheism,* ch. 4, Sect. 5, pp. 136–137; Boyle, *A Free Inquiry into the Vulgarly received notion of Nature, Works,* V, pp. 197–198, 211, 216.

[102] *A Free Inquiry, Works,* V, pp. 163–164.

[103] *Some Considerations, Works,* IV, pp. 161–162 (italics mine).

It will be remembered that this example of the miraculous survival of Daniel's three companions, Shadrach, Meshach and Abednego, after they had been thrown into the Babylonian furnace, was the very example which Ockham himself had used to illustrate much the same point, and the recurrence of this particular Biblical illustration may serve as the final and clinching evidence for the validity of our thesis that the scientific idea of divinely imposed laws of nature had its origin in a living theological tradition which went back to the last years of the thirteenth century. For this very Biblical example, used to illustrate this same point concerning the power of God, is to be found, not only here and in two other works of Boyle, but also in the works of Luther, Melanchthon, Suarez, Perkins, Preston, Ames, Shepard, Norton, Increase Mather and Willard [104]—that is to say, in the works of a high percentage of those very authors whom we have seen to subscribe to the voluntarist theory of natural law and of the laws of nature.[105]

[104] Boyle, *Some physico-theological considerations about the possibility of the Resurrection, Works,* IV, pp. 201–202; *A Disquisition about Final Causes, Works,* V, pp. 412–414; Luther, *Werke,* 43, p. 71; Melanchthon, *Opera Omnia,* XIII, p. 207; Suarez, *Met. Disp.,* I, Disp. XXII, p. 552; Perkins, *An exposition of the Symbole, Works,* I, p. 159, *A Resolution to the Countreyman, Workes,* III, p. 657, *A Discourse of the Damned Art of Witchcraft, Workes,* III, p. 609; Preston, *Life Eternall,* Part I, p. 32, Part II, p. 200; Ames, *Marrow,* Bk. 1, ch. 9, p. 40; Shepard, *Three Valuable Pieces,* pp. 9–10; Norton, *Orthodox Evangelist,* ch. 5, p. 124; Increase Mather, *Doctrine of Divine Providence,* Serm. I, pp. 23–24, Serm. II, pp. 53–54; Willard, *Compleat Body,* Qu. XI, Serm. XLVI, p. 144.

[105] It is perhaps worthy of note that many of these authors also make use of another distinction related to that which they drew between the absolute and ordained powers of God. This distinction concerned the order of salvation and was drawn between what Calvinist theologians usually referred to as the *secret* will and the *revealed* will of God, but which the Scholastics called *voluntas beneplaciti* and *voluntas signi.* Its history can be traced back as far as the *De Sacramentis Christianae Fidei* of Hugh of St. Victor (1096–1141)—Bk. I, Part 4, ch. 8 (*Patrologia latina,* ed. J-P. Migne, 176 [Paris, 1854], col. 237), but it consorted very profoundly with the voluntarism of the Ockhamists and became a commonplace of Protestant thought. It was cited, for example, by Hubmaier—*Spiritual and Anabaptist Writers,* pp. 132–133; William Perkins, *A Treatise of God's free grace, Workes,* I, pp. 704–705; Ames, *Marrow,* Bk. I, ch. 7. §§ 52–54, pp. 30–31; John Norton, *Orthodox Evangelist,* ch.. 4, p. 92; Hobbes, *The Questions concerning liberty, necessity and chance clearly stated and debated between Dr. Bramhall Bishop of Derry, and Thomas Hobbes of Malmesbury* (London, 1656), pp. 10 and 78. It was used, among the members of the Royal Society, not only by the staunchly Calvinist John Wallis—*A brief and easie explanation of the Shorter Catechism* (London, 1662), E 4—but also by Charle-

In the light, therefore, of these considerations, there can remain little room for doubt either that the voluntarist conception of natural law attained a wide currency in the sixteenth and seventeenth centuries, or that it was directly descended from the similar theory hammered out by the nominalist theologians in the years after the condemnations of 1277. It was conceived both with a juristic and a scientific sense,[106] and, being the result of a crucial shift in the direction of the "simplified view of nature" which was later to be adopted by Galileo, Descartes and Newton, was eminently compatible with this view. If, therefore, we ask ourselves why, in the seventeenth century, the Semitic concept of divinely imposed laws of nature burst into scientific prominence, it is unnecessary, and, indeed, misleading to postulate the influence of social and political analogies—for the influence was, if anything, exerted in the opposite direction. When Descartes spoke of a God who put laws into nature, he did not have to create such a God. He did not, as Zilsel suggests, have to apotheosize Bodin's sovereign. He did not even have to transfer the idea from the juridical and moral realm into the world of natural causation. All he had to do was to employ the theological conception of a legislating God whose most striking attribute was his irresistible power, a conception which had its principal source in the Old Testament, which was clearly formulated and fully elaborated by his philosophizing predecessors of the later Middle Ages, and which lay at the heart of the natural theology, not only of many of the Catholic theologians of his own day, but also of perhaps the majority of their Protestant counterparts.

III

Some years ago, E. A. Burtt noticed that "Newton, in common with the whole voluntaristic British tradition in medieval and modern philosophy, tended to subordinate, in God, the intellect to the will," [107] and in the light of the above findings, it must now seem that when he did so he had noticed something of far greater signifi-

ton, *Darkness of Atheism*, ch. 10, 4, p. 354. Cf. also Sanderson, *De oblig. consc.*, Prael. quarta, p. 97.

106 Hardly surprising for, according to d'Ailly, "just as the divine will is the first efficient cause in the genus of efficient causality, so also is it the first obligating rule or law in the genus of obligating law"—*Sent.* I, qu. 14, art. 3 Q, fol. 173r.

107 *Metaphysical Foundations of Modern Physical Science*, p. 294.

cance than an interesting similarity. It now remains, briefly and in conclusion, to attempt to assess the fundamental significance of these findings.

When scientists today speak of the laws of nature, no element of command attaches to the expression. It is regarded, perhaps most often, as "indicating statistical regularities, valid only in given times and places." [108] On this ground it might, perhaps, be argued that the historical application of the legal metaphor to mechanical regularities, experimentally established and mathematically formulated, was productive less of scientific progress than of a terminological inexactitude prolific in misconceptions. Such an assertion would ignore, however, the theological assumptions which we have seen the legal metaphor to involve and because of which it was adopted.

As long ago as 1883 Ernst Mach pointed out that an undue preoccupation with "the conflict between science and theology" could be extremely misleading because, in his considered opinion, many of the conceptions "which completely dominate modern physics" actually "arose under the influence of theological ideas." [109] Mach's warning does not seem to have attracted a great deal of notice, but in 1926 and 1945, respectively, Whitehead and Collingwood again drew attention to the importance of Christian beliefs for the development of the classical or Newtonian science. The most complete statement of this point of view, however, was made in 1934–5 by Michael Foster in two lucid and penetrating articles which, after a lapse of some years, have now begun to command the interest they so richly deserve.[110] His general thesis, put very roughly, is this: in the first place, that the early modern philosophers, from Descartes to Leibniz, ascribed to the world of nature, in advance of the actual establishment of the modern natural science, the very character which constituted it a possible object of that science; secondly, that in so doing, they were putting forward a new theory of nature, not

[108] Needham, *Science and Civilization,* II, p. 582.

[109] *Science of Mechanics,* trans. T. J. McCormack (London, 1942), pp. 542, 551–552; cf. Mortimer Taube, *Causation, Freedom and Determinism* (London, 1936), pp. 108–109.

[110] A. N. Whitehead, *Science and the Modern World* (New York, 1958), p. 14; R. G. Collingwood, *Idea of Nature,* pp. 3–9; Foster, "The Christian doctrine of Creation and the rise of Modern Natural Science," *Mind,* XLIII (1934), pp. 446–468, "Christian Theology and Modern Science of Nature," *Mind,* XLV (1936), pp. 1–28. Cf. e.g. E. L. Mascall, *Christian Theology and Natural Science* (London, 1956), pp. 93–100.

upon any grounds of proven expediency, but because their thinking was shaped by elements which were not of Greek origin and which consorted ill, therefore, with the Greek idea of nature; finally, that the source of these non-Greek elements must have been the Christian revelation, and in particular the Christian doctrine of creation —presupposing, as it did, the idea of an omnipotent God from whom the world did not proceed by any necessary emanation, but who called it into being by the autonomous *fiat* of his will. Foster attempts to show, therefore:

> that the method of natural science depends upon the presuppositions which are held about nature, and the presuppositions about nature in turn upon the doctrine of God. Modern natural science could begin only when the modern presuppositions about nature displaced the Greek . . . ; but this displacement itself was possible only when the Christian concept of God had displaced the pagan, as the object . . . of systematic understanding. To achieve this primary displacement was the work of Medieval theology, which thus laid the foundations both of much else in the modern world which is specifically modern and of modern natural science.[111]

The arguments which he uses to establish his claim need not detain us here—suffice it to say that they are philosophical rather than historical in character. But herein, it may be suggested, lies the central significance of our own findings. For they go at least some of the way towards providing the complementary historical arguments, some of the way towards establishing that what Foster, after an examination of theological and philosophical positions, claimed *must* have been the case, *was* in fact the case. For the reappearance in the later Middle Ages of the crucial idea of imposed laws of nature, along with the view of the universe most eminently compatible with it, was the outcome of a reaction on the part of Christian theologians against the pagan necessitarianism of Greek thought. The exact significance of this becomes even more apparent if we bear in mind Needham's parallel conclusion that one of the crucial reasons for the failure of the Chinese to develop a natural science comparable with that of the West was their prior failure to produce a comparable concept of laws imposed upon nature, and that this latter failure was, in turn, the outcome of their lack of any conception of a personal, legislating Creator-God.[112] Speaking of

[111] *Mind,* XLIII (1934), p. 465.
[112] *Science and Civilization,* II, pp. 578–583.

the Taoist thinkers he says that "with their appreciation of the relativism and subtlety and immensity of the universe they were groping after an Einsteinian world-picture, without having laid the foundations for a Newtonian one," and that "by that path science could not develop."[113] It was not that the Chinese lacked the idea of an order in the universe, but that they regarded it as an "harmonious co-operation of all beings" arising "not from the orders of a superior authority external to themselves, but from the fact that they were all parts in a hierarchy of wholes forming a cosmic pattern, and what they obeyed were the internal dictates of their own reason."[114]

Such a view of the world is not unfamiliar. It clearly has much in common, not only with the thinking of the Stoics, but also with the scholastic view as propounded by Aquinas and the *realists*. Assuming, therefore, that the abrogation of this view was one of the metaphysical adjustments necessary for the inception of the classical of Newtonian science, I am led to propose the following general conclusion: that the prime mover in this process of adjustment was the renewed and disturbing pressure upon Greek modes of thought of the Semitic idea of an omnipotent Creator-God. So that, paradoxically, if it is possible to argue that philosophy suffered because of the condemnations of 1277, it must surely be admitted that the physical sciences, in the long run, undoubtedly gained.[115]

[113] *Ibid.*, p. 543.

[114] *Ibid.*, p. 582—Needham adds that "Modern Science and the philosophy of organism, with its integrative levels, have come back to his wisdom, fortified by a new understanding of cosmic, biological and social evolution. Yet who shall say that the Newtonian phase was not an essential one."

[115] As long ago as 1909 Pierre Duhem drew attention to the importance of these condemnations for the history of science—*Etudes sur Léonard de Vinci,* II (Paris, 1909), pp. 411 ff. He did so, however, because he believed that the utterances of the Bishop of Paris on specific points such as the possibility of the existence of a plurality of worlds marked the starting point of the development of modern science, and Alexandre Koyré has convincingly exposed the lack of evidence to support such a belief—"Le vide et l'espace infini au XIVe siècle," *Archives d'hist. doct. et litt. du Moyen Age,* 24 (1949), pp. 45–91. But if the condemnations and the theological reaction to which they witnessed were unimportant in the realm of specific scientific discoveries, this was far from being the case in the realm of philosophical assumptions about nature—a point which Koyré apparently failed to perceive.

CHAPTER 4

What Accelerated Technological Progress in the Western Middle Ages?

LYNN WHITE, JR.

In *The Cambridge Historical Journal* for 1955,[1] A. G. Keller called attention to a letter of Bessarion which poses a major problem in the history of technical innovation. About 1444, the Cardinal wrote to Constantine Palaeologus, despot of the Morea and the best hope of Greek resurgence against the Turks, urging him to send young men to Italy to learn the practical arts. Bessarion had been impressed not only by Western textiles, glass and metallurgy, and by improved arms and ships: he was particularly struck by the use of water-power to eliminate hand labour, for example in sawing timbers and for working the bellows of furnaces. Evidently he had seen nothing of the sort in the Byzantine realm, and I know of no firm evidence that water or wind power was applied at that time to any industry other than milling grain either in Byzantium or in Islam. Yet by 1444 such machinery had long been used and was common in the West. To be specific, the first water-powered saw-mill appears about 1235 in Villard de Honnecourt's sketchbook,[2] while the earliest evi-

[1] A. G. Keller, "A Byzantine admirer of 'Western' progress: Cardinal Bessarion", *Cambridge Historical Journal*, XI (1955) 343–8.

[2] *The Sketchbook of Villard de Honnecourt*, ed. T. Bowie (Bloomington, 1959) plate 58. On the problem of the powered marble saws in *Mosella*, cf. below p. 282.

dence of powered bellows for a furnace comes in 1214 from the Trentino.[3]

We are only beginning to understand that the Europe which has hitherto been envisaged as chiefly occupied with scholastic debates and building Gothic cathedrals was likewise plunging headlong into the age of power technology. By about 1322 a chronicler of St. Mary's of Pipewell in Northamptonshire could record that one of the chief reasons for deforestation was the search for timbers for the vanes of windmills.[4] The conclusion is inescapable that, whatever the fecundity of the medieval East in other realms of culture, modern technology was born of the Western Middle Ages.

I

The contrast between the technological mood and movement in the medieval West and those in its sister cultures of the Greek and Muslim East is the more curious because communications were generally good and parallel developments frequent even in technology. For example, the first Christian to fly mechanically was the Anglo-Saxon monk Eilmer of Malmesbury who, some time between 1000 and 1010, built wings with which he flew some six hundred yards before crashing, as he said, because he had forgotten to add a tail. Yet in either 1003 or 1008 the famous Iranian student of Arabic philology al-Jauharī met his death attempting flight in some apparatus from the roof of the old mosque of Nishapur in Khorasan. Since, to judge by finds of coins in Scandinavia, by about 985 nomadic activity had temporarily severed the old trade route from the Northern Seas down the Volga to the Caspian and on to Persia, it is unlikely that Eilmer had heard of al-Jauharī, or the latter of Eilmer. But it is entirely possible, in terms of roads and sea lanes then open and frequented, that both had heard of the successful glider flight of Abu'l-Qāsim 'Abbās b. Firnās in Cordoba about A.D. 875.[5]

As Ibn Firnās and al-Jauharī illustrate, technical impulses were

[3] W. Kuhn, "Das Spätmittelalter als technisches Zeitalter", *Ostdeutsche Wissenschaft,* I (1954) 73: "laborare ad unam rotam . . . cum uno furno."

[4] "Et quot virgae molendinorum venticorum dabantur in temporibus diversorum abbatum nemo novit nisi Deus cui omnia patent"; W. Dugdale, *Monasticon anglicanum* (2nd ed., London, 1682) I, 816.

[5] L. White, Jr., "Eilmer of Malmesbury, an eleventh-century aviator. A case study of technological innovation, its context and tradition", *Technology and Culture,* II (1961) 97–111.

by no means lacking in the Near East, and the West's eventual superiority is the more surprising because both Byzantium and Islam, together with the West, had inherited the full equipment of the Roman-Hellenistic world. There is no evidence that any significant techniques were lost during the transition from Antiquity to the Middle Ages. In the Levant there was complete continuity and vitality of culture. In the more turbulent Occident, political disintegration and economic decay made engineering on the old Roman scale infrequent. Yet even there the full technology of Antiquity was available when required: the 276-ton monolith which crowns the tomb of Theodoric the Ostrogoth was brought to Ravenna from Istria and was lowered with fantastic accuracy on to a high drum of masonry.[6] More than two centuries later Charlemagne transported not only sizeable columns but also a great equestrian statue of Zeno across the Alps from Ravenna to Aachen.[7] As for the Roman method of building roads: it appears that neither Islam nor Byzantium chose to retain it any more than the West. The cost of maintenance was out of all proportion to benefits derived, and once the surface of a Roman road began to disintegrate, an unsurfaced road was preferable.[8] Similarly, the hypocaust would seem to have been wasteful of fuel. It remained in use only until Europe invented the more economical and efficient fireplace with chimney-mantel, and then the hot-air stove.[9]

When a seemingly desirable technique vanished, the reason was generally technological advance rather than regression. For example, the Gallo-Roman toothed grain harvester powered by an animal was ingenious, yet was unknown during the Middle Ages. Its defect in medieval eyes was that it wasted the straw, and was therefore appropriate only to a regime of cereals little related to animal hus-

[6] A. Gotsmich, "Das Grabmal Theoderichs in Ravenna", *Universitas,* XII (1957) 1183–94.

[7] Agnellus, *Liber pontificalis ecclesiae ravennatis,* C. 94, ed. O. Holder-Egger in *Monumenta Germaniae historica, Scriptores rerum langobardicarum et italicarum, saec. VI–IX* (Hanover, 1878) 338; Einhard, *Vita Karoli Magni,* C. 26, ed. G. H. Pertz in ibid., *Scriptores,* II (1829) 457.

[8] P. Fustier, "Notes sur la constitution des voies romaines en Italie", *Revue des études anciennes,* LX (1958) 85.

[9] R. J. Forbes, *Studies in Ancient Technology,* VI (Leiden, 1958) 36–57; for the medieval developments, A. Dachler, "Die Ausbildung der Beheizung bis ins Mittelalter", *Berichte und Mitteilungen des Altertums-Vereins zu Wien,* XL (1906) 141–62, remains useful.

bandry.[10] As we shall see, one of the great agrarian advances in Northern Europe during the early Middle Ages was the development of a much more intensive and productive agricultural system combining grain with stock raising. In such a complex, straw had great value, and the Gallo-Roman harvester was worthless.

Again, historians of numismatics have habitually lamented a post-classical decay of the art of minting, virtue being represented, in their opinion, by the magnificent sculptural relief of the best Greek and Roman coins. Not only Western medieval but also Byzantine and Islamic currencies are much flatter. But for bankers, money-changers and merchants, these later coins had a new convenience: they would stack.

We are learning to view the early Middle Ages in new ways. What our grandfathers regarded as decay may indicate merely a shift of interest. In judging our own time we recognize that Picasso's purposes are not those of Ingres; so in contrasting a Roman carved gem with the Sutton Hoo enamels we are today less prone to detect evidence of decline. Changing tastes and conditions may lead to the degeneration of a few techniques or skills in a period when technology as a whole is advancing. The technology of torture,[11] for example, reached new perfection during the Renaissance; its decline in the Age of Reason did not mean that eighteenth-century technology as a whole was degenerating.

But in trying to understand Western medieval technology, it is not enough to probe into the classical inheritance and into the technologies of the medieval Greeks and Muslims. Below the level of the written records, in the subhistory where most of mankind, including the lower classes of Europe, have dwelled until very recently, there was a vast technical osmosis extending over the entire Old World. Joseph Needham[12] is in process of demonstrating in detail such relations between the West and the Far East, while in a brief article[13] I have indicated similar diffusions from Central and South

[10] J. Kolendo, "La moissonneuse antique en Gaule romaine", *Annales: economies, sociétés, civilisations,* XV (1960) 1102–3.

[11] While there is a large literature on the legal aspects of torture, there is little on its changing mechanics. One aspect is handled by W. Treue, *Kulturgeschichte der Schraube* (Munich, 1955).

[12] *Science and Civilization in China* (3 volumes to date, Cambridge, 1954–9).

[13] L. White, Jr., "Tibet, India and Malaya as sources of Western medieval technology", *American Historical Review,* LXV (1960) 515–26.

Asian areas to which our medieval ancestors are usually thought to have had no debt.

Exchanges of technological ideas between the Mediterranean-European peoples and those south of the Ethiopian highlands and the Sahara have scarcely been examined. My colleague in Los Angeles, the geographer Joseph E. Spencer, who has been tracing the very curious global distribution of the agricultural invention of terracing, believes that terraces reached the Niger region from Western North Africa, but that they never penetrated to the zone of heavy rainfall along the Guinea Coast, although terraces have elsewhere proved very useful in similar terrains and climates.[14] The trigger of Benin crossbows is so similar to that used quite recently by Norwegian whalers, that it is assumed to have been introduced by Danish, Dutch or English sailors in the early sixteenth century.[15] But an analogous possible transmission in archery, this time through Arab traders along the East Coast of Africa, warns us that the connexion may be earlier. In the National Gallery, Hieronymus Bosch's *The Crowning with Thorns* (of the very late fifteenth century) shows one of Christ's tormentors wearing, thrust in the folds of his Infidel turban, an arrow with a chisel-shaped head[16] almost identical with one excavated in Uganda from a site thought to date likewise from the fifteenth century.[17]

Even the New World was not entirely removed from medieval technology. It is now clear that by the thirteenth century the Greenland Eskimos had borrowed the art of cooperage from the Norse settlements.[18] Claims that they also adopted the holding screw from the Vikings as a means of attaching bone points to shafts have been doubted. The discussion is not, however, closed: an arrowhead with a holding screw was excavated in north-western Greenland in a

[14] J. E. Spencer and G. A. Hale, "The origin, nature and distribution of agricultural terracing", *Pacific Viewpoint* (Wellington), II (1961) 34.

[15] H. Balfour, "The origin of West African crossbows", *Annual Report of the Smithsonian Institution* (1910) 635–50.

[16] L. Baldass, *Hieronimus Bosch* (2nd ed., Vienna, 1959), plate 110.

[17] P. L. Shinnie, "Excavations at Bigo, Uganda", *Antiquity,* XXXIII (1959) 57, fig. 3b.

[18] E. Holtved, "Archaeological investigations of the Thule district", *Meddelelser om Grønland,* CXLI (1944), Part 2, pp. 14–15, 18, 26, 54; T. Mathiassen, "Inugsuk, a medieval Eskimo settlement in Upernivik district, West Greenland", ibid., LXXVII (1930) 237–9, 295–6.

stratum of the sixteenth century, or earlier than any Eskimo contact with Europeans other than the Norse.[19]

Clearly, in a world teeming with ideas and far more open to their transmission than we have been accustomed to think, technological originality must be understood not only as capacity to generate new concepts and skills but also as the penchant for seizing imported techniques and developing them to new levels of efficiency and types of application.

Such, then, is the context within which we must discuss technological acceleration during the Western Middle Ages. It is a problem which naturally divides into two questions. First, how early and in what ways did the West begin to show its distinctive originality in technological matters and its velocity of technical change? Second, for what reasons did this happen and continue to happen?

II [20]

(1) Between the first half of the sixth century and the end of the ninth century Northern Europe created or received a series of inventions which quickly coalesced into an entirely novel system of agriculture. In terms of a peasant's labour, this was by far the most productive which the world had seen. The earliest new item, the heavy plough, was derived from some Northern peasant society as yet unidentified. The three-field system of rotation, appearing in the later eighth century, was a hybridization of the Mediterranean autumn planting with the ancient Baltic spring planting. The development of open fields aided cattle raising in conjunction with agriculture. Modern harness, arriving probably from Central Asia and first appearing *c.* 800 in the Trier *Apocalypse* (f. 58r), made the horse commonly available in Northern Europe for farm labour. Finally, the nailed horseshoe, emerging simultaneously in Siberia, Byzantium and the West at the end of the ninth century, greatly confirmed the horse's economic uses.

As the various elements in this new system were perfected and diffused, more food became available, and population rose. New supplies of proteins were made available by the stress on dairy

[19] Holtved, op. cit., Part 1, p. 214, Plate 11.30; Part 2, pp. 46, 74, 78.

[20] The documentation for this section will be found in my *Medieval Technology and Social Change* (Oxford, Clarendon Press, 1962).

products, and by the large part which legumes played in the spring planting of the three-field rotation of crops. Moreover the surplus of oats and barley from the spring planting gradually enabled most northern peasants to shift from the ox to the more efficient horse for ploughing and hauling. Mediterranean peasants, in a climate which did not permit extensive spring plantings, continued to plod behind the ox. In the north the greater speed of the horse enabled peasants to live further from their fields, and this led to the decay of small hamlets and the growth of large agricultural villages with a type of life which was almost urban. And the new productivity of each northern peasant enabled more of them to leave the land for the cities, industry and commerce.

More than any other single factor, this agricultural revolution of the early Middle Ages helps us to understand the shift of Europe's focus from the Mediterranean to the Northern plains. In general, the lands of ancient civilization continued to prosper using the Roman methods of agricultural production. But the surge forward of the new agrarian technology of Northern Europe provided the basis for late medieval and early modern civilization.

(2) Moreover in the early eighth century Western Europe seized the initiative in improving methods of warfare, and created a novel military technology so superior that its foes had no alternative but to adopt it.

The stirrup was the most important military invention prior to the cannon. Before the stirrup, a horseman's spear was held at the end of his arm, and the blow was struck with the strength of his biceps. When the saddle with a high pommel and cantle was supplemented with stirrups, a warrior could lay his spear at rest, held between his upper arm and body. Now the blow was delivered not by his arm but by the weight of a charging stallion and rider. The increase of impact altered warfare fundamentally.

The stirrup emerged in India in the late second century B.C. as the big-toe stirrup. By the fifth century A.D. the boot-wearing Chinese had expanded it into the foot stirrup. In the sixth century it is found among the rider peoples of the Altai. In A.D. 694 the Muslim armies fighting in Northern Iran received it from Turkistan. About A.D. 730 it reached Gaul. The Franks were, then, almost the last nation using horses to learn of the stirrup, yet they were the first fully to realize its implications for warfare. In 732, the year before he fought off the Arabs at Poitiers (a battle which, since 1955, has been redated 733), Charles Martel decided drastically to renovate the Frankish host in terms of the new mode of fighting. He began seizing Church lands and distributing them to retainers, and from this military revolution the feudal system developed, as well as the chivalric stratum of European society.

The new violence of the lance at rest called for heavier armour, which in turn produced the crossbow as an 'anti-tank gun'. The shield became pointed at the bottom to offer better protection to the knight's left leg. Heraldic devices grew up to permit identification of the warrior under his carapace. With a lag of about a century, most of the features of Frankish warfare were taken over by both Byzantines and Saracens. It is significant that by 1087, before the First Crusade, the pointed shield is found in Cairo. The Muslims of Andalusia particularly complained that, whereas in Morocco one could fight with light equipment, in Spain they were compelled to assume the heavy armour, the long lances held at rest, the bucklers, the pennons and surcoats of their Frankish adversaries. Moreover they armed their Muslim infantry with the crossbow. Thus, having seized the leadership in agrarian methods in the sixth century, the medieval West did the same in military technology two hundred years later, and thereafter radiated to surrounding cultures much more than it absorbed in matters of warfare.

(3) Finally, by the year 1000, the West had begun that process of saving human labour by applying natural power to industry which so captured Bessarion's imagination over four centuries later. By 983 there may have been a fulling mill on the banks of the Serchio in Tuscany, while a document of 1008 almost certainly indicates others along a stream in Milan. The appearance of the place-name Schmidmülen in the Oberpfalz in 1010 can only mean that water-driven trip-hammers were then sounding in the forges of Germany. Before the end of the eleventh century we have evidence of the use of water-power in the metal and textile trades from the Pyrenees to Britain.

In 1185 the first horizontal-axle windmill appears. Within seven years this new device is found from Yorkshire to Syria, whither it was taken by German Crusaders. In the thirteenth century, one hundred and twenty windmills were built in the vicinity of Ypres alone. In the same period the application of water-power to fulling became so general that, as E. M. Carus-Wilson has shown, the centre of English textile manufacturing shifted from the south-east to the north-west where mill sites were more plentiful. And in general the Continent seems to have anticipated England in such matters. By the early fourteenth century, mills for tanning and laundering, mills for sawing, for crushing anything from olives to ore, mills for operating the bellows of blastfurnaces, the hammers of forges or the grindstones to finish and polish tools, weapons and armour, mills for reducing pigments for paint, or pulp for paper, or the mash for beer, were in ever vaster numbers to be found all over Europe. This medieval industrial revolution powered by water and wind reached its ultimate refinement ninety years after Bessarion's letter when, in 1534, the Italian Matteo del Nassaro set up a mill on the Seine at Paris to polish diamonds, emeralds and the like—a mill taken over by the royal mint in 1552 for the production of the first 'milled' coins. The Europe which followed Columbus and Vasco da Gama into the oceanic routes had had five centuries of growing experience with power technology in industry. No other civilization, not even the Chinese, was nearly so well equipped. The world hegemony of the West during the subsequent five hundred years—now terminating—may partly be understood in this context.

But if the West seized the initiative in agricultural systems in the sixth century, in military methods in the eighth, and in industrial production in the eleventh, how are we to account for this distinctive talent of the European Middle Ages for technological progress? And why did Europe differ so markedly in this respect from its two sister cultures of Byzantium and Islam?

III

No historian in our time dares use the word *cause*. Historical understanding is arrived at, these days, less in terms of causes, in the vernacular sense, than through the isolation of various elements in an historical situation which seem to exert a "gravitational" influence upon each other and to move in a cluster in the direction of the movement which we are trying to comprehend.

(1) The transition from Antiquity to the Middle Ages is best seen as the reassertion of dominance by the native elements in each of the three chief parts of the Roman Empire. The bland cosmopolitan culture of Imperial times—itself a blend of Latin, Greek and Levantine ingredients—began to differentiate once more into vigorous localisms. A distinctive feature of the Islamic world, or of Byzan-

tium, or of the West, may therefore be partly intelligible as the re-emergence of an indigenous trait.

The heart of the Western Middle Ages lay between the Loire and the Rhine. In a remarkable study of Gallo-Roman tombs, J. J. Hatt, the Director of the Archaeological Museum at Strassburg, has shown that from *c.* A.D. 100–275 the sepulchral art of the region of Trier and the Rhineland, the valleys of the Saône and Seine, and Aquitaine, illustrates craftsmen at work with their distinctive tools (of which he gives an inventory) in a way which far exceeds the incidence and elaboration of such scenes in any other province of the Empire.[21] The men who lay beneath these stones had had no sense of inferiority because they laboured with their hands. They wanted posterity to remember them as good workers.

And who were these craftsmen? They were Celts, and thought of themselves as Celts. Hatt has tabulated the occurrence of Celtic names in funerary inscriptions both by period and by region. Our traditional notion that the civilizing of Gaul was identical with its Latinizing must be revised: the Romans planted the cities, but thereby created a Celtic urbanism. Hatt shows that there is a consistent and very marked increase in the percentage of Celtic names in the second and third centuries as compared with the first century. Clearly, Celtic peasants were migrating to the cities and becoming the artisan class; but they continued to prize their Celtic identity, as their names show. Moreover, the highest proportion of Celtic names appear in the parts of Gaul where depictions of craftsmen with their tools are most common.[22]

This is not coincidence. Northern Gaul was a centre of marked technical innovation in Roman times. Any etymological dictionary will show that an astonishing number of Latin terms for carts and wagons (e.g. *cisium, reda, carrus, carruca*) are of Celtic derivation. Presumably the Germans got the heavy horse from the Celts since in the eighth century their laws call it *marach,*[23] a Celtic word. The marvellous technique of forging 'damascened' swords from faggots or rods of iron and steel of different qualities was perhaps invented by Celts under Roman rule.[24] Not only the powered grain-harvester

[21] J. J. Hatt, *La tombe gallo-romaine* (Paris, 1951) 192–4, 246, 293–5.
[22] Ibid. pp. 26–31.
[23] *Monumenta Germaniae historica, Leges,* III, 69, 317; cf. A. Holder, *Altceltischer Sprachschatz* (Leipzig, 1904) II, 417.
[24] É. Salin, *La civilisation mérovingienne,* III (Paris, 1957) 109.

mentioned above, but also the scythe, the hinged flail and the most advanced form of vineyardist's pruning knife seem to be Gallo-Roman.[25] The barrel, a most ingenious application in wood of the principle of the masonry vault, is quite clearly Celtic in origin.[26] Finally, the most puzzling and spectacular item credited to Roman technology appears in the heart of the Celtic area: the water-powered marble saws mentioned in Ausonius's *Mosella*. An unpenetrated jungle of difficulties surrounds this poem.[27] The *Mosella*—a work so much superior to anything else from Ausonius's stylus as to arouse immediate suspicion—is not found in the oldest MSS of his works, or in any MS earlier than the tenth century. There is no marble in the Moselle region: the only marketable stone is slate, which cannot be sawed. There is no other known powered saw until that of Villard already mentioned. I personally incline to regard the *Mosella* as a tenth-century forgery. But if it is authentic and of the late fourth century, its saws are prime evidence of a powerful technological impulse in the area which was to become the centre of Western medieval vitality.

(2) In 1952 the Californian sociologist Margaret Hodgen published *Change and History: a study of dated distributions of technological innovations in England, A.D. 1000–1899*, an investigation of what she calls "the crucial phenomenon of the acceptance of the new". With incredible labour she had studied the history of over twelve thousand English parishes, and concluded that even neighbouring parishes have had surprisingly different histories of technical change. The chief factor making for innovation in a community is prior innovation.

Applying this hypothesis to the Middle Ages as a whole, it would appear that to some extent the greater originality of the West is related to the fact that Latin Christendom was far more profoundly shaken than the East ever was by wave after wave of barbarian invasion, extending, with interruptions, from the third century into the tenth. The Orient indeed experienced turmoil, but was spared

[25] C. Parain, "Das Problem der tatsächlichen Verbreitung der technischen Fortschritte in der römische Landwirtschaft", *Zeitschrift für Geschichtswissenschaft*, VIII (1960) 364–5.

[26] F. M. Feldhaus, *Die Technik der Vorzeit, der geschichtlichen Zeit und der Naturvolker* (Leipzig, 1914) 285.

[27] Cf. *Isis*, XLVI (1955) 291–2.

the degree and prolongation of chaos so characteristic of Europe during the Early Middle Ages. And Byzantium in particular retained a sense of Roman majesty, and an Hellenic contempt for things outlandish, which made it psychologically a bit hostile to innovation. The West, in contrast, was a molten society, ready to flow into new moulds. It was singularly open to change, and agreeable to it.

(3) A third major reason for the technical dynamism of the Western Middle Ages is a fundamental change in the attitude towards nature which occurred with the spread of the new religion. Sambursky is correct in declaring that "the last traces of the old Greek mythological subservience to the cosmos were eliminated by the influence of Christianity",[28] as is Forbes in holding that "Christianity, by its opposition to animism, opened the door to a rational use of the forces of nature".[29] Nevertheless, exactly how the high dogmas of the new faith affected the ordinary peasant and artisan remains obscure: we know strangely little of the history of popular piety. It has long been said that small change occurred: the local *genii* were renamed after local saints, and paganism continued in Christian garb.

Quite the contrary, the shift from animism to the cult of saints was seismic. The spirit of a tree or waterfall or lake was in the natural object, part of it, guarding it, and only partly anthropomorphic. Such a spirit was not like ourselves. A saint, on the other hand, was entirely a human being, on our side as against the phenomena of nature. When saint replaced animistic sprite as the most frequent and intimate object of popular religious concern, our race's earthly monopoly on "spirit" was confirmed, and man was liberated to exploit nature as he wished. The cult of saints smashed animism and provided the cornerstone for the naturalistic (but not necessarily irreligious) view of the world which is essential to a highly developed technology.

The cult of saints was common to all Christendom. It helps us to understand the medieval West, but not in contrast to the medieval East. However, the change in man's attitude towards nature which was inherent in adoption of the cult of saints was greatly reinforced

[28] S. Sambursky, *The Physical World of the Greeks* (New York, 1956) 241.
[29] R. J. Forbes, "Power", in C. Singer et al., *A History of Technology* (Oxford, 1956) II, 606.

by a distinctive development in Northern Europe about the time of Charlemagne.

From the earliest times land had been distributed among peasants in allotments sufficient to support a family: the assumption was subsistence farming, plus enough to pay rent or taxes. Then, as I have said, in Northern Europe and there alone, a great change occurred in methods of farming. Beginning in the early sixth century, the new heavy plough began to spread, equipped with a mouldboard to turn the sod. Friction with the soil was so much greater than in the case of the older two-ox scratch-plough that normally eight oxen were needed. But no peasant had eight oxen of his own. So the peasants began to combine their ox-teams to work a single plough, each taking strips of ploughed land in proportion to his contribution. Thus the standard of land distribution in much of the north ceased to be the needs of a family and became the ability of a new power-engine to till the earth. No more fundamental change in the idea of man's relation to the soil can be imagined: once man had been part of nature; now he became her exploiter.

This new attitude was reflected in Charlemagne's effort to replace the old 'passive' names of the months with new names describing human assaults upon nature: June was to be "Ploughing Month"; July, "Haying Month"; August, "Harvest Month".[30] But also the new orientation emerges in the change in illustrated calendars which begins shortly before 830.[31] The old Roman calendars had occasionally shown genre scenes of human activity, but the dominant tradition (which continued in Byzantium) was to depict the months as static personifications bearing symbolic attributes. The new Carolingian calendars, which set the pattern for the Western Middle Ages, are very different: they show a coercive attitude towards natural resources. The pictures change to scenes of ploughing, harvesting, wood-chopping, people knocking down acorns for the pigs, pig-slaughtering. Man and nature are two things, and man is master. Now, with the old underbrush of animism cleared away, the new attitude provided a soil far more favourable than the old for the sprouting of technological innovations.

(4) Our problem, then, seems partly to be explained by Celtic

[30] Einhard, op. cit. C. 29, ed. cit. II, 458.

[31] H. Stern, *Le calendrier de 354* (Paris, 1953) 356–7; also his masterly "Poésies et représentations carolingiens et byzantins des mois", *Revue archéologique*, XLVI (1955) 164–6.

cultural genes in the West, partly by the fluid attitudes induced by centuries of turmoil, and partly by the emergence of a novel psychological relationship with the physical environment—a relationship produced to some extent by a new attitude towards the supernatural and to some extent by an improvement in agrarian methods in Northern Europe. But I believe that a fourth factor is to be found in the distinctive temper of Latin monasticism.

While Graeco-Roman society had by no means entirely rested on the backs of slaves, and while the effect of slavery in retarding technological advance has certainly been exaggerated, nevertheless manual labour was so associated with slavery in late Antiquity that any free man who dirtied his hands with it, even in the most casual way, demeaned himself.[32] Socrates was a stone-cutter and unabashed about it; but his disciple Plato was more typical in his time.[33] Plato once sharply rebuked two Greeks who had constructed apparatus to help solve geometrical problems: they were contaminating thought.[34] Plutarch tells us that Archimedes was ashamed of the machines he built.[35] Whatever may have been the Syracusan's sentiments, Plutarch's are clear. In the later classical tradition there is scarcely a hint of the dignity and potential for serenity inherent in labour.

The seeds of a very different view of work were to be found in the Jewish community. The fourth Commandment from Sinai said, "Six days shalt thou labour" and this was as religiously binding as the injunction to rest on the seventh day. Rabbi Nathan II taught that "Like the Sabbath, work is commanded. . . . Like the Torah, so

[32] M. J. Finley, "Was Greek civilisation based on slave labour?", *Historia,* VIII (1959) 145–64, provides a thoughtful introduction to a vast literature of controversy on the nature and effects of ancient slavery. On the social and intellectual context of classical technology, see especially L. Edelstein, "Recent interpretations of ancient science", *Journal of the History of Ideas,* XIII (1952) 579–85, R. Mondolfo, "The Greek attitude to manual labour", *Past and Present,* VI (1954) 1–5, and K. D. White, "Technology and industry in the Roman Empire", *Acta classica: Proceedings of the South African Classical Association,* II (1959) 78–89.

[33] P. M. Schuhl, "Remarques sur Platon et la technologie", *Revue des études grecques,* LXVI (1953) 465–72, shows that Plato was well informed about certain technical matters, but does not deny his basic attitude towards manual labour.

[34] Plutarch, *Marcellus,* XIV.

[35] Ibid. XVII.

work is given as a covenant".[36] Many great rabbis worked habitually as woodcutters, shoemakers, tailors, carpenters, and the like.[37] One recalls that the highly educated St. Paul, who had sat at the feet of Gamaliel and who boasted Roman citizenship, not only was a tentmaker but at times supported himself by his trade during his evangelistic missions (Acts, xviii: 3). Moreover, until the fourth century, the Jewish heresy called Christianity remained largely a proletarian faith. By proclaiming that (as St. Peter put it) "God is no respecter of persons" (Acts x: 34) the new religion gave dignity to the humble, and, by implication, to their banausic activities.

But once the persecutions were ended, once the Emperor Constantine himself had been converted and the *labarum* had displaced the eagle as the symbol of Roman might, the Church was flooded by conformists trying to make the best of the new religious situation with minimal inconvenience to themselves. It seemed to many that Constantine had merely managed to paganize Christianity.

The result was monasticism: the effort to retrieve the supposed purity and simplicity of the apostolic church. Integral to monasticism, in both East and West, was the Jewish idea that labour with the hands is not merely a mortification of the flesh, or a practical economic necessity, or even a means of providing charity to one's neighbour: it is a service to God himself, a form of prayer, a joyful oblation.[38] Surprisingly, a concept of work as pure penance for sin, unconnected with prayer and praise, seems to have appeared only

[36] S. Kalischer, "Die Wertschätzung der Arbeit in Bibel und Talmud", in *Judaica: Festschrift zu Hermann Cohens siebzigstem Geburtstage* (Berlin, 1912) 583.

[37] *Authorized Daily Prayer Book*, ed. Joseph H. Hertz (New York, 1954) 630, note; Kalischer, op. cit. p. 605.

[38] J. Leroi, "La reforme studite," in *Il monachesimo orientale* (*Orientalia christiana analecta*, CLIII, Rome, 1958) 194, correctly points to the lack of an adequate history of manual labour in monasticism, which is more deplorable because "aucune observance ne peut mieux servir à définer l'orientation profonde d'un type de vie monastique, ou d'une école spirituelle dans l'histoire du monachisme". Much material, but embedded in a matrix of rhetoric, is to be found in L. Redonet y López Dóriga, *El trabajo manual en las reglas monásticas* (Madrid, 1919). More satisfactory are H. B. de Warren, "Le travail manuel chez les moines à travers les siècles", *La vie spirituelle* LII (1937), 80–123, A. T. Geoghegan, *The Attitudes towards Labor in Early Christianity and Ancient Culture* (Washington, 1945), and E. Delaruelle, "Le travail dans les règles monastiques occidentales due IVe au IXe siècle", *Journal de psychologie normale et pathologique*, XLI (1948), 51–64.

once in Christian monasticism: in St. Columba's Irish rule of the seventh century.[39] Otherwise, with amazing consistency in theory, and only slightly less in practice, the monks of the first millennium both in the Greek East and in the Latin West worked as a form of worship. In doing so they defied the classical attitude towards manual labour which continued to be sustained by the aristocratic society which was their context. So great was the general respect for the labouring monk that we can scarcely escape the conclusion that the attitudes of peasants and artisans towards their own labours, and towards the moral value of labour, were improved. Here we can identify another post-Roman psychic innovation favourable to the vigorous expansion of technology.

But since both Greek and Latin monks shared an identical *mystique* of labour,[40] this does not help us to account for the greater technical acceleration in the West as compared with Byzantium. We must look for significant regional modulations of the common melody.

Monks, both Eastern and Western, held that, in addition to manual labour, the reading of pious books was an essential part of the spiritual life. In theory at least, all monks were literate, and in every generation no small number of them were good scholars. In late Antiquity, with rare exceptions, learned men did not work, and workers were not learned. The monks were the first large group of intellectuals to get dirt under their fingernails: surely a fact related to the growth of technology.

Yet very early a contrast began to develop between the types of erudition fostered in Benedictine abbeys and in those following the

39 Delaruelle, op. cit. p. 61.

40 Indeed, one might argue that Eastern ascetics were even more convinced than Western of the spiritual value of work with the hands, since the Greek abbeys never developed lay brothers, *conversi*, especially designated for manual labor and distinguished from choir monks whose prime duty was *opus Dei;* cf. P. de Meester, *De monachico statu iuxta disciplinam byzantinam* (Vatican City, 1942), 93–5. The elaboration of Benedictine liturgies from the ninth century onward made such a division of function inevitable; cf. P. Schmitz, "L'influence de saint Benoît d'Aniane dans l'histoire de l'Ordre de saint Benoît," *Settimane di studio del Centro Italiano di Studi sull' Alto Medioevo:* V, *Il monachesimo* (Spoleto, 1957), 401–15. According to K. Hallinger, "Woher kammen die Laienbruder?", *Analecta sacri Ordinis cisterciensis,* XII (1956) 38, *conversi* are found in many places in the eleventh century, but not at Cluny before 1100.

tradition of St. Basil. St. Benedict of Nursia had not thought of his disciples as extending their studies beyond the precincts of divinity,[41] but men like his younger contemporary Cassiodorus saw that if anything not only of sacred but of secular learning was to survive in the turbulent West, it would be in the monasteries. In the Greek realm, a literate laity made it unnecessary for monks to devote much attention to worldly writings. Even on such a frontier of Byzantine culture as Calabria, where the Hellenic tradition had long been under Latin attack, by 1457 the sixteen hundred MSS of its Greek abbeys included only six secular items: two Homers—one a fragment—a part of Aristophanes, the *Hecuba* of Euripedes, Galen's treatise on medicaments, and the Greek *Physiologus*. Moreover all five of the literary MSS (excluding Galen) are listed in only two of the seventy-eight monasteries, Seminara and Mesiano, and these were located no more than twenty miles apart.[42] Throughout the Western Middle Ages, monastic libraries and monastic learning had a much higher secular component.[43] While religious studies, quite naturally, were dominant, the pagan Latin authors were sedulously copied and perused. Benedictines were no less devout than 'Basilians', but the cultural environment of their labours had sunk to so low a level that it became part of their religious duty to cultivate all learning, sacred and secular alike. The catastrophes which overwhelmed the West prevented the working intellectuals in the abbeys from withdrawing themselves from worldly concerns as completely as was possible for the Oriental monks. Thus the high valuation of manual labour which was common to both Greek and Latin monasticism was able to permeate Western medieval society more freely than the society of the Byzantine Empire. The viability and continuing economic importance of the idea that *laborare est orare* is nowhere better seen than in the latest and most distinctive form of Occidental ascetism, Puritanism, in which to work not only

[41] "Certes temporibus occupari debent fratres in labore manuum, certis iterum horis in lectione divina": *Sancti Benedicti Regula monachorum: textus critico-practicus secundum Cod. sangall. 914, ed.* P. Schmitz (Maredsous, 1955), § XLVIII, p. 109.

[42] *Le "Liber visitationis" d'Athanase Chalkéopoulos* (1457–1458), ed. M. H. Laurent and A. Guillon (*Studi e testi,* CCVI, Vatican City, 1960) 47, 107, 111. There is no indication that these libraries had yet been looted by the neo-Hellenic enthusiasts then emerging in Northern Italy.

[43] Cf. M. L. W. Laistner, *Thought and Letters in Western Europe, A.D. 500 to 900* (Ithaca, 1957) 228–35.

in but *through* one's 'calling' became both the prime moral necessity and the chief means of serving and praising God.[44]

(5) There is another contrast between the Greek and the Latin Middle Ages which helps to illuminate the different practical effects in these two regions of an identical monkish doctrine of labour. Historians of theology and philosophy have long pointed to two very different moods which seem to pervade the thought of the two great segments of Christendom: emphasis on *theoria,* contemplation, intellectual or mystical understanding in the East; emphasis on *praxis,* activity, the disciplining of the will by good works in the West. In the past such contrasts between Latin voluntarism and Greek intellectualism have been based on what authors have said. The historian must ask not only what they said, but the extent to which they really meant what they said.

Fortunately a new school of historians of exegesis, by using methods somewhat like those of art historians, is penetrating not only the convictions but also the religious tastes of the past: they are exposing the subliminal mind. For our purposes the exegesis of the Martha-Mary pericope (Luke x: 38–42) is of particular significance. Since the first great crisis in the history of the Church was the Petrine-Pauline confrontation, inevitably Martha was identified with the synagogue and observance of the Mosaic law, whereas Mary represented the Church and the freedom of the New Covenant. But as soon as Christianity had definitely seceded from Judaism this exegesis vanished, and, in keeping with the Hellenizing of Christian thought, Origen took Martha to represent the active and Mary the contemplative life.[45] Thenceforth in the Greek Church it became customary to regard this episode as giving Christ's sanction to the contemplative rather than the practical life, to the monastic rather than the secular.

One discovers, however, a quite different style of exegesis in the West. St. Ambrose, himself formerly a high Roman official, looks at the sisters of Bethany and feels that they represent *actio* and *inten-*

[44] E. Troeltsch, *Social Teaching of the Christian Churches* (New York, 1931) 609–12.

[45] T. Camelot, "Action et contemplation dans la tradition chrétienne", *La vie spirituelle,* LXXVIII (1948) 275. It is notable that St. Ephraem Syrus, writing in Syriac and almost uninfluenced by Platonic tendencies, adopts elaborate stratagems to avoid ranking Martha's activism below Mary's contemplative bent; cf. I. Hausherr, "Utrum sanctus Ephraem Mariam Marthae plus aequo anteposuerit", *Orientalia christiana,* XXX (1933) 153–63.

tio: they are both essential, and the one cannot rightly be called superior to the other.[46] Then Augustine, with his devastating originality, inverts the Greek exegesis and the structure of values which pervades it. His constant preoccupation is the contrast between time and timelessness, between Church Militant and Church Triumphant: a contrast which makes each of his writings, almost each of his sentences, an antiphon of praise. To him, Mary and Martha are symbols of two stages in the perfect life: Martha the life of the soul in the context of time and space; Mary, in the context of eternity. To be sure, by grace the elect soul may catch occasional glimpses, foretastes, of timeless blessedness, but for practical purposes we must be Marthas troubled about many things: "In Martha erat imago praesentium, in Maria futurorum. Quod agebat Martha, ibi sumus; quod agebat Maria, hoc speramus."[47] Whereas in the Greek Orthodox world activity was something to be transcended, in the Latin Catholic world it was a spiritual obligation. In this Western atmosphere, technology could thrive.

Until after 1100 at least, the activity and attitudes of the monastic orders so permeated every tissue of the medieval organism that one would not expect the technological adventure of that era to be confined to the abbeys, or perhaps even centered there. Nevertheless, the monks maintained interest and at times leadership in the field. In the twelfth century, for example, the Cistercians set the pace in applying water-power to a variety of industrial processes: in St. Bernard's own abbey of Clairvaux there were three waterwheels powering different shops devoted to grinding grain and sifting the flour mechanically, to fulling and to tanning, all of which is recounted with great satisfaction in a contemporary life of the Saint.[48]

(6) A sixth and final aid to our understanding of the acceleration of Western medieval technology is found in Christian theology as enunciated with a Latin intonation. Christianity, both Eastern and Western, in theory at least ascribes infinite worth to even the lowliest of human beings as potentially "children of God; and if children then heirs . . . and joint-heirs with Christ" (Romans viii: 16–17). Despite the rigidity of class structures, spiritual egalitarianism con-

[46] D. A. Csányi, "Optima pars", *Studia monastica,* II (1960) 56–7.
[47] *Sermo* 104: 4, cited by A. M. de la Bonnardière, "Marthe et Marie, figures de l'église d'après saint Augustin", *La vie spirituelle,* LXXXVI (1952) 425.
[48] Cited in Singer et alii, op. cit. II (1956) 650.

tinued to resound in the churches with every chanting of the *Magnificat,* while through the centuries preachers and commentators like Isidore of Seville noted with interest that God's foster-father, St. Joseph, was a blacksmith, while the Prince of the Apostles was a fisherman.[49] But the Greek East, with its more contemplative bent, its tendency to abstraction, has felt less impulse than the West to make faith concrete in works.[50] Only in the West does one find a religious urge to substitute a power machine for a man where the required motion is so severe and monotonous that it seems unworthy of a child of God. As early as the sixth century an abbot in Gaul, troubled by the sight of his monks grinding grain in hand mills, built a water-driven mill, "hoc opere laborem monachorum relevans".[51]

Human history is not mathematical. Valid results are at times achieved on the basis of wrong assumptions. The New World is not abolished by the fact that Columbus sailed westward to find the East Indies and died thinking that he had succeeded. To deny or minimize the culturally desirable products of Christianity because one may consider Christianity to be a fabric of illusions, is as subjective as to argue that Christianity is true because some of its effects seem salutary.

The nineteenth-century revulsion against abuses symbolized in Blake's "dark Satanic mills" has blinded historians to the fact that Western labour-saving power technology is profoundly humane in intent, and is largely rooted in religious attitudes. Its ideology is the Christian doctrine of man as developed not in the context of Greek contemplative intellectualism but rather in the framework of Latin voluntarism.[52] The power machines of the Western Middle Ages

[49] "Joseph justus, cui virgo Maria desponsata exstitit, faber ferrarius fuit . . . et Petrus princeps apostolorum piscatoris officium gessit"; Isidore, *Regula monachorum,* V, 2, in J. P. Migne, *Patrologia latina,* LXXXIII (Paris, 1862) 873.
[50] R. E. Sullivan, "Early medieval missionary activity: a comparative study of Eastern and Western methods", *Church History,* XXII (1954) 17–35, shows that while the Greek evangelists in the Slavic north were very theological in their emphasis and seldom supported themselves economically, the Western missionary was not only a preacher but a "farmer, builder and technician" who introduced not only a new religion but new crops and skills. Moreover, Western preaching was less concerned with doctrine than with ethics.
[51] Gregory of Tours, *Vitae patrum,* C. 18:2, ed. B. Krusch in *Monumenta Germaniae historia, Scriptores rerum merovingicarum,* I (Hanover, 1885) 735.
[52] Lynn White, Jr., "Dynamo and Virgin Reconsidered", *American Scholar,* XVII (1958) 183–94.

which amazed Bessarion were produced in part by a spiritual repugnance towards subjecting anyone to drudgery which seems less than human in that it requires the exercise neither of intelligence nor of choice. The Western Middle Ages, believing that the Heavenly Jerusalem contains no temple (Rev. xxi: 22), began to explore the practical implications of this profoundly Christian paradox. Although to labour is to pray, the goal of labour is to end labour.

PART II

Man

CHAPTER 5

Introduction: The Human and the Divine

DANIEL O'CONNOR

The most fundamental impact of the idea of creation on the theory of man can be very simply formulated: man is not divine nor part of the divine. It is the unanimous verdict of the religious philosophies of the ancient world that man or at least a part of man shares essentially in the divine nature. But this claim is radically negated by the doctrine of creation. The Hebrews alone among ancient peoples were able to entertain a notion of "secular man." We saw in Part One that the doctrine of creation permits, indeed requires, a desacralization of nature: nature is not to be confused with God; it is the result of the divine creative *fiat*—not a necessary emanation from the divine substance, not an "alienation" and externalization of the divine Idea, but a created world, wholly separate from God and utterly dependent upon Him. Similarly, man is not a part of the divine substance which has fallen into the dark prison of matter, and not the divine spirit as it becomes self-conscious, but a created and incarnate spirit, conscious and free, made "in the image and likeness of God."

This point is so central that we must take some pains to establish it by consulting the ancient texts. In the typical cosmogonies of the Near East the creation myth presents man as fashioned from the body of a god or generated by divine parentage. In the Babylonian *Enûma Elish*, for example, man is fashioned out of the blood of the evil deity, Kingu.[1] In the *Orphic Fragments* Zeus is depicted as fashioning man from the ashes of the Titans, whom he had destroyed with one of his thunderbolts. Their crime had been to dismember and devour the infant-god, Dionysus.[2] Man has thus a two-fold divine inheritance. Particles of the divine Dionysus in each human soul are engaged in a life-long struggle with the dark Titanic element. The object of the Orphic rituals and purifications was to ensure the escape of the Dionysian element and its reunion with the god.

If the soul is essentially divine, how account for its present condition? The answer given in varying formulations by all the myths is: by a primordial fall. The theme of the primordial fall of the soul runs through most of the mythopoeic and philosophical writing of the ancient world. Professor Claude Tresmontant has recently published a comprehensive study of this theme in pagan writers together with the responses given to it by early Christian authors.[3] His account traces the theme in the Upanishads, the Orphic writers, the pre-Socratics, Plato, the Gnostics, and Plotinus. There is, of course, considerable variation in the details and the elaboration of the theme and, among the philosophers, important differences in the reasons offered to support the theme. But the common core might be formulated as follows: the soul was originally part of the divine essence, the One. Owing either to a fault on the part of the soul or to a necessary process of self-elaboration on the part of the One, multiplicity is introduced. Souls are individualized by being cast down into material bodies which are compared to "prisons" and "tombs." The whole object of life is to free this divine element from the degrading effects of its temporary union with a body. By passing through many such embodiments (including animal and vegetable, in many versions) or by passing back through progressively purer emanations, the divine spark will be finally reunited with the eternal conflagration of the One.

Such myths had great influence in religious cults and in the popular imagination. But it was their translation into philosophical

[1] VI, 1–38, in A. Heidel, *The Babylonian Genesis* (Chicago: University of Chicago Press, 1951), pp. 46–7.

[2] *Orphicorum Fragmenta*, 220–221, cited in W. K. Guthrie, *Orpheus and Greek Religion* (London: Methuen, 1935), pp. 107–9.

[3] C. Tresmontant, *La Métaphysique du Christianisme* (Paris: Editions du Seuil, 1961).

language which had more direct influence on the history of ideas. In order to exhibit the impact of the biblical idea of creation we must, therefore, briefly consider some of these philosophical translations.

The philosopher, Empedocles, writing about the middle of the fifth century B.C., gives a vivid statement of the myth:

> There is an oracle of Necessity, an ancient decree of the gods, eternal, sealed fast with broad oaths, that when one of the divine spirits whose portion is long life sinfully stains his own limbs with bloodshed, and following Hate has sworn a false oath—these must wander for thrice ten thousand seasons far from the company of the blessed, being born throughout the period into all kinds of mortal shapes, which exchange one hard way of life for another. . . . Of this number am I too now, a fugitive from heaven and a wanderer, because I trusted in raging Hate. . . . For by now I have been born as boy, girl, plant, bird, and dumb sea-fish.[4]

From the surviving fragments of his writings, we can gather that Empedocles attempted to fit this picture of human being into a general theory of the cosmos, of which the principal feature is a continual fusion and separation of elements in an eternal, cyclical pattern.

Plato frequently mentions the doctrine of the divine soul and its primordial fall,[5] and he uses it to express his most profound and cherished convictions. It is true that he sometimes exhibits a skeptical, even a playful, attitude towards the details of the myth,[6] but there is no doubt about his adherence to its general content: the divine character of the soul and its natural immortality.[7] In the *Phaedo,* for example, the argument reaches a climax in the following passage:

> Now, Cebes, he said, see whether this is our conclusion from all that we have said. The soul is most like that which is divine, immortal, intelligible, uniform, indissoluble, and ever self-consistent and invari-

[4] Frag. 115, 117 in K. Freeman, *Ancilla to the Pre-Socratic Philosophers* (Oxford: Blackwell, 1956) p. 65.

[5] *Cf. Phaedo* 66 b seq.; *Gorgias* 493 a; *Meno* 81 a–d; *Cratylus* 400 c; *Phaedrus* 246 b–250 d; *Republic* 614 b–621 d; and *Statesman* 272 d–273 c.

[6] In *Phaedrus* 247 e and *Gorgias* 493 a, for instance, but not in the *Phaedo* and the *Republic.*

[7] I am accepting here Guthrie's interpretation of Plato's use of myth in general and of the Orphic myth in particular. See *op. cit.,* pp. 239–244.

> able, whereas body is most like that which is human, mortal, multiform, unintelligible, dissoluble, and never self-consistent.[8]

In the *Phaedrus* the myth is used to explain the possibility of true knowledge even in our present confused condition of dependence on bodily powers of sense. True knowledge is a recollection of that clarity of vision we once possessed in the primordial state.

> Now, as we have said, every human soul has, by reason of her nature, had contemplation of true being; . . . but to be put in mind thereof by things here is not easy for every soul. Some, when they had the vision, had it but for a moment; some when they had fallen to earth consorted unhappily with such as led them to deeds of unrighteousness, wherefore they forgot the holy objects of their vision. Few indeed are left that can still remember much, but when these discern some likeness of the things yonder, they are amazed, and no longer masters of themselves, and know not what is come upon them by reason of their perception being dim.[9]

The soul is uncreated, immortal by nature, divine—that is Plato's conviction. But the biblical account of the creation of man is flatly opposed to the Platonic doctrine.

> And God said, Let us make man, wearing our own image and likeness; let us put him in command of the fishes in the sea, and all that flies through the air, and the cattle, and the whole earth, and all the creeping things that move on earth. So God made man in his own image, made him in the image of God. Man and woman both, he created them.[10]

Couched in poetic and figurative language, to be sure, but there is no mistaking the point that man is created and does not share the divine essence. If he is to enjoy immortality, that, like his very being, will be the free gift of the Creator.

As we can readily verify in Tresmontant's collection of texts,[11] the early Christian writers were quick to see that their beliefs were incompatible with the myth of the divine soul and its fall into matter. With some exceptions, these early Christians were admirers of Greek culture, many of them had been trained in the classical *paideia*. The cultivated men among them were particularly sensi-

[8] *Phaedo*, 80 b (Tredennick trans.).
[9] *Phaedrus*, 250 a (Hackforth trans.).
[10] Gen. I, 26–27 (Knox trans.).
[11] Tresmontant, *op. cit.*, pp. 370–518.

tive to the intellectual beauty and elevated morality of Platonism.[12] Yet they were fully aware that their belief in creation led them to formulate a novel anthropology. From the very beginnings of Christian literature the adherents of the new faith knew that they had to rethink the theory of man. St. Paul's insistence on the resurrection of the body—a concept quite foreign to Greek thought—would be a case in point. But it is among the early apologists, writers who explicitly undertook to meet the challenges of Greek thought, that we may clearly see the formation of a new theory of human nature. Justin Martyr, for example, just after the middle of the second century, seeks to refute Plato's claim in the *Phaedrus* that the soul has a natural affinity with the divine and that it is by nature immortal.[13]

Two decades later, Irenaeus is still more explicit on the point. Dealing with a Gnostic version of the doctrine, he remarks:

> For if it is on account of their nature that all souls attain to the place of enjoyment, and all belong to the intermediate place simply because they are souls, as being thus of the same nature with it, then it follows that faith is altogether superfluous, as was also the descent of the Saviour (to this world). If, on the other hand, it is on account of their righteousness (that they attain to such a place of rest), then it is no longer because they are *souls*, but because they are *righteous*. . . . For if nature and substance are the means of salvation, then all souls shall be saved; but if righteousness and faith, why should these not save those bodies which, equally with the soul, will enter into immortality?[14]

One can also see in this text a linking of the freedom and responsibility of man with faith in creation. This introduces a considerable novelty in comparison with the various forms of the myth of the fall. On the Christian view man bears the final responsibility for his own destiny, and his free and final choice is irrevocable. In all the variants of the myth of the fall, though there is a link-up between man's actions and his fate (e.g. in the chain of reincarna-

[12] See É. Gilson, *A History of Christian Philosophy in the Middle Ages* (New York: Random House, Inc., 1955) for the attitudes of individual Fathers. W. Jaeger has written an interesting account of the relations of some of the Fathers to Greek thought in his *Early Christianity and Greek Paideia* (Cambridge, Mass.: Harvard University Press, 1961).

[13] *Dialogue with Trypho*, Chaps. IV–VI.

[14] *Against Heresies*. II, xxix, in Ante-Nicene Christian Library (Edinburgh: T. & T. Clark, 1868) Vol. V, p. 229.

tions nobler status is assigned to the soul who has acquitted himself well in the previous incarnation), in the end, *all* the soul-fragments return to the One. None are finally lost and the possibility of their destruction is never raised. It seems fair to say that in those systems of thought, man's freedom is, at most, a resistance—temporary and futile—to the necessary and inevitable process of exile and return. We will come back to this point later.

The criticism which nearly all the Fathers heaped upon the myth of the divine soul and its fall did not eliminate it from the history of thought. In fact, that system of thought which gives the myth its most impressive and coherent treatment, the *Enneads* of Plotinus, was written in the middle of the third century, well into the Christian era.[15] Once again, this new treatment of the myth called forth a series of responses from Christian authors, of which that by Augustine in his *City of God* was the most sustained and powerful. From that same book, which sums up the thought of the Greek and Latin Fathers, we can document the idea of human nature which early Christianity, conscious of its novelty, presented to the world.

The human being is not part of the divine nature but wholly separate and created; it had no preexistence in some other life, but was born into this world at a definite moment, though promised the gift of subsequent immortality.[16] Its birth is not a punishment, nor the result of a fall, but rather the beneficent gift of a personal history in which man will be offered the choice of union with God, a choice which is his to accept or reject.[17] Matter, including the human body and its activities, are also created; they are therefore good and will share in the promise of eternal life.[18] Life is thus a drama of human freedom with a determinate result and not an endless cycle of exile and return.[19]

Such in merest outline are the fundamentals of the new idea of man based on the doctrine of creation. The purpose of this second Part is to draw out a few of the most important implications of these fundamental tenets and to show their novelty against the background of classical thought. The three essays which follow

[15] For a treatment of the *Enneads* from the standpoint of the myth of the divine soul, see Tresmontant, *op. cit.*, pp. 319–359, for its revival in Spinoza, Fichte, Schelling, and Hegel, see the same, pp. 709–746.

[16] *City of God*, X, 31.

[17] *Ibid.*, XI, 17, 22, 23.

[18] *Ibid.*, XIV, 5; XXII, 4, 5.

[19] *Ibid.*, XII, 13, 17, 20.

deal separately with temporality, human freedom, and the question of good and evil. It might not be out of place here to dwell on the interconnection of these ideas.

In some ways the most surprising of these themes in the present context is the theme of temporality. We take for granted the representation of time as an upward sloping line. We are used to thinking of historical change, of novel developments, of decline and progress. A *linear* conception of time comes naturally to us. We may be willing to concede difficulties in thinking about the nature of time and the relationship between the abstract uniform time of science, on the one hand, and the vagaries of lived time, on the other. We might also admit to some confusion about the notions of the beginning and the end of time. Difficulties in our linear concept might thus be admitted. But we are likely to be surprised when we are forced to recognize that an *alternative* concept is possible and was, in fact, dominant in the classical world until the advent of Christianity.

Greek philosophers, quite generally, held that the cosmos was eternal. With few exceptions, they regarded the cosmos as an organic whole wherein each phenomenon could be understood and explained only through its relations to other phenomena. The fundamental principle of such an explanation is formulated by Empedocles in two characteristically pointed fragments:

> Fools!—for they have no long-sighted thoughts, since they imagine that what previously did not exist comes into being, or that a thing dies and is utterly destroyed. From what in no wise exists, it is impossible for anything to come into being; and for Being to perish completely is incapable of fulfillment and unthinkable. . . .[20]

Being is eternal. *Ex nihilo nihil fit*—nothing comes of nothing.[21] Nature, for the Greeks, is an eternal process.

[20] Frag. 11, 12 (Freeman trans. p. 52).

[21] This is not just a Greek axiom, it is an axiom of scientific explanation. All phenomena are causally linked to other phenomena in which their explanation is to be found. The idea of a spontaneous beginning, without activity of the same phenomenal kind, cannot therefore fit into a scientific explanation. As Kant convincingly demonstrates, scientific explanations deal only with connections between phenomena *within* an indefinite series. No scientific statements can be made about the beginning, the end, or the whole of the series. (This is another way of saying that "creation" is not a scientific idea; it is an idea of the imagination to which one must adhere by faith, not understanding.)

Aristotle is only summing up the dominant tradition in Greek philosophy when he argues that motion is, by nature, eternal, since to initiate motion or to destroy it would itself require motion.[22] But an eternal, continuous motion, he argues, must be circular. The world process as a whole, then, must be conceived as perpetual cycle in which, since the number of possibilities is finite and the duration infinite, all possibilities will be not only realized but repeated *ad infinitum.*[23] This is the notion of the "eternal recurrence of the same" which haunted the ancient world.[24]

The idea was represented in different forms and with different degrees of radicalness. The reincarnation of souls in an otherwise stable universe is a mild variant. More radical is the notion of a periodic loss and recovery of all knowledge, suggested by Plato and Aristotle.[25] Perhaps only in the Stoic doctrine of the world-periods do we find a consistent and fully radical position. At definite intervals, variously computed, the whole universe is generated out of the eternal Divine Fire. At the end of the period the universe is completely destroyed in a general conflagration and then begun anew. All the personalities, actions and events of the cycle are repeated in exact detail. Once again Zeno will meet with his pupils on the Painted Porch to teach them the doctrine of world cycles. Strictly speaking, there is no novelty in the endless series; the world epoch is like a film which will be rerun forever. For the rational soul, itself a part of the Divine Fire, wisdom and right conduct consist in acquiescing gracefully, even joyfully, in this inexorable fate. Not all thinkers reached this radical conclusion, of course, nor saw its consequences if they did. Yet the conclusion seems to follow from the premises of the eternity and self-sufficiency of the cosmos, which were quite generally upheld by Greek philosophers.[26]

[22] *Physics,* Book VIII.

[23] *Cf.* W. Jaeger, *Aristotle* (New York: Oxford University Press, 2nd. ed., 1948), p. 389. In the *De anima,* however, Aristotle rejected the idea of transmigration as incompatible with his theory of *psyche* as the form of the body. (I, 3; 407 b 13).

[24] See M. Eliade, *Cosmos and History: The Myth of the Eternal Return* (New York: Harper and Row, 1959), for a general and introductory discussion.

[25] Jaeger, *Aristotle,* pp. 133 ff.

[26] It is Nietzsche who insists on the logical implication and also on the corresponding ethical doctrine of *amor fati.* See the discussion in W. Kaufman, *Nietzsche* (New York: Meridian Books, 1956), pp. 274–286.

Prescinding from the details and variations of the different Greek writers, it seems fair to say that, in general, Greek thought does not distinguish history from nature. Human affairs are likened to the eternal movements of the celestial bodies. The "history" of mankind is part of the one natural process of the cosmos.

The doctrine of creation, by contrast, forces a distinction between nature and history, between the recurring patterns of celestial movements and terrestrial seasons, on the one hand, and the irreversible course of individual and societal destiny, on the other. In place of the Greek circle we have the biblical *historia* with beginning and end. With the advent of Christianity there emerges also a midpoint, the appearance of Christ, which to the believer clarifies the direction and meaning of historical development.

In his contributing essay, Emil Brunner forcefully draws out the full impact made by the doctrine of creation on the idea of temporality. To his account I would add only one emphasis which clarifies the connection between the ideas of temporality and freedom.

Greek thought paid little attention to the idea of individual personality as a unique reality, a qualitative unit which cannot be treated as a mere quantum nor replaced by other units without a discernible difference. This conception of personality, now a firm possession of the Western mind, was foreign to the Greeks. Two theories conspired against its emergence in the classical world: firstly, the cyclical theory of time already discussed. That theory obviously denies the uniqueness and importance of individual events and, by extension, of individual persons. Everything shall be repeated again, the trivial, the absurd, the banal, as well as the momentous. No event stands out as incomparable. To the Greek intellectual the notion of attaching infinite significance to a historical event was senseless and absurd, as St. Paul discovered when he attempted to preach the gospel in Athens.[27]

The second reason for the lack of an idea of individual personality is the principle of Greek epistemology that the individual is unknowable, ineffable, a surd factor. Knowledge is of the general, the formal and the typical. To know the human being is to know the form or essence of humanity as it is differentiated in a natural hierarchy of excellence or as it is specified from other forms of life

[27] Acts 17: 16–23.

by determinate faculties and potentialities. The individual as such is apprehended by the senses alone and cannot enter *as* individual into the objects of knowledge. A striking illustration of this attitude is given in the Platonic speculation of the reincarnation of man in animal form,[28] which later Platonists defended on the ground that all souls are of one essence and form—human, animal, and vegetative alike.[29] A similar example is offered by Aristotle's difficult speculations on immortality in his *De anima* which, in the most plausible interpretation, confer that status on one active intellect which is shared by all men, in other words, on an impersonal faculty.[30] It would be foolish to deny that there were mighty personalities in the Greek world, in particular the philosophers themselves, or to fail to see that the high moral earnestness of most Greek philosophy encouraged individuals to strive for self-knowledge and self-fulfillment. The point is only that, according to the theories, the standard of such striving was an eternal archetype which did not distinguish between persons.

But where there is no clear notion of individual personality there can be no affirmation of freedom in the full sense. Here too the doctrine of eternal cycles works against an idea which has become common property in the West. This is clearly pointed out by Origen in his polemic against the pagan philosopher, Celsus.

> [Celsus asserts] that the period of mortal life is similar from beginning to end, and it is inevitable that according to the determined cycles the same things always have happened, are now happening, and will happen. If this is true, free will is destroyed. . . . Socrates will always be a philosopher and be accused of introducing new deities and of corrupting the youth; Anytus and Meletus will always be accusing him, and the council on the Areopagus will vote for his condemnation to death by hemlock. . . . Jesus will again come to visit this life and will do the same things He has done, not just once but an infinite number of times according to the cycles. . . . And again Celsus will write his book, though he has written before an infinite number of times.[31]

[28] *Phaedo* 81 e, *Republic* 620 a.
[29] *Cf.* H. Chadwick, *Early Christian Thought and the Classical Tradition* (New York: Oxford University Press, 1966), p. 116 and note 85 on p. 167.
[30] Aristotle, *De anima,* III, 5: for a discussion of the various interpretations see the introduction to Hick's edition (New York: Cambridge University Press, 1907), pp. lxiv–lxix.
[31] *Contra Celsum,* IV, 67. Ed. by H. Chadwick (New York: Cambridge University Press, 1965), p. 237.

But long before Origen, the Stoic sages had insisted that there is no escape from the iron ring of necessity present in the eternal cycles. And, more generally, we can see that there is a relation of implication between the ideas of the eternal cycles, the divinity and reincarnation of souls, and determinism. But conversely, we must also admit a reciprocal implication and a solidarity between the ideas of an irreversible sequence of events, individual personality, and human freedom.

Erich Frank's essay on "Letter and Spirit" deepens and strengthens a conviction of this solidarity. The essay is difficult and densely packed; yet it deserves and rewards a close study, not overlooking the important footnotes. With respect to the idea of freedom, Frank is making essentially two points: 1) the idea of freedom latent in the doctrine of creation and fully emergent only in the Christian era is absolutely new and unprecedented in Greek philosophy, and 2) this new idea has still not fully established itself in philosophical thought because of a continuing struggle with that Greek idea which it seeks to replace.

The very kernel of Greek ideas of freedom is *order:* the eternal, rational order of nature in which every thing and every man has its place. In Greek philosophical thought human freedom is always dependent on reason, understood as the power to discern that fixed order of nature. Indeed, freedom is in effect equated with this power of true vision. Knowledge lifts the scales from man's eyes and he discerns his place in the natural hierarchy. Conversely, lack of freedom stems from ignorance; it reflects a disorder within the human soul or within society. This conception is given a powerful and definitive statement in Plato's *Republic.* In the Greek view, the power of God does not stand above the natural order; in fact, where the divine is admitted in Greek philosophy, it is equated with the eternal, rational order. God does not transcend nature. Even in Plato's *Timaeus,* where Greek thought comes closest to the biblical concept of transcendence, the "father and maker of all this universe" shapes it according to "the eternal pattern of the unchangeable." [32] His function is to impose the rational order upon a not wholly tractable chaos or "receptacle." [33]

In practice, the conception of freedom in Greek society also turned on the idea of natural order. Freedom was an objective status, a name for certain ranks in society. That man is free whose

[32] *Timaeus,* 28 c–29 b.
[33] *Timaeus,* 48 e–51 c.

human needs have been secured, who has the necessary leisure to devote himself to a public life in the affairs of the city.[34]

In the Christian view, by contrast, man is free because God is free. The creation of the world is the result of God's free will, subject to no necessity. The order of the world reflects His intelligence and wisdom but He stands above it, freely ordaining its continuation or its suspension. Man, made in "the image of God," shares in this power of creative will. In his will, even more than in his reason, man bears the divine likeness. Since man's power is not absolute, his freedom is conditioned. Nevertheless, it is much more than the power to choose between presented alternatives. Within its limits, it is the power to create genuine novelty, to introduce something new into the otherwise regular course of nature. In the prologue to the second part of the *Summa Theologica,* the treatise on man, Thomas Aquinas gives concise expression to this point:

> Since, as Damascene states, man is said to be made in God's image, in so far as the image implies an intelligent being endowed with free-will and self-movement; now that we have treated of the exemplar, i.e., God, and of those things which come forth from the power of God in accordance with His will, it remains for us to treat of His image, i.e., man, inasmuch as he too is the principle of his actions, as having free-will and control of his actions.[35]

The last of our three themes, represented here by Étienne Gilson's essay "Christian Optimism," is that of good and evil. Here, too, the doctrine of creation is rich in consequences. In a non-created universe the problem of evil can be solved by singling out some feature of the universe as the source and principle of evil. In the metaphysical theories of the ancient world this role inevitably fell to matter. But in a created world such a solution is possible only if we attribute malice to the Creator. If the Creator is good, what He creates—all reality—must be good. Evidently, then, we cannot regard evil as a created reality, as if it were something that could have been left out of the universe. We must regard it as the result of a tendency unavoidably present in all creatures, a tendency towards that nothingness from which only the creative power restrains them. Since the Creator has chosen to call forth

[34] I am here relying on H. Arendt's interesting account in *The Human Condition* (New York: Doubleday Anchor Books, 1959).
[35] I–II, *Prologus* (Dominican translation).

from that nothingness a creature made in His own image, i.e., endowed with will and freedom, the possibility is raised, over and above the passive tendency towards nonbeing, of an active choice of the lesser good and, in the extreme case, a choice of nothingness. The creation of man constitutes a risk. In that risk, the value of a conscious affirmation of being has been measured against the refusal of all value, nihilism. Belief in a created world, this is Gilson's theme, is the expression of a profound optimism, not denying the presence of evil, but dwelling instead on the emergence of good. It is, we might say, a specifically *humanistic* optimism because it is the acceptance of the possibility of evil as a necessary condition for free man, and the assertion of man as the highest created value.[36]

[36] For an interesting discussion of the idea and the history of Christian humanism, see G. MacGregor, *The Hemlock and The Cross* (Philadelphia: Lippincott Co., 1963).

CHAPTER 6

The Problem of Time

EMIL BRUNNER

The relation of man to time is an essential factor determining the character of existence for the individual, as well as for whole epochs and different civilisations. Everyone knows that the haste and rush which characterise our life are something typically modern, and probably a symptom of a deep-seated disease. But there are few who take account of the basic elements which determine man's relation to time. It is not because modern man has watches and time-saving machinery that his life shows an ever-increasing speed; modern man has watches and time-saving machinery because he has a certain relation to time, which expresses itself most crudely in that often heard phrase: I don't have time! Now that even children in the nursery use this phrase, we can no longer postpone investigating the roots of the apparent time-disease of the present world.

All who have travelled in the East with open eyes and an impressionable mind are at one in finding an immense contrast between the quiet of the Orient and the unrest of the West. Although we cannot deny that certain external elements of technical civilisation contribute towards this striking difference, its real cause does not lie on this superficial level, but in a different relation to time. The Orient has a conception of time entirely different from that of the

West, and this difference belongs to the religious and metaphysical sphere. In all Oriental philosophy and religion, time is something irrelevant and illusory compared with eternity, although the individual interpretations of this basic conception may differ. Reality is beyond and above the time-process. Change means imperfection. Just as a man looking for change does so because he is not satisfied with what he has, so nothing that is subject to change can be looked upon as true being. That which exists must have duration, persistence; it must be changeless, being satisfied with itself. It is not possessed by an urge to get what it does not have, to become what it is not yet. True being is eternal. This idea is common to the whole Eastern world, however differently this eternal being may be interpreted. The radical expression of this idea is again found in India. The world of change is unreal. Reality is—as we heard in a previous lecture—the One and All which cannot change, and therefore has no relation to time. It is timeless, motionless, self-satisfied eternity; therefore it is the deepest desire of the Indian thinker to enter into or to share in that motionless eternal being, in Nirvana.

This conception, however, was not foreign to ancient Greece. We find it in its most daring expression in the system of Parmenides, and in a less extreme form in Plato's idealism. The ὄντως ὄν, the true being of the world of ideas, is distinguished from mere appearance or the half-reality of the world of sensations by this very fact, that it is timeless eternity beyond all change. This world of sensible experience, however, is taken up with an incessant stream of change and becoming. There is a clear-cut opposition between eternity and the temporal world. Eternity is the negation of time: time is the negation of eternity. How this time-world came into being, and what kind of being it has, is a question which can hardly be answered satisfactorily from Plato's presuppositions. On the one hand, Plato wants to get away from the blunt negation of the temporal world as represented by Parmenides; on the other hand, he does not seem to succeed in giving the world of time and becoming its proper place. Neoplatonism which, as we have already seen, is so important for the formation of the mediaeval world, tried to solve the problem by the concept of emanation, emanation meaning at the same time a kind of degeneration. By a process of flowing out or going down, a whole hierarchy of half-realities is established between the eternal, true being and absolute nothingness. In this hierarchy the distance of each step from the eternal is also its distance from true being or the measure of its approach to nothingness. Thus a continuum reaching from eternal true being to zero is conceived, which forms a parallel to the modern concept of evolution but runs in the opposite direction.

Modern man's understanding of time is quite different from this conception. To him the temporal is the real. Whether there is anything eternal is uncertain; but that the things in time are, is beyond question. But what is his concept of time? As it is quantity which determines his concept of reality, time also is a quantum—measurable time, time which consists of time-units, time-atoms. The second hand of the watch is the symbol of modern man's understanding of time. He looks for reality in the present moment, but the present moment is the smallest indivisible element or fraction of time. Life, then, cannot be but the sum or addition of such fractional time-entities, of time-atoms. This quantified physical time has completely lost its distinctiveness from space; it has become a fourth dimension of space.[1] Quantified time is spatialised time. Time dwindles away into space. It has no quality of its own. It is interchangeable with the dimensions of space, and is therefore always about to pass into zero.

It is this conception—not the watch or the telephone or the aeroplane—which is the cause of man's not having time. Time was lost to him metaphysically long before he had overcome it technically. The exact time-signal on the radio, which every decent citizen notes in order to set his watch correct to the second, the wrist watch, which at any moment shows him the exact time—all these devices have been invented because man wants them, because time vanishes under his fingers, because he does not have time any longer. We have reached here the opposite pole from the Oriental view. Reality is pulverised temporality. It is in vain that Faust wishes to see that moment to which he can say: "Verweile doch, Du bist so schön!" It is in vain that Nietzsche exclaims in a superb poem: "Denn alle Lust will Ewigkeit, will tiefe, tiefe,

[1] Of course Bergson's idea of *durée réelle* was an attempt to overcome this spatialisation of time; just as, in a very different way, was Heidegger's conception of *Dasein* (*Sein und Zeit*). But both solutions of the time problem are very different from that of Christianity, Bergson's *durée* being a pantheistic or mystical mixture of temporality and eternity, Heidegger's *Dasein*, on the other hand, being correlative to life-unto-death, without a Beyond. But it is highly important that the leading philosophers of our age are dealing with the problem of time much more intensively than any previous school of philosophy.

Ewigkeit". If once you have declared your option for the moment, the fate of your reality as radical temporality is determined, and radical temporality is vanishing time. Time dwindles away, constantly approaching zero.

It is for this reason that modern man wants to snatch as much of this time as possible, to get as much "into his time" as he can. He begins, so to say, a race with time, and in this race man is inevitably the loser, because it is the last moment which decides, and the last moment is death. Man races death, but death wins. Over the whole of life there looms this certainty of a lost race with death. But no one likes to face it. The thought of it is avoided, because man's chances are so absolutely hopeless. Modern man puts out of sight as well as he can all reminders of death; he does not want to hear of it, because the thought reminds him of his being the loser. All the same, the remembrance of death stands behind him with its whip like a slave-driver and urges him on. This —and this—and this I must have, cries man, before it is too late, before the door closes for ever. It is the panic of the closed door. This panic explains many of the features which are typical of modern life: man's hasty enjoyment, his all-dominating craving for security, to which finally he sacrifies freedom and his soul.

The Christian understanding of time and its relation to eternity stands midway between, but also above and beyond, the opposing views of East and West. At first sight it seems much more similar to the Eastern than to the Western concept, its main thesis being that God is eternal, and that therefore true reality is eternity. Is not the Gospel the promise of eternal life? Is it not said that God is unchangeable? "With Him there can be no variation, neither shadow that is cast by turning." [2] He is the same yesterday, to-day and in eternity. "For a thousand years in Thy sight are but as yesterday, when it is past." The time-process in its totality, from beginning to end, is present in Him. For Him there is no surprise. Everything that happens does so according to His eternal decree. God is eternal.

But the relation of this eternal God to temporal being and becoming is totally different from what it is in Indian thought or in the systems of Parmenides, Plato or the Neoplatonists. God creates the time, He *gives* time. As He, the Almighty, gives man room for his freedom, so He creates time for him, for his becoming and for

[2] James I, 17.

his free action. Temporality is not an approach to nothingness any more than the created world is unreal. God has created time together with the world, He has set a beginning to time and will set an end of time. He gives every man his time, with a beginning and an end to his temporal existence, but the end of time and the beginning are not the same. The time-process does not come back to its beginning. Between these two points, the start and the finish, something happens, which even for God is real and significant. There is history, an individual and a universal human history, in which God is infinitely interested. He is so intensely concerned with this history that He not only looks down on the scene of human life like an interested spectator, but He Himself intervenes in it. Even more, at a certain point in this time-process, He Himself enters the scenery of temporal life; He, the eternal, appears in the shape of a historical person and, as such, performs, once and for all, the decisive act of all history. The incarnation of the word of God is at once the insertion into time of the eternal God: "When the fulness of time came, God sent forth His son".[3] And in Him He revealed unto us the eternal secret of His will.[4]

This event charges the time of man's history with an extreme tension.[5] It is the time of expectation of the end, that end which is not the closed door, but the open door. It is the expectation of fulfilment. Time conceived in that fashion is the time of decision and probation. It is that time in which the eternal fate of the individual is decided. Therefore this sense of time is as remote from Oriental indifference to the temporal as from that time-panic of the modern Westerner. It is of the utmost significance, because it is within time that everything is decided for us, and every moment is a moment of decision. In every moment we have to keep faith; the servants must be awake all the time, for they do not know the day and the hour when the Lord comes; they do know, however, that if the Lord finds them sleeping they are lost, and that it will be said to them, as to those foolish virgins battering in vain on the closed door of the wedding-feast, "I know you not".[6]

All the same, in spite of the tremendous tension and the weight of decision involved, this temporality is not the ultimate reality; it

[3] Gal. IV, 4.
[4] Eph. I, 9.
[5] *Cf.* my article, "Das Einmalige und der Existenzcharakter", in *Deutsche Blätter für Philosophie,* 1929; and *Die christliche Lehre von Gott,* S. 285 ff.
[6] Matt. XXV, 12.

is an intermezzo between divine election in the beginning and eternal perfection beyond time, beyond the limit of death, beyond this historical movement.

These two aspects of time enable us to understand the Christian concept of history. As has often been observed, neither in Oriental nor in classical Greek thought does the problem of history play any rôle. For the Oriental as well as for the Greek—and, we may say, for all humanity outside of Biblical revelation—the image of temporal happening is that of the circle. Temporality, as far as it has any reality and any significance, is a circular movement, always returning on itself. It is the same movement which we observe in nature: day and night, summer and winter, birth and death in perpetual rotation. This movement, then, has no climax; it leads nowhere. It is therefore not worth while making it a problem of thought. This is why Greek philosophy, to which everything else has become a problem, never made history an object of philosophic reflection.

The theme of history as a topic of thought is Judeo-Christian, brought into our consciousness by the Old Testament prophets and by the New Testament Gospel. Here history is no circular movement. History is full of new things, because God works in it and reveals Himself in it. The historical time-process leads somewhere. The line of time is no longer a circle, but a straight line, with a beginning, a middle and an end. This is so because—if I may use a simile—God Himself has entered this circular time at a certain point, and with His whole weight of eternity has stretched out this time-circle and given the time-line a beginning and an end, and so a direction. By this incarnation or "intemporation" of the word of God, time has been charged with an immense intensity. It has become, as we have said, the time of waiting, of decision and probation. Thus history has become interesting as a theme even for the thinker. It is now worth while for a thinker of the highest calibre, like St. Augustine, to write his *De Civitate Dei* as a kind of Christian philosophy of history, in fact the first philosophy of history ever written.[7]

We have been speaking of the tension of temporality. Compar-

[7] Of course it is true that Augustine's *De Civitate Dei* is no *philosophy* of history as Troeltsch points out (*Der Historismus und seine Probleme,* S. 14 and note, S. 15). The question is whether anything which Troeltsch would have acknowledged as *philosophy* would be able to deal with that which a Christian would acknowledge as *history*.

ing, however, the Christian existence with that of the panic-stricken modern man, we could also speak of a removal of tension. "For I am persuaded, that neither death nor life . . . nor things present, nor things to come . . . shall be able to separate us from the love of God, which is in Christ Jesus our Lord." [8] "For I reckon that the sufferings of this present time are not worthy to be compared with the glory which shall be revealed in us." [9] Christian man, through his faith in Christ Jesus, is time-superior, time-exempt; he lives already in the coming eternity. Important as earthly events may be in his life and that of other men, the all-important, the true decision has already been made in Christ, and the believer's life consists only in living on the basis of this earlier decision. This is what is meant by "Living by faith".

The Christian conception of time, then, permits and even obliges us to partake in temporal happenings with the utmost intensity—the picture presented by the New Testament being usually that of an athlete on the race-course, spending his last energy to reach the goal—and at the same time to be free from the haste and over-excitement created by the panic of the closed door. Those who live in faith are seriously intent on something going forward on this earth, something being bettered, so that the will of the Creator may be more fully expressed in His creation than it is now, under the domination of evil. But at the same time the life-feeling of the Christian is not dependent on whether or not this earthly goal is reached. He knows that whatever he can do for the realisation of God's will is at best something relative. He knows that whatever goes on within this temporality is encircled by the limits of death and fragility. And yet this insight into the insurmountable barrier does not make him resigned. His true, ultimate hope is not based on what can be achieved within temporal history, but upon that realisation of the divine purpose, which is neither dependent on man's action, nor happens within time, but sets an end to the temporal world, and which is not *a* goal, but *the* goal, the ultimate τέλος, the perfection of all things, which God gives and effects in bringing about life eternal.

The Christian understanding of history and its goal is sharply distinct from the idea of progress and evolution, which is characteristic of our era. Such a concept of universal evolution is un-

[8] Rom. VIII, 38.
[9] Rom. VIII, 18.

known not only in the Eastern world but also in the West, so far as regards antiquity, the Middle Ages, and the period from the Reformation right up to the 18th century. Where the totality of temporal reality is interpreted by the symbol of a circle, there is no room for the idea of universal progress. Neither Heraclitus' *πάντα ῥεῖ*, nor Aristotle's entelechy means anything like a directed time-process. The stream of happenings of which Heraclitus speaks is a movement without direction and goal, an eternal fluctuation comparable to the moving sea. But neither does Aristotle's entelechial movement have any reference to history. It is an eternal movement without beginning or end. No Greek thinker ever conceived the Cosmos in such a way that it represents a movement in time directed towards a goal, so that the later generations of time are somehow better off than the previous ones. If there is anything like a universal direction in this time-process, it is a movement downwards rather than upwards, a decline or degeneration rather than an evolution or progress. Such is the mythical concept of the successive world-epochs, as we find it in Hesiod, and a similar consequence might be drawn from Neoplatonic metaphysics.

The idea of evolution is, however, also entirely unknown within early Christianity. It is true that the basic conception of the coming kingdom of God includes the idea of a goal of history. It is also true that within this historical, temporal world a hidden germ of this kingdom of God is growing, intensively and extensively. Still, the idea of universal progress is impossible within this Christian conception because, alongside this growth of the kingdom, there is the concurrent growth of the evil powers and their influence within this temporal world. The tares are growing together with the wheat.[10] The opposition to the kingdom is growing at the same rate as the kingdom itself, so that the later generations are in no way better off than the earlier ones. On the contrary—it is in the last days that the conflict between good and evil forces reaches a climax. The goal of history is reached not by an immanent growth or progress, but by a revolutionary change of the human situation at the end of history, brought about not by man's action, but by divine intervention—an intervention similar to that of incarnation, namely the *παρουσία*, the advent of the Lord, the resurrection of the dead, the coming of the eternal world. That this end of human history is utterly distinct from continuity and immanent growth is

[10] Matt. xiii, 30.

most clearly expressed in the idea of the *dies irae*, the day of the Last Judgment, which puts an end to human history. The framework of this Universe is broken, death—"the last enemy", and the characteristic feature of the temporal world—is overcome and annihilated, and the eternal world is established. There is no room in this picture for the idea of universal progress and evolution.

On the other hand, the popular belief that the idea of evolution and progress was first worked out within natural science, and thence affected the conception of history, is false. The reverse is true: the idea has been transplanted from an evolutionary conception of history into natural science. Lamarck and Darwin are not the pioneers but the heirs of this modern idea. The real pioneers are men like Rousseau, Lessing, Herder, Hegel. The idea of progress and evolution is a child of the optimistic philosophy of the Enlightenment.

Its basis is an optimistic evaluation of human nature and, as its negative consequence, the repudiation of the fundamental Christian ideas of the Fall and of original sin. Human nature as such is good; at least, it is raw material fit to be shaped into something good, into true humanity. This anthropology seems to be based not on axiomatic speculation but on observation, on facts. History does begin with primitive man; he is the raw material out of which perfect humanity can be shaped. He it is whose mental capacities are not yet developed, whose cultural life has not yet begun. Civilisation and culture are acquired only in the course of a process extending through thousands of years, growing from generation to generation. It is this undeniable fact of the continuous growth of the benefits of civilisation, and of a progressive use of man's mental capacities, which is the backbone of the 18th-century idea of the universal progress of humanity.

This idea, however, is possible only by using a very dubious equation, *i.e.* the supposition that the more developed human life is in the cultural sense, the more human or good it is in the ethical sense; that moral evil is therefore only the primitive, the not-yet-developed; and that the good, the truly human is identical with the no-longer-primitive, the developed. Or—to express the same from the negative angle—the idea of universal progress is made possible only by denying the Christian conception of evil as sin, *i.e.* egoistic self-will and self-affirmation contradicting and opposing the will of God and the moral law. According to the Christian conception, there is continuity between the primitive state of mind and the developed one, but between the morally good and the morally evil there is no continuity but merely contradiction. Moral evil, understood as sin, is not that which is not yet good, but that which is no longer good. Sin is not undeveloped good, but spoilt and perverted good. It is not something which is not yet there, but it is a present reality of a negative character, the antagonism of men's will to the will of God. It is therefore only by substituting for the contradiction, for the Yes-and-No relation, the merely relative contrast of less and more, that the idea of universal progress is possible. As a consequence, the Christian idea of redemption is replaced by the idea of cultural development. The more man is trained to use his mental faculties, the more he gains power over the outside world and over his own forces, the more human he becomes, so the more evil disappears. This is the basic illusion of this favourite and most influential idea of modern man.

But where did 18th-century philosophy get the idea of a goal towards which history moves—an idea which was utterly foreign to rational philosophy in pre-Christian times? The answer, I think, is obvious, and the proof for it can easily be found in thinkers like Lessing and Herder. The idea of a universal goal of history is a Christian heritage, although completely transformed in context. Whilst, in the Christian view of history, this goal is transcendent in character, namely the world of resurrection and eternal life, it has now become immanent, being here identified with an imaginary terminus of the movement which leads from the primitive to civilised cultural life. In this fashion was formed that inspiring—not to say intoxicating—idea of idealistic progressivism which has taken hold of the best minds since the middle of the 18th century. It is the bastard offspring of an optimistic anthropology and Christian eschatology. Humanity as a whole is involved in a unique process, leading upwards from primitive beginnings, from a more or less animal start, to the loftiest peaks of true spiritual humanity, a process which is far from being finished, in which our generation is involved; one which perhaps will never be finished, but the end of which we are steadily approaching.[11]

[11] The first idealist philosophy of history is Lessing's *Erziehung des Menschengeschlechts,* 1777 and 1780, soon followed by Herder's *Ideen zur Philosophie der Geschichte der Menschheit,* 1784–90. I do not know any system of philosophy of history, not even Hegel's, which shows more clearly the traits of this

It is this idea of evolution which modern natural science inherited and which it had only to supplement, to support and substantiate by its own means. From this idealistic conception Lamarck, Lyell and Darwin drew their ideas of an all-embracing evolution of life on this globe. The scientific evolutionism of the later 19th century is composed of two elements: this idealistic idea of progress, combined with certain observations in the field of biology. What 18th-century philosophy had worked out in the limited field of human history was now brought into a much larger context. The history of the forms of organic life on our planet seemed to corroborate such an optimistic idea of a universal development. Was it not a fact that everywhere the primitive, undifferentiated forms precede the differentiated, the higher forms of organisation? Therefore it would appear that life is moving onward to unknown heights. Again, it was not seen that this naturalistic form of evolutionism is based on an unjustified identification, namely that the more "differentiated" in the biological sense is the "higher" in the human or spiritual sense.

But, once taken for granted, this idea of evolution seemed to give a new value to temporal becoming, which in the thought of the ancient world was a merely negative concept. In the course of becoming the perfect seems to emerge gradually.[12] The splendour of the idea of perfection, which in ancient philosophy had been identified with the transcendent and timeless world of ideas, and which in Christian thought had been reserved for the divine, supernatural sphere, then seemed to have shifted over to the historical world and to natural forces. From then on it seemed to be possible to believe in perfection on the basis of purely secular, natural, even material, principles. Since the idea of progress had come into the

optimistic evolutionism than Schleiermacher's, embedded in his "philosophische Ethik".

[12] The typical and most influential representative of this optimistic evolutionism is Auguste Comte in his *Cours de Philosophie Positive* and *Système de Politique Positive, ou traité de sociologie, instituant la religion de l'humanité, 1830–54.* Whilst in Comte's system the faith in science is combined with a spiritual, although entirely immanent element, Herbert Spencer's evolutionist philosophy has got rid even of this remainder of religion or idealism. Spencer puts his faith in evolution entirely on the natural process of "differentiation" and "integration" and on the rôle of utilitarian thinking. The more recent idea of "emergent evolution"—as, *e.g.* expounded in Laird's Gifford Lectures (*Theism and Cosmology*) is a combination of speculative idealism and naturalistic evolutionism following Bergson's neo-Schellingian idea of *évolution créatrice.*

wide field of natural science, it seemed to have become independent of all metaphysical and religious presuppositions. It had become an instrument of natural explanation.

This was certainly not the conception of Rousseau, Lessing, Herder and Hegel. When they were speaking of evolution, they meant something which was at the same time immanent and transcendent, natural and divine. For them evolution was not merely a causal process of differentiation, but in the literal sense an evolution, *i.e.* the disclosure of something divine hidden in the natural. To them the time-process was at once both natural and supernatural and certainly, in any case, teleological and spiritual, not merely causal and material. But with Darwin's theory of selection, teleology seemed to be superseded. The one principle of causality was sufficient not only to explain a process as such, but to explain a progress, *i.e.* a process with a certain definite direction. Now it was possible to have finality without a principle of finality, to have teleology on the basis of causality, to have a direction of history by merely natural forces—in a word, automatic progress.

This new phenomenon—the idea of evolution and progress—is not only important from the point of view of becoming, but also as an element in that feature which we found so characteristic of our age, the temporalisation of existence. By means of the idea of evolution it seemed possible to repudiate eternity and still keep all those values which in previous times had been connected with the eternal. The eternal is no more necessary to give meaning to life. Temporal life, interpreted in terms of evolution, had meaning, direction and finality in itself. For that reason evolutionism became one of the most potent factors of temporalisation, of radical repudiation of the idea of eternity within the conception of human existence.

But I am constrained to offer some observations which lead to a different conclusion:—

1. Even granted that the idea of universal progress is correct—which we never should admit—it is undeniable that the result of this progress means very little to the individual. One has to think in generations, in centuries. This means that the interest moves away from the personal to the collective. The individual and his fate, his future, become irrelevant. It is only the totality which counts; or rather it is an abstract humanity forming, so to say, the subject of this evolution.

2. Therefore this present existence has no meaning and value of its own. It is merely a point of transition, a rung on the ladder which leads upward. Its own value—if you ask for such estimate—must be left indefinite, and is therefore open to question.
3. But these factors lead in the direction which we have been calling the dwindling-away of time. The real, existing man appears to himself like a snapshot, a fraction of a large reel of film—a picture which, taken by itself, is as meaningless as a single frame cut from a movie strip and as absurd as a slow motion film. So this idea of evolution must—once its first intoxicating effect is over—take the whole substance away from life. It means that life is, as it were, eaten away from the inside.

Needless to say, this idea of a universal progress of such a natural upward movement is irreconcilable with Christian faith. This does not mean that the Christian cannot acknowledge certain aspects of the evolutionary theory of natural science. From the point of view of Christianity, there is no reason to deny that life on earth has a long history, spanning millions of years; that it has passed through many transformations; that the origins of mankind lie far back in prehistoric, primitive beginnings, presumably in animal forms. Within the limits which conscientious scientists have set for themselves, the evolutionist theory is not in conflict with Christian faith.

Two elements of this evolutionist thought, however, must be unconditionally rejected from the Christian point of view: first, the identification of moral evil or sin with the primitive; and, second, the assumption that the development of human intelligence, technical skill and cultural enrichment mean in themselves a progress in the sense of the truly human. The Christian conception of man includes the belief that the higher differentiation of intellectual powers, as well as the increase of the means of civilisation, is most ambiguous with regard to goodness and to the truly human. It can mean an increase of moral evil, of destructive inhumanity, just as much as the opposite. Civilised man, with the highest scientific and technical training, and commanding the accumulated wealth of ages of civilised life, may still be morally bad, even devilish, and if he is, he is so much the more dangerous. The highly developed human mind and the highly developed human civilisation may come to a point where they are capable of destroying all gains and goods in one frantic moment of diabolical madness.

This is why the modern identification of the idea of progress with the Biblical message of the kingdom of God is a demonstrable error which has most fatal effects. The idea of progress means a movement from here to there, from below to above, reaching more or less steadily towards a point in the far future, in which perfection is conceived of as materialised. The Christian message of the coming kingdom, however, means just the opposite movement—a movement coming down from above to below, from "heaven", *i.e.* from the transcendent, to earth. Where it reaches the historical plane, it breaks the framework of this temporal, earthly existence. That is what is meant by resurrection, *parousia,* eternal life. The New Testament knows nothing whatever of a kingdom of God which develops according to the idea of progress, slowly, immanently, from below upward. This so-called kingdom of God is simply an invention of the 19th century, read into the Bible, but not to be found there. It is a mixture of the New Testament message and modern evolutionism, out of which nothing good can come, but only illusion, disillusionment and final despair.

One last question has not yet been touched: From the point of view of Christian faith and hope, what is the result and value of the historical process? This question cannot be answered by a simple scheme. The Christian expectation of the coming kingdom first of all places everything historical under the radical negation of the divine judgment. All human history is flesh, taking the word in its Biblical sense. Therefore it is transient. From the texture of history the two dark threads of sin and death cannot be eliminated anywhere, from the beginning to the end. They belong to the picture of historic life. History in its process already performs part of this judgment upon its own creations. "Die Weltgeschichte ist das Weltgericht." History devours its own children; whatever it brings forth passes away some day. This, however, is only one side of the picture. There is also continuity, there is tradition, there is historical heritage. Not every epoch begins anew from nothing. We all live from the stored-up wealth of previous ages. Eternal life is not only the negation, but also the fulfillment of this earthly life. It is not only a new world, but also the perfection of this world. Even our body, which seems to be particularly perishable and unfit to inherit the eternal, will be not simply destroyed, but transformed into a completely obedient organ and expression of the life of the spirit.

If, however, we ask whether there is any part of this reality, any element of our present experience, which as such shall be deemed worthy to enter into the perfect eternal existence, the answer must be, Yes indeed, there is one element which, whilst being an experience within the Christian life, will also be *the* element of eternal life, namely love in the New Testament sense of Agapé. Neither the State, nor culture and civilisation, nor even faith and hope, are that element which remains in eternity, but love alone. For God Himself is Love. That is why it is said that whilst all other things pass away, including faith, knowledge, language and hope, love alone remains, and this love is the principle of true humanity.

CHAPTER 7

Letter and Spirit

ERICH FRANK

The idea of creative freedom is a religious conception. It is unverifiable by reason, and yet, only on the supposition of such a freedom can man find truth and destiny in history. Throughout these lectures, belief has proved to be the ultimate ground of fundamental philosophical concepts. Our task has been to elucidate philosophy through belief and belief through philosophical reason. In interpreting the true meaning of religious and philosophical ideas we have tried to grasp the spirit which is behind the letter.

Plato described the task of the philosopher as the endeavour to read the script of the world and to understand its true meaning.[1]

[1] Plato's metaphorical use of the word 'letter' has a distinct philosophical meaning: To him the invention of the alphabet is a symbolic example of a logical analysis (*diaeresis*). This discovery proved to man that even the infinite variety of speech sounds can be reduced to a finite number of general constituents. Thus the Greek word for 'letter' (στοιχεῖον, Latin *elementum*) gained the philosophical meaning of 'element.' In this sense already Democritus seems to have called his atoms 'letters,' 'elements.' For as the word (Greek *logos*) which represents reality consists of ever-recurring constituent parts, so the whole universe consists of simple substances and can be represented through a corresponding combination of these 'elements.' (Cf. Aristotle, *Metaphysics,* I, 4, p. 985b4; *Gen. et Corr.* I, 2, p. 315b14; Lucretius I, 196, 912, II, 1013; H. Diels, *Elementum,* Leipzig, 1899, p. 16 f.; O. Lagercrantz, *Elementum,* Uppsala, 1911, pp. 11 ff.; and my book, *Plato und die sogenannten Pythagoreer,* 1923, pp. 169 ff.)

But is this not precisely the aim of the religious thinker as well? St. Paul, in formulating the ultimate secret of Christianity, uses the metaphor of letter and spirit.[2] Yet, the significance of his expression surpasses all that philosophers before him had ever thought; it indicates an entirely new understanding of truth, which resulted from the religious experience of the Christian. Greek philosophers, and again modern thinkers, have considered religious ideas as mere letters, figurative expressions to be interpreted in terms of a rational understanding of the world.[3] For St. Paul, the relation between letter and spirit is just the opposite: mundane reality is the letter, which must be read in the spirit of a more sublime truth. To him, everything in the world—man, philosophy, and even morality—is without meaning unless it is taken as a symbol.

In Christianity, interpretation therefore acquired an importance that it had never had before. One may even say that the struggle to ascertain true interpretation epitomizes the whole history of Christian faith. To curb the unrestrained freedom of a merely personal

In an analogous way Plato compared his primary principles, the 'Ideas,' with the letters of the alphabet: The philosopher by means of a *diaeresis* divides reality into its logical 'elements' and represents its original unity through a reciprocal synthesis. Thus his method of dialectic is modelled after the art of writing and reading. (Cf. Plato, *Philebus,* pp. 17A ff.; *Sophistes,* pp. 253A ff.; *Theaetetus,* pp. 20E ff.; *Politicus,* pp. 278A ff.; *Cratylus,* p. 423E and in Diog. Laert. III, 19; Aristotle, *Metaphysics,* pp. 1053a12 ff., 1014a26; 1041b12 etc.) This is a concept of logical procedure which was revived by Leibniz in his plans for a 'Characteristica Universalis' and which through him is effective even in our time. In a general sense then the word 'letter' can be regarded as a symbol for any universal concept, gained through logical analysis, and it is in this sense that I use the word 'letter': to denote the opposite of original unity, of the 'spirit,' which gives the letter its proper meaning.

[2] Second Epistle to the Corinthians 3. 6: 'Who also hath made us able ministers of the new testament; not of the letter, but of the spirit: for the letter killeth, but the spirit giveth life.' Cf. below notes 16 and 33.

[3] The Greek philosophers considered the gods of popular religion as merely mythical expressions of those rational principles which they understood as the 'true elements' of the world (cf. notes 17 ff. to ch. II). But the same method of allegoric interpretation has also been applied by modern philosophers in order to justify the ideas of their religion. According to Kant and to most modern thinkers the true meaning of Christ's teaching is not different from the moral law of reason. Philosophers like Hegel or Whitehead interpret religion in terms of their metaphysics (cf. note 45 to ch. IV, and note 40 to ch. V). But no such 'allegoric' interpretation can do justice to the particularity and profundity of religious thought. Long ago Plato ridiculed such a naïve procedure (*Phaedrus,* 229 ff.).

and subjective exegesis, the Church was obliged to establish an objective canon and a strict dogma. In support of its letter, it developed a new rational philosophy based on the Christian spirit. The authority of tradition and the independence of thought were in constant opposition, and by this conflict all Church disputes, among Catholics and Protestants alike, were determined.[4]

Out of this striving after truth arose the sense of intellectual integrity and freedom which led eventually to a repudiation of all religion. It was Nietzsche, the most radical antagonist of the faith, the self-styled anti-Christ, who admitted: 'We atheists, we godless foes of metaphysics, we too take our fire from that conflagration which was kindled by a thousand-year-old faith, from that Christian belief . . . the belief that God is the truth, that truth is *divine*.'[5] Indeed, the philosophical ideas which form the natural and unquestioned presuppositions of the modern sceptic originated in Christianity. Augustine was the first to formulate them in trying to express rationally the Christian spirit as he had found it in himself. He established the new concepts of the conscious ego as opposed to the outside world, of personality, of time and of history; he raised the problems of free will and of inward truth; in short he laid the philosophical foundation of modern thought.[6]

[4] The modern methods of historical hermeneutic have their origin chiefly in the discussions of the Protestants and Catholics about the correct interpretation of the Bible. The Council of Trent (1545-63) occupied itself with these problems. In 1567 appeared the Protestant standard work, the *Clavis Scripturae Sacrae* by M. Flacius, and in 1581 R. F. Bellarmin formulated the Catholic principles of exegesis in a polemical treatise which was intended to refute Flacius. (W. Dilthey, *Werke*, vol. v, 324 ff.; II, 110 ff.; cf. also J. Wach, *Das Verstehen*, 3 vols., Leipzig, 1926 ff.)

[5] Nietzsche, *The Genealogy of Morals*, III, 24, Engl. transl., 1910, p. 197, cf. p. 194: 'These solitaries and deniers of today; these fanatics in one thing, in their claim to intellectual integrity; all these pale atheists, anti-Christians, immoralists, Nihilists; these sceptics . . . these supreme idealists of knowledge—in point of fact they believe themselves as far away as possible from the ascetic ideal [of Christianity] . . . And yet they represent it nowadays and perhaps no one else, they themselves are its most spiritual products.'

[6] Cf. my paper, *St. Augustine and Greek Thought*, 1942. To be sure, Greek philosophers such as Stoics, Sceptics and Neoplatonists had prepared the ground for Augustine's subjectivism (cf. note 28). The Jewish philosopher Philo had tried to ascertain the meaning of biblical concepts like that of free will. (Cf. H. A. Wolfson, *Harvard Theological Review*, 1942, pp. 131 ff. and note 31.) The principle of voluntaristic metaphysics had been developed by the Christian Neoplatonist Marius Victorinus, by whom Augustine undoubtedly

No matter how far present-day man may have deviated from Christianity, liberty, will, love—*these* he is not willing to renounce. More than that: it is precisely his insistence on freedom, his feeling of sovereignty, which is the driving force of modern philosophy. This we find with Descartes, in his indubitable *cogito,* which expresses the basic assumption of the new age, the independence of reason and the supremacy of man over nature; we find it in Kant's principle of autonomous morality; we find it in Marx and in Bolshevism, for which social revolution means the collective liberation of man; we find it in pragmatism; and we find it in modern Democracy, where the freedom of the individual forms the basis of all political activity. Even in the most secularized forms of modern thinking, then, free will and sovereign personality have remained pre-eminent ideals.[7]

These principles, however, by which the modern philosopher is led, are entirely at variance with that criterion by which he would test the truth of his ideas. Modern philosophy has endeavoured in vain to establish the freedom of will through either positivistic or rationalistic postulates. The Positivist declares that this problem is merely illusory: We may observe the psychological fact that we will, but we shall never be able to prove that this experience has a correlate in reality.[8] Free will transcends indeed all that we can perceive, and can never be proved by the evidence of the senses. Modern rationalists, on the other hand, have argued that man finds his autonomy precisely in reason, in his concurring with his own rational laws, but this argument obviously is a vicious circle.[9]

was influenced (cf. Benz, *Marius Victorinus,* Stuttgart, 1932). Nevertheless Augustine must be considered the true originator of all these ideas. (Cf. note 30.)

[7] Cf. the notes 45 f. to ch. v.

[8] Cf. the formulation of Bertrand Russell, *Mysticism and Logic,* New York, 1929, p. 208.

[9] Cf. note 47 to ch. v. Kant was fully aware of the danger of a vicious circle in such a theory of freedom. He says: 'It must be freely admitted that there is a sort of circle here from which it seems impossible to escape . . . There was indeed a latent circle involved in our reasoning from freedom to autonomy: viz. we lay down the idea of freedom because of the moral law only that we might afterwards in turn infer the latter from freedom . . . Consequently we could present it as a *petitio principii.*' (Cf. *Fundamental Principles of the Metaphysics of Morals,* London, 1926, pp. 83 and 87.) Although he tried to evade the vicious circle through subtle distinctions, one may doubt that he succeeded. St. Augustine and St. Thomas, on the other hand, did not have to

Freedom of will does not mean only choice between given possibilities, rather it means the very creation of such possibilities. Free will is the power to act in accordance with one's own thought, that is, the sovereign power to change given facts, to reshape factual reality, and to control it. It remains inexplicable to human reason; and yet, without such freedom of will and thought, truth itself would be impossible. We cannot renounce these ideas, even if they are not substantiated by objective facts.

Although modern man regards nature as the only proper object of understanding, and passionately rejects all other-worldliness, he is no longer able to look at the world as naïvely as the Greek philosopher was wont to do; he no longer feels thoroughly satisfied within its bounds. For the Greek philosopher, the world was not mute, not senseless. If in all the charm of its beauty it seemed to him to be divine, this was possible because he could not conceive of anything beyond it, he did not know of any higher value.[10] Modern man, however, who has passed through the experience of Christianity, knows of something else even though, or rather just because, he may most emphatically deny it. He clings desperately to this world—not because it seems sufficient to him, but rather because he no longer finds satisfaction in religion. He attributes to empirical reality an increased weight, a new dimension, as it were, unknown in former times.

This new enthusiasm for empirical reality finds expression everywhere today, in philosophy, in the fine arts, in poetry, and even in politics. The pictures of Van Gogh have no perspective into any Beyond. And yet, the reality he depicts is not merely factual; it is surcharged with vital forces which, although they do not break through the surface, still seem to be driving towards an unknown goal. In writers like D. H. Lawrence, Rilke, or James Joyce we observe a similar struggling to describe reality, which in its merely empirical presence seems to acquire an almost mythical meaning.[11]

face this difficulty, for neither of them considered the idea of free will (*liberum arbitrium*) as a merely rational concept. (Cf. below, note 30.)

[10] Cf. note 15 to ch. II and Aristotle's expression: 'Nature and God' (*On the Heaven,* I, 4, p. 271a33, where the latter term may be taken as explaining the former: 'Nature that is God.'

[11] Cf. H. Miller's interpretation of D. H. Lawrence's thought in *The Wisdom of the Heart,* 1941, pp. 159 ff., and *The Cosmological Eye,* 1939, pp. 65 ff. James Joyce speaks of 'the *perverted transcendentalism* to which Mr. S. Dedalus' (*Div. Scep.*) contentions would appear to prove him pretty badly addicted'

Even thinkers like Dostoevski and Kierkegaard, who wish to re-establish the truth of religion, try to substantiate Christian faith by psychological or other objective phenomena.[12] The various political movements of today likewise understand their own ideologies as a mythical expression of the dynamic forces of life; and the political mythus is meant to replace religion.[13] Modern philosophers of all shades, Positivists and Metaphysicians alike, are inspired by the same ardent longing and admiration for this reality.[14]

Every endeavour to reach out past this world, every suggestion of the idea of a Beyond is considered treacherous by modern man. But by this very longing for reality he betrays to what small extent he is actually absorbed in it, how ill-satisfied he is with the world as it is, how badly he suffers from this self-imposed taboo of transcendence. The spirit of freedom which transcends reality is still

(*Ulysses*, p. 397). R. M. Rilke sings of the mysterious presence of 'things':

> O house, O sloping field, O setting sun . . .
> One space spreads through all creatures equally—
> Inner-world space. O, I that want to grow
> The tree I look outside at's growing in me.

[*Later Poems*, transl. by J. B. Leishman, London, 1932, p. 128]

And Proust: 'Les Choses ont autant de vie que les hommes' (*A Propos du Style de Flaubert*). In similar terms Evelyn Underhill (*Mysticism*, London, 1912, p. 360) describes mystic contemplation: 'The object of our contemplation may be almost everything we please: a picture, a statue, a tree; . . . you will become aware of a heightened significance and intensified existence in this thing at which you look; . . . seen thus, a thistle has celestial qualities. Our great comrades, the trees, the clouds, the rivers initiate us into mighty secrets.' (Cf. the penetrating analysis of this modern attitude in K. Jaspers's *Philosophie*, vol. III, Berlin, 1932, pp. 133 ff.)

[12] Dostoevski (*Letters*, transl. by E. L. Maync, London, 1904, p. 4): 'Balzac is great—not the spirit of the age but whole millenniums have worked toward such development and liberation in the soul of man.' (Cf. p. 93 and note 27 to ch. IV; in regard to Kierkegaard, cf. note 26 to ch I.)

[13] Cf. George Sorel's theory of the political mythus in his *Reflections on Violence* (transl. by T. E. Hulme, London, 1925); his thought is inspired by Bergson's philosophy. The influence of Sorel's ideas on Mussolini and his theory of Fascism is well known. Cf. note 17 f. and *Enciclopedia Italiana*, vol. 32, 1936, p. 159.

[14] A. N. Whitehead, *Process and Reality* (Cambridge, 1929, e.g. p. 497): 'In this way, the insistent craving is justified—the insistent craving, that zest for existence be refreshed by the everpresent unfading importance of our immediate actions which perish and yet live for ever more.' Cf. the similar idea in P. Weiss, *Reality*, Princeton, 1938, *passim*, esp. pp. 17 ff.

alive in him; it determines all his actions and his whole existence, although in his theories he does not acknowledge it.

In Positivism modern realism surpasses itself. Since the Positivist regards as true and meaningful those concepts alone which can be verified by observable facts, there remain literally for him only 'letters,' namely the conventional characters of science or the symbols of mathematics.[15] Even those ideas which stand for the modern consciousness of man, such as will, freedom, and personality, become meaningless. Thus the development of modern philosophy has led to the paradoxical result, that in terms of his own philosophy modern man no longer understands himself. This situation seems to attest to the truth of that thought which St. Paul tried to express by his metaphor of spirit and letter: for him who seeks sufficiency in himself, the world and man become mere letter. This is the meaning of the passage in Corinthians: 'Not that we are sufficient of ourselves to think anything as of ourselves; but our sufficiency is of God; Who also hath made us able ministers of the new testament; not of the letter but of the spirit: for the letter killeth, but the spirit giveth life.' And then St. Paul continues: 'Therefore if any man be in Christ, he is a new creature: old things are passed away; behold, all things are become new.'[16]

With the religious experience of Christianity something actually new came into the world, a new man was created; and the fundamental structure of this 'new creature' who finds his truth in the freedom of spirit and personality has remained evident even in present-day man and his most secularized forms of life. Of St. Paul's religious idea of a new creation Schelling has given a striking rational interpretation. He says: 'Christ returns into the supersensible world and in place of himself he proclaims the spirit. It is as though he put an end to the past age—he is the last God—after him comes the spirit, the ideal principle, the soul that rules over the new world.'[17] Is it not an historical fact that Christ was the

[15] One may take symbolic logic as a further example.

[16] 2 Corinthians 3. 5 ff. and 5. 17. St. Augustine wrote an important treatise 'On the Spirit and the Letter.' Cf. note 33. Concerning the expression 'ministers of the new testament' the modern commentators remark that the Greek word translated here as well as in the Septuagint by 'testament' is intended to render the Hebrew for 'covenant.' See also Theodoret's interpretation of our passage in Migne, *Patrologia Graeca*, vol. 82, Paris, 1859, pp. 392 ff.

[17] Schelling, 'Lectures on the Philosophy of Art,' 1804 (in *Werke*, part 1, vol. v, Stuttgart, 1859, p. 432). The same spiritualistic interpretation of Christian

last God? Is it not true that since His time the history of European religion has become the history of the spirit? And yet, Schelling's words are only a secularized version of a medieval thought; Joachim of Floris, the renowned theologian and philosopher of the twelfth century, first had such a vision of the history of mankind. He saw it divided into three periods of dispensations: the age of

faith is characteristic of Hegel (cf. note 34 to ch. v), with whom Schelling at that time was still on friendly terms. In his later years Schelling elaborated on this principle in a '*Philosophy of Revelation*,' in which he envisages a historical scheme of three ages: after a long period of polytheism humanity rises to Jewish monotheism and then to Christianity. Within the history of the church he assumes again three periods: the Apostles Peter, Paul, and John represent the age of Catholicism, the age of Protestantism, and the future age of a universal religion of perfected humanity. In the years 1841 and 1844 Schelling expounded this philosophy of history in his lectures at the University of Berlin. A motley crowd from all European countries filled lecture room no. 6, eager to hear from Schelling the new philosophical revelation which was to overthrow Hegel's system. Among the audience were Engels, Kierkegaard, Bakunin and other representatives of the younger generation (cf. Marx-Engels, *Gesamtausgabe,* 1930, pp. XLII ff., 173 ff.). The lectures, however, greatly disappointed the students, and their disappointment contributed to their turning from idealism to a radical realism: Kierkegaard conceived his idea of an existential philosophy and theology; Bakunin became the founder of Russian Anarchism, and Engels turned from the worship of God to the worship of human society. Marx and Engels now found in the every-day world of human relations the truth which they had looked for in Hegel's 'Idea.' Yet, however far Marxism may have deviated from its Schelling-Hegelian origins, even today Bolshevism draws its propagandistic force and its Messianic aspirations from the vision of a future age of freedom which will bring humanity to perfection. (Cf. note 45 to ch. v.) Thus from Schelling's lecture room philosophical ideas issued, which were to have a tremendous effect on the history of mankind.

It was a still smaller room in which sixty years later the instigators of a very different movement gathered: the editorial office of the 'Cahiers de la Quinzaine,' in the Rue de Sorbonne in Paris, where Charles Péguy received his friends every Thursday. Under the influence of Bergson's philosophy these revolutionary socialists, among them Sorel, initiated the revolt against their contemporaries' dogmatic confidence in progress, democracy, and modern science. Péguy became Nationalist, Traditionalist, Christian: 'It was through a persistent heart-searching, not at all through a development or a movement backwards that I found the way back to Christianity.' In defence of his conviction he died on the battlefield, in September 1914. (Cf. Charles Péguy, *Basic Verities,* transl. by Ann and Julian Green, New York, 1943, pp. 33 ff., 40, 170 ff.; and J. Maritain in his introduction to H. Iswolsky's *Light before Dusk,* New York, 1942, pp. 3 ff.) In Sorel's mind on the other hand, those ideas took shape which later influenced Mussolini in his political action and thought and

the Law or the Father (relating to the Old Testament); the age of the Gospel or the Son (relating to the New Testament); and the age of the Spirit. This 'Third Empire,' he thought, would bring all temporal ages to an end and be the sabbath of humanity. The Church of St. Peter would be purified, and the new Church would be an *ecclesia contemplativa.* The Gospel of Christ would be superseded by the Gospel of the Spirit, which would be final and everlasting.[18]

This apocalyptic vision of a third empire, the age of the Spirit, was to be of tremendous influence on later religious as well as political speculations up to the present time.[19] Joachim's idea marks the

through him Hitler. (Cf. G. Sorel, *Les Illusions du Progrés,* Paris, 1908; *La Décomposition du Marxism,* Paris, 1908; *Reflexions sur la Violence, Paris,* 1908; *De l'Utilité du Pragmatism,* Paris, 1921). In the present war all these antagonistic ideologies are locked in a violent struggle to determine the future of the human race.

[18] Joachim of Floris lived from 1145 to 1202. When Schelling worked out his doctrine of the three ages, which was so similar to that of Joachim, he did not know of this medieval thinker. It was not until 1841, the time of his Berlin lectures, that he encountered Joachim in his reading of Neander's *History of Christian Religion and Church* (vol. v, 1, 1841, pp. 220 ff.; Engl. transl. Boston, 1871, vol. IV, p. 236). He was greatly surprised and delighted to find that this notion of his had been anticipated and developed 'in the writings of a man so significant and so prominent in the history of the church' ('Lectures on the Philosophy of Revelation' in *Werke,* part II, vol. 4, p. 298, note). Owing to the political development of the last decades, the interest in Joachim has steadily increased, and a great number of books on this thinker have been published in various countries: Henry Bett, *Joachim of Flora,* London, 1931; Rufus M. Jones. *The Eternal Gospel,* New York, 1938; E. Buonaiuti, *G. da Fiori,* Rome, 1931; H. Grundmann, *J. von Floris,* Leipzig, 1927; E. Benz, *Ecclesia Spiritualis,* Stuttgart, 1934, etc.

[19] In Joachim's prophecy the religious fervour of his age found its most characteristic expression. It was a time when the Christians became aware of the discrepancy between the existing order of things and the teachings of the Gospel and were longing for a reformation of church and state, for a regeneration of the soul of man. Joachim prophesied that the time was near when the religion of the 'letter' would be replaced by the Eternal Gospel of the 'Spirit' and when the order of force and justice would be supplanted by the order of love. Soon would come the 'Novus Dux,' the Messianic leader, to introduce the new Third Age, the realm of the Spirit, just as Christ had been the 'Dux' (Matthew 2. 6, Vulgate), whose birth brought into the world the second age, that of the Son. Joachim's later contemporary, St. Francis, (1182–1226), was stirred by a similar spirit: the Franciscan Spirituals saw in the life and work of their saint the fulfilment of Joachim's prophecy of the 'new Dux.' It is Joachim's

beginning of that trend of thought which at first led to an ever more rationalized interpretation of Christianity and which later in a secular form brought about an abstract philosophical spiritual-

prophecy which gave to the terrific ecclesiastical, political, and social conflicts of the period an eschatological aspect. Dante (*Paradiso,* IX, 33) sings the praise of St. Francis and St. Dominic as the 'princes' whom providence ordained to save the church, and he introduces St. Bonaventura and St. Thomas as the philosophical representatives of the Franciscan spirit and that of the Dominicans. But beside them 'shines the Calabrian Abbot Joachim' (*Paradiso,* XII, 140). Thus for the medieval poet even the philosophical thought of his time reflects this spiritual revival. In another famous passage (*Purgatorio,* XXXIII, 43) Dante enigmatically prophesies the DVX who, sent by God, would save Empire and Church. A century later Cola di Rienzo styled himself 'soldier and knight of the Holy Spirit,' destined to regenerate Rome, and with Rome the whole of Christendom: As the new DVX he compared himself even with Christ (cf. his letter, no. 57, 507 ff., ed. Burdach and Piur, part III, pp. 250 ff., V, pp. 308 f.) and it was the poet Petrarch who encouraged him in his belief in a millennial mission.

Never before or after had Europe envisaged a higher goal of secular history or struggled to achieve its ideal with greater expectations than in this period of the Middle Ages. Modern scholars are entirely justified in tracing the origin of the ideas of 'Reformation' and 'Renaissance' to this epoch. (K. Burdach, *Reformation, Renaissance, Humanismus,* Berlin, 1926; cf. M. E. Cosenza, *F. Petrarca in the Revolution of C. di Rienzo,* Chicago, 1913; P. Piur, *Cola di Rienzo,* Vienna, 1931, pp. 108 ff., 119 ff.; G. A. Greenway, *Arnold of Brescia,* Cambridge, 1931.) The vision of a new age of the Spirit which would bring about paradise on earth and perfection for humanity remained the inspiring force of Europe throughout its history, even if this idea later became more and more secularized and trivial. In seventeenth-century England, Joachim's original idea of an Eternal Gospel was revived by the sect of the Philadelphians, who were led by the prophetess Jane Lead (1623–1704). Her writings, translated into many languages, made a great impression on the Continent. In Italy since Cola di Rienzo, the Joachimite tradition has always been closely connected with the political dream of a new Rome, liberated from her tyrants. Thus the Italy of the Risorgimento was called 'La Terza Italia' by Carducci in his ode to Mazzini (1872):

> With Gracchus' heart and Dante's thought expand
> Glimmering in heaven the Third Italy
> He sees . . .
>
> (Transl. by E. A. Tribe, London, 1921, p. 10.)

Later Mussolini dubbed himself 'Duce,' adopting the traditional idea of a Messianic leader. In our day the most consequential literary revival of Joachim's vision is to be found in the works of the outstanding Russian author Merezhkovski, who lived in exile in Paris from 1905 to 1941. In his prophecy of a third Empire of the Spirit which would bring the final union of *Logos* and *Cosmos,* of Religion and Culture, he strangely blended the Joachimite idea

ism. This idealistic conception of the Spirit finally turned into the plain materialism of today.[20]

In view of the critical situation following from this modern misunderstanding of spirit and freedom, we may ask what the idea of spirit originally meant in the passage quoted from St. Paul. Spirit and freedom, to him, were just the opposite of what they came to mean in modern philosophy; for they could not be found in individual sovereignty, but rather in the consciousness 'that we are not sufficient of ourselves to think anything as of ourselves; but that our sufficiency is of God.' Spirit, as understood by St. Paul, is not the same as soul or mind; it is the true manifestation of God. It diffuses itself throughout man's existence; his inmost heart is full of the transcendent God who gives form to his life, who reshapes his body as well as his soul, who henceforth dwells within him as his true essence. By taking part in this creative spirit, man understands everything anew; he can read the script of his own existence, which is 'written not with ink, but with the spirit of the living God, not in tablets of stone, but in fleshy tablets of the heart.'[21] Thus, he becomes transparent to himself and understands himself in his true

with Dostoevski's mystic and political vision of Russia's mission. (Prince Mirskii, *Contemporary Russian Literature*, New York, 1926, pp. 156 ff.; Williams, *Russia of the Russians*, pp. 204 ff.; H. Bett, op. cit. p. 179.) In Paris, A. Moeller van den Bruck, a Russo-German litterateur, was closely connected with Merezhkovski. Together they edited the German translation of Dostoevski (1906–15), and Merezhkovski contributed the introduction to Dostoevski's important *Political Writings*. Moeller van den Bruck later returned to Germany and after the last war wrote *Germany's Third Empire* (Engl. transl. by E. O. Lorimer, London, 1934), undoubtedly influenced by the philosophical thought of his friend. It is from the title of this book that Hitler took the term *Drittes Reich*.

[20] The rationalistic spirtualism of modern philosophy reached its climax in the thought of Hegel, who identified Spirit with philosophical reason and made this 'Spirit' the fundamental principle of his whole system (cf. note 47). Within the Hegelian school, especially with Feuerbach and Marx, this abstract spiritualism immediately turned into materialism. The crisis is marked by the year 1841, when Feuerbach's *Essence of Christianity* appeared and Schelling gave his lectures in Berlin. (Cf. note 17; K. Löwith, *Von Hegel bis Nietzsche*, Zuerich, 1941; Sidney Hook, *From Hegel to Marx*, London, 1936.) P. Tillich, *The Interpretation of History*, New York, 1936; the same, 'Existential Philosophy,' in *History of Ideas*, 1944. Cf. note 42 to ch. IV.

[21] 2 Corinthians 3. 3. By the 'tables of stone' the Law of Sinai is meant (cf. Exodus 24. 12; 31. 18; and Jeremiah 38 [31]. 33): the Decalogue, although written by the finger of God, is visibly written by means of *letters*, whereas the

significance. Regarded in this new light, man himself and all objects reveal an eternal, a spiritual content behind their outward appearance. This is 'the ministration of the spirit' of which St. Paul speaks in this passage. But as soon as man, bereaved of the spirit, seeks sufficiency in himself, 'and thinks everything as of himself,' his own existence as well as that of all things in the world become mere letter, dead and meaningless. Man and world, if separated from the spirit, mean 'ministration of death and condemnation.' Never in the history of religion have the remoteness from God and the nearness to Him, His transcendence and immanence, been felt simultaneously with as much fervour as in Christianity.

In the tension of this contradictory experience all words and concepts took on a new meaning. First of all 'spirit' itself. For the Greeks, *pneuma* was the gift of the Muses or the Gods which inspired the poet and the seer to perceive the world in all its beauty and its truth, as it really is, and as the Gods themselves saw it.[22] In Judaism, spirit is the true essence of God, as it is revealed in His Creation and His Law; but only in Christianity does man find in his own heart the whole profundity of the spirit. Or, as St. Paul says: 'In the Old Testament the veil is still upon their hearts which veil is done away in Christ.' Spirit manifests itself only in spirit, in the very core of man's personal existence, in that which is peculiarly his own. Although the spirit is divine, although it is universal, still it is not what is common to everything, like the world-soul or the all-being in the philosophical systems of the

epistle of Christ is an inspiration of the heart (cf. Pascal in note 39 to ch. II). But this does not mean that a merely subjective feeling is a sufficient criterion of truth. Therefore St. Paul immediately adds: 'Not that we are sufficient of ourselves to think any thing as of ourselves . . .' (Cf. 2 Corinthians 3. 5, quoted above, p. 152.

[22] Concerning the Greek religious concept of spirit see I. G. van der Leeuw, *Religion in Essence and Manifestation,* Engl. transl. 1938, p. 304 etc.; the same, *Schoepfung,* 1927; H. Leisegang, *Hagion Pneuma,* Leipzig, 1932, pp. 32 ff., the same, *Der Heilige Geist,* 1919, pp. 132 ff.; R. Reitzenstein, *Hellenist. Mysterien-Religionen,* 3rd ed. 1927, p. 184 and *passim.* Characteristic of the original Greek notion of spirit are passages like that of Hesiod; 'They [the Muses] gave me a staff of lusty olive, . . . and breathed in me a voice divine, that I might celebrate the things that shall be and the things that were aforetime' (*Theogony,* v. 31, transl. by A. W. Mair, Oxford, 1908, p. 32). In regard to the Jewish notion of spirit, see G. F. Moore, *Judaism* (vol. I 1927, pp. 237 ff.); *Jewish Encyclopedia,* VI, p. 445; and Leisegang's interpretation of Philo in the treatises quoted above.

Pantheists: Spirit is not an external presence but becomes man's inward being, the centre of his personality.

It is precisely for this reason that to St. Paul spirit, *pneuma,* does not mean soul, or mind, or reason, as it has been understood by the Greeks and again by modern philosophers from Descartes to Hegel.[23] To St. Paul, spirit is far above soul and even 'Nous.'[24] What for the Greeks and for the modern rationalists belongs to soul or mind in contrast to body, in St. Paul's view still belongs to the flesh. For flesh, to him, is by no means the same as body, or 'matter,' which is a philosophical abstraction created by the Greeks.[25] Flesh means body *and* soul, the whole human being, so far as he thinks himself 'sufficient of himself,' so far as he is mere letter as opposed to living spirit. But if spirit is neither mind, nor soul, where can we grasp it? Nowhere, except in the experience of freedom. For, as St. Paul says: 'Where the spirit of the Lord is, there is liberty.' These are the memorable words which mark the beginning of a new era.[26]

[23] It is characteristic of the Greek philosophers that they replaced the religious notion of *pneuma* by the philosophical concept of *nous* (reason), thus restricting the meaning of *pneuma* to the animating vital spirit, the breath of life. (Concerning Aristotle, cf. W. Jaeger in *Hermes,* 1913, p. 279 ff., and in regard to the Stoics, E. Zeller, *The Stoics* etc., Engl. transl. London, 1870, pp. 141 ff.) The Jewish and Christian thinkers of late antiquity already show the tendency to interpret the Spirit of Scripture in terms of rational philosophy, and this tendency has increased in modern times. In regard to Hegel's 'Spirit,' cf. notes 47 and 20.

[24] Concerning the Hellenistic background of St. Paul's distinction between *pneuma* and *psyche,* see T. Wilson, *St. Paul and Paganism,* Edinburgh, 1927, p. 79; Reitzenstein, op. cit. pp. 70 ff., 175 ff., etc.

[25] The philosophical concept of an abstract body seems first to have been formulated by Democritus (or by Leucippus). The definition of an abstract 'soul' in opposition to such a 'body' can hardly be found before Plato or the Pythagoreans (cf. U. von Wilamowitz-Moellendorf, *Glaube der Hellenen,* Berlin, 1931, vol. I, pp. 370–75). The word 'matter' (*hyle*), however, is still used by Plato in its literal sense of 'wood' or 'raw, unwrought material.' It is Aristotle who coined the abstract concept of 'matter,' which is fundamental for his whole philosophy in opposition to that of Plato (cf. *Physics,* Book I, 6 ff., C. Baeumker, *Materie,* 1890, p. 210). Concerning St. Paul's concept of Flesh, cf. W. Schauf, *Sarx,* 1924; H. Lietzmann, *Commentary on the Epistle to the Romans,* 7. 13, and note 29.

[26] 2 Corinthians 3. 17: By 'liberty' St. Paul means spiritual freedom as opposed to the limitation of him who 'has still a veil on the heart.' This 'veil is done away in Christ' (2 Corinthians 3. 14). It is this freedom of the Spirit which alone gives the frankness and 'plainness of speech' (*parrhesia*), the possibility

In his religious experience of Spirit, the Christian then finds a new meaning of freedom. For the Greek, it meant the liberation of the soul and the intellect from their bondage to body and senses. The philosopher's independence of all emotions and passions, ataraxia or impassiveness, was considered the highest moral ideal.[27] The same can be claimed of modern thinkers like Descartes, Spinoza, or Kant, not to mention those more recent, all of whom understand the freedom of man as the sovereignty of his thought and the autonomy of his moral will, in other words, of his conscious ego.[28] For St. Paul, on the contrary, true liberty of the spirit signifies man's liberation from the narrowness of his ego: 'The adoption for which we are waiting is the redemption of our body.'[29]

of giving expression to one's whole heart (E. Peterson, *Parrhesia,* 1927; H. Schlier, *Theolog. Woerterbuch,* vol. II, pp. 484 ff.).

[27] This is true of all Greek philosophers, of Socrates and Plato (especially in the *Phaedo*) as well as of the Stoics (cf. E. Zeller, *The Stoics,* etc., Engl. transl. pp. 206 ff.; W. H. S. Jones, *Greek Morality,* London, 1906, pp. 26, 59 ff., etc.; A. Bonhoeffer, *Epiktet und das Neue Testament,* Giessen, 1911, pp. 164 ff.; R. Bultmann, *Z. N. T. Wft.,* 1912, p. 97; R. Hirzel, *Themis, Dike,* etc., 1907, pp. 25 ff.).

[28] It is the Stoic attitude which has been revived in modern rational ethics, in Descartes and Spinoza, as well as in Kant and more recent philosophers. That modern thought is greatly indebted to the Stoics also in other fields, especially in epistemology, logic, and psychology, has rightly been emphasized by W. Dilthey (*Werke, passim,* e.g. vol II, 1929, pp. 107 ff., 268). Stoic philosophy is much more in keeping with the subjective tendency of modern thinkers than is the thought of Plato and Aristotle. Thus Stoic ideas such as 'criterion of knowledge,' 'the assent given by the mind to its perceptions' (i.e. subjective consciousness), 'fantasy,' 'substance' (i.e. material substance), etc. were infiltrated into modern philosophy, transmitted mainly through Cicero, who up to the nineteenth century was widely read by the educated.

[29] Romans 8. 23. According to John Chrysostom (*The Homilies on the Romans,* Engl. transl. Oxford, 1861, p. 248) and other Fathers, the redemption of the body means 'full redemption, the change of the body and along with it the change of the whole world.' Through its redemption the body becomes free of all its defects and shall be glorified and elevated to the incorruptible body similar to the glorified body of Christ (cf. Philippians 3. 21; 1 Corinthians 15. 54; 7. 31; 2 Corinthians 5. 2, and the modern commentators, esp. E. Kaesemann, *Leib Christi,* 1933). Thus Christian faith implies an entirely new conception of the body. Augustine attacked the Greek philosophers, Plato as well as the Gnostics, for their belief that every evil, every suffering of the soul, originates in its union with the body and the senses. The human body and the senses cannot be evil, since they were created by God and restored to their original dignity through the union of divinity with humanity in Christ. Through the Christian doctrine of incarnation, the life of the individual, the principle

This new concept of liberty implied an entirely new meaning of free will, the like of which had never been envisaged before. Greek philosophy possessed no such idea of will, since reason was considered to be the ultimate criterion of truth. God as well as man had merely the choice between various given possibilities which were dependent upon the unalterable order of the universe, and it was reason that enabled God as well as man, to recognize the best among them.[30] In the Old Testament, however, the idea of a free moral will is indicated for the first time: if God created the world with all its laws, not because this was the best possible world, but because out of His own unfathomable volition He wanted it thus, He must also have the power through His own free will to break these rational laws; to put it differently, He must be able to work miracles. Man, who is created in the image of God, reflects this miraculous power in his free moral will, which considers itself superior to all other forces in the world. In this sense the concept of free will was first understood, at any rate, when a Jewish philosopher, Philo, tried to grasp and to interpret in rational terms the idea of creation as he found it in Scripture.[31]

of personality, gained new importance. (Augustine, e.g. *De Civitate Dei*, XIV, 5; X, 29; *De Natura Boni*, 18; *Retract.* I, 5, 3; Cf. E. Frank, *St. Augustine and Greek Thought*, p. 9.)

[30] Aristotle had not yet a concept of the truly free will, but only that of free choice (*prohairesis*) between given possiblities, which presupposes the activity of reason and intellect (cf. *Nic. Eth.*, book III, 2; *Moralia*, book I, 17 ff., and the passage quoted from Galen above, ch. III, p. 60). It was not until the thirteenth century that the Christian philosophers became acquainted with Aristotle's intellectualistic theory of freedom, but they had been familiar with the Christian notions of free will (*liberum arbitrium*) from the beginning. For this concept had been formulated by the Fathers, above all by Augustine, in their interpretation of Scripture. It is characteristic that Thomas Aquinas in his philosophical Ethics restricts himself to Aristotle's theory. Only in the theological parts of his *Summa* does he deal with the problems of free will (*liberum arbitrium*)—that is, in close connection with Grace and Creation, which he discusses in terms of the old Augustinian tradition. This fact makes it quite clear that our idea of free will is a religious, not a rational, concept, that its origin is to be found in Scripture and in the Fathers, esp. in Augustine; cf. M. Wittmann, *Ethik des heiligen Thomas*, Muenchen, 1933, pp. 109 ff., where the origin of the doctrine of free will is traced. (See also J. Auer, *Willensfreiheit bei Thomas, und Duns Scotus*, Muenchen, 1938.) Modern philosophers, who since Descartes have tried to prove the existence of free will in a rationalistic way, are therefore bound to fail.

[31] H. A. Wolfson, op. cit. pp. 131 ff. (cf. note 6), makes it evident that Philo was the first philosopher who in his interpretation of the Old Testament formulated the concept of free will.

This idea of free moral will was far surpassed by St. Paul's conception of freedom. For him, to be truly free means to be able to will what one wants to do, that is, to have the freedom of the spirit: 'For to will is present with me, but how to perform that which is good, I find not. For the good that I would I do not: but the evil which I would not, that I do.'[32] These Pauline words serve to express man's experience of the insufficiency of his moral will; they stress the psychological fact that it is precisely the autonomous will which creates the disparity between intention and accomplishment and thwarts the achievement of true morality.[33] Spirit alone can free man from the meshes of this net in which his sovereign volition gets him forever entangled, proving thereby that even the power of conscious will belongs to the sphere of the letter, of the flesh.[34] St.

[32] Romans 7. 18 ff. St. Paul continues: 'Now if I do that which I will not, it is no more "I" that do it, but sin that dwelleth in me. I find then a law, that when I have a will to do good, evil is present with me.' Cf. St. Augustine's interpretation of this passage in *Opus Imperfectum Contra Julianum* IV, 103. (Concerning the meaning of 'will' in the New Testament, cf. H. Riesenfeld in the *Publications of the Seminar for the New Testament in Uppsala*, 1936.)

[33] St. Augustine, *On the Spirit and the Letter*, ch. 4, 6 (transl. by P. Holmes, p. 161), gives the following interpretation of the Pauline passage: 'When he says "the letter killeth but the spirit gives life," this prescribes not to take in the literal sense any figurative phrase which in the proper meaning would only produce nonsense . . . The Apostle's principle, however, is not to be confined to this limited application but it must also—and indeed mostly—be regarded as equivalent to what he says elsewhere in the plainest words: "I had not known lust, except the law had said, Thou shalt not covet" [Romans 7. 7]; . . . the Apostle, indeed, purposely selected this general precept in which he embraced everything as if this were the voice of the Law. And the Law which prohibits this is a good and praiseworthy law. Still, when the Holy Spirit withholds his help which diffuses love in our hearts, that law, however good in itself, only augments the evil desire by forbidding it. Just like the rush of water which flows incessantly in a particular direction, it becomes more violent when it meets with any impediment; and when it has overcome the stoppage it falls in a greater bulk, and with increased impetuosity hurries forward in its downward course. I know not how it is, but the very object which we covet becomes all the more pleasant and desired by being forbidden.' Cf. Romans 2. 27 ff. and 7. 6: 'But now we are delivered [Vulgate: *soluti;* loosed, *released*] from the law of death wherein we are detained, that we should serve in newness of spirit and not in the oldness of the letter.'

[34] Cf. Kierkegaard's realistic analysis of the psychological phenomenon, which he calls the 'Demoniacal' (cf. *Concept of Dread* and *Sickness to Death*). One may think also of Freud's analysis of the compulsions to which according to him the conscious will easily leads: 'All these things combine to bring about an ever

Paul, in his most exalted state of true spiritual freedom, exclaims: 'Wherefore henceforth I know no man after the flesh; yea, though we have known Christ after the flesh, yet, now henceforth know we Him no more; therefore if any man be in Christ, he is a new creature.' [35] Thus man gains an entirely new understanding of himself and of his true essence. In experiencing this spiritual freedom, he discovers within himself a power which liberates him, which takes him beyond the narrow limits of the world and of his conscious ego to which he was formerly restricted.

This absolutely novel and unprecedented Christian conception of spiritual freedom led to another, that of free personality. In Greek philosophy, this idea was unknown; individuality was expressed mainly in physical appearance, and the Greek word for 'body' frequently occurs where we would expect 'person.' Yet, it was not the individual body, but rather its universal 'form,' the living soul, in which the Greeks saw the true nature of man, just as of all other things in the world.[36] Plato, in order to express the essence of a thing, chose the word 'Idea,' '*eidos*,' which means 'form.' [37] To the

increasing indecisiveness, loss of energy and curtailment of freedom; and that although the obsessional neurotic is originally always a person of a very energetic disposition, often highly opinionated, and as a rule intellectually gifted above the average.' (*Introductory Lectures on Psycho-Analysis,* transl. by J. Rivière, London, 1922, p. 220.) Cf. note 26 to ch. I.

[35] 2 Corinthians 5. 17 ff. With reference to this passage St. Augustine (*Homilies on St. John,* 94. 4, transl. H. Browne, Oxford, 1849, p. 887) says: "This surely our Good Master would intimate, in saying, "for if I depart not, the Comforter will not come unto you: but if I depart, I will send Him unto you" [St. John 16. 7, see above note 34 to ch. v].' Cf. the similar passages Romans 8, 9 and Galatians 2, 20.

[36] The Greek word *soma* originally means the living body, even life and personal freedom, and person, especially in legal language. Body as opposite to soul first appears with Plato (e.g. *Gorgias,* p. 493A, *Phaedo,* 91C, where the Pythagorean origin of this concept seems to be suggested; cf. above note 25). For Aristotle 'the soul of animals is the general form and the essence of a body of a certain kind.' But when we come to the individual, Socrates is composed of ultimate individual matter (*Metaph.* VII, 8, pp. 1035b14 ff. and VII, 11, pp. 1037a5 ff.; cf. *On the Soul,* II, 1, p. 412a19). Thus for Aristotle as well as for Plato the individuality of a person like Socrates derives from the body rather than from the soul. To both philosophers matter is the very *principium individuationis* (cf. Plato, *Philebus,* p. 24C; *Timaeus,* p. 52A; *Phaedo,* p. 105D).

[37] The Greek word for form (*eidos*) specifically means the form of a living body. If a body is dead its form is called no longer *eidos* but *schema* (like that of a geometrical figure). Plato himself uses the terms *eidos* or 'Idea' only rarely

Greek philosopher, only the universal form had part in eternal truth; the subjective ego, like everything else that was shapeless and indefinite, belonged to the realm of the perishable.

Personality in the Christian sense of the word first occurs in the discussions of the Church Fathers about the true nature of God.[38] For it is through Christ that God reveals Himself in His true nature, that is as personality; God as spirit is essentially this. Man seeks a personal relation to the divinity and on it the whole Christian religion rests. By interpreting his conscious ego in terms of his relation to God, the Christian individual becomes a free personality.[39] Modern Man, on the other hand, understands by personality a distinctive individuality expressing itself in actual deeds or in particular characteristics. This is a merely psychological definition of personality, whereas the true idea of it involves much more, namely the responsibility of the conscious ego towards a higher authority.[40] The adequate conception of personality, there-

for what are called his 'Ideas' (viz. the universal essence [*ousia*] of things). Cf. U. von Wilamowitz-Moellendorf, *Plato,* 1918, vol. II, 248; C. M. Gillespie in *Classical Quart.* 1912, p. 179; A. E. Taylor, *Varia Socratica,* Oxford, 1911, p. 178; C. Ritter, *Neue Untersuchungen,* 1910, and note 8 to ch. III.

38 Concerning the origin and the history of our concept of personality, cf. U. von Wilamowitz-Moellendorff, op. cit.; A. Trendelenburg in *Kantstudien,* 1908, p. 1 ff.; S. Schlossmann, *Persona, Kiliae,* 1906; H. Rheinfelder, *Persona,* Halle, 1928; R. Hirzel in *SB der Bayer. Akad., der Wiss.,* 1914, p. 28; F. Altheim, *Persona, Archiv f. Relig. Wft.,* 1929, pp. 35 ff.

39 To St. Augustine the Latin word *persona* still means primarily human person, so that he tries to avoid the term in his discussion of the dogma of the Trinity (Sermon 232, ed. by Migne, vol. 39, p. 2173). Boethius is the first to give a philosophical definition of *persona:* 'Persona is the indivisible [individual] substance of a rational nature.' This definition was generally accepted by the medieval philosophers. (Cf. St. Thomas, *Summa Theologica,* part 1, qu. 39, art. 1.) In modern philosophy the concept of personality again has been confined to man. In English the word personality, as popularly used, means distinction or excellence of individual and social traits. Kant defines personality as the power which 'elevates man above himself and above the mechanism of nature.' According to him it is through his personality that 'man is an end in himself and maintains humanity in its proper dignity in his own person' (*Critique of Practical Reason,* p. 180 ff.).

40 John Laird (*Problems of the Self,* London, 1917, p. 82): 'Personality, in the current acceptation, implies a certain degree of intellectual and moral development. A person is responsible and cannot be responsible without the power of making deliberate and reflective choice. Personality, in short, is a legal and ethical notion which applies only to beings of a complex and developed type of psychical life.' For a psychological interpretation of personality cf. e.g. G. W. Allport, *Personality,* New York, 1937.

fore, comprises two other ideas, conscience and repentance, which were indeed of fundamental moral importance in the New Testament.

True, it is the Greeks who formed the concept 'conscience' (*syneidesis*), which originally meant awareness of something and only later on came to signify awareness of oneself.[41] For the Stoics, it implied that man is witness or judge of his own actions. But any symptom of divided personality, such as repentance or shame, was considered by them as a sign of moral inferiority.[42] To the Christian, on the other hand, the soul is split in two, and it is precisely in this cleavage and duality that he discovers his true self and becomes a free personality. He liberates himself from everything that constituted his former objective existence. Through repentance he becomes aware of his genuine ego; he envisions a new and higher Self, which he must actualize in his life. The penitent, by trying to rid his inmost personality of guilt, strives to overcome his limited psychological ego and his preoccupation with his subjective self. The ego, which in stubborn defiance held to its empirical individuality, now opens up, as it were, to an ideal existence, and in this way a new self is born.[43]

Modern man does not accept such a concept of repentance. He is prone to say: let us not repent, let us rather amend our wrongs.[44]

[41] Concerning the concept of Conscience in Greek philosophy and in the New Testament see: P. Ewald, *De Vocis 'syneideseos' Vi,* Lipsiae, 1883; F. Zucker, *Syneidesis-Conscientia,* Jena, 1928; B. Snell in *Gnomon,* 1930, p. 21; H. Osborne, *Classical Review,* 1931, p. 8, and the literature quoted in W. Bauer's *Dictionary, s.v.*

[42] Concerning the Greek attitude towards repentance and shame, see Aristotle: 'The wicked are always full of repentance' (*Nic. Eth.* IX, 4, p. 1166b24); 'The virtuous man does not feel shame' (ibid. IV, 9, p. 1128b22); the Stoic Chrysippus: 'The sensible man does not repent or regret' (*Fragment* 548, Arn.); Epictetus: 'He [the philosopher] must not reproach himself, not struggle with himself, nor repent' (*Dissert.* II, 22, 35; *Enchir.* 34) etc. See A. H. Dirksen, *Metanoia,* Washington, 1932; E. F. Thompson in *Historical and Lingual Studies relative to the New Testament,* vol. 1, Chicago, 1908; A. Bonhoeffer, *Epiktet und das Neue Testament,* Giessen, 1911, pp. 107, 225 ff.; E. Norden, *Agnostos Theos,* Leipzig, 1913, p. 134 f.

[43] See Kierkegaard's Analysis of the 'Demoniacal,' especially in his *Concept of Dread,* ch. 3. Cf. notes 25 and 42 to ch. v.

[44] E.g. Spinoza, *Ethics,* IV, 54, or Descartes, *The Passions of the Soul,* III, art. 191. Both philosophers are only reproducing formulations of Aristotle and the Stoics (notes 28, 42; cf. H. A. Wolfson, *Spinoza,* Cambridge, Mass., 1934, vol. II, pp. 254 ff.). The same is true of Nietzsche. Cf. e.g. *Human, All-too-Human,* II (The Wanderer and His Shadow) Engl. transl. Edinburgh, 1911, no. 323;

Thus ancient and modern philosophers alike have failed to understand that true repentance does not concern our various actions only, but is aimed at a complete change in our very essence. Repentance means that process through which man is transformed into his true self by renouncing the stubborn resistance of his merely particular and subjective personality.[45] Through conscience and repentance man acquires a new dimension, that of depth—a new awareness of himself and his own freedom.

Yet it is the essence of personality, as conceived by Christianity, that the individual cannot exist by himself but becomes real only in communication with others. Man as a personality is not isolated, like a Greek statue, is not that harmonious and plastic individuality which was the loftiest ideal of Greek ethics.[46] Quite the opposite; he throws his soul open to others, renouncing his aloofness. By thus imparting himself, he regains a richer being.[47] It is this spiritual community with others which in Christian terms is love. This, which also constitutes the true essence of God, is altogether different from what Greek philosophers, and after them many among the

'Never allow repentance free play but say at once to yourself: "That would be adding a second piece of folly to the first."

[45] Cf. Max Scheler's analysis of repentance and rebirth in *Vom Ewigen im Menschen*, Leipzig, 1923, vol. I, pp. 5 ff.

[46] It is Aristotle who compares the *ethos* which man attempts to achieve in his life with a statue carved out in stone by a sculptor. A similar idea is expressed in Plato's *Philebus*. Cf. also W. Jaeger, *Paideia*, vol. II, New York, 1943, p. 277, who refers to *Republic*, p. 500E.

[47] Cf. Hegel, *Philosophy of Religion* (vol. III, p. 24): 'Morality, love, just mean the giving up of particularity or of the particular personality and its extension to universality, and so, too, is it with the family and friendship . . . In friendship and love I give up my abstract personality and in this way win it back as concrete personality. It is just that winning back of personality by the act of absorption, by the being absorbed into the other which constitutes the true nature of personality . . . If [abstract] personality is not cancelled, then we have evil, for personality which does not yield itself up to the absolute Idea is evil.' One cannot understand Hegel's philosophy, and especially his Dialectic without being aware of the fact that the concept of personality, as defined in this passage, is the ultimate category even of his Logic. So he says in *Science of Logic* (vol. II, p. 483): 'The highest and acutest point is simple personality, which by virtue alone of the absolute Dialectic which is its nature, equally holds and comprehends everything within itself, because it perfectly liberates itself.' This principle is what he calls 'The Absolute Idea of Spirit.' Cf. note 20. Kierkegaard's interpretation of human existence and through him to contemporary existential philosophers such as Jaspers.

moderns, have understood by love. To the Christian, it is not merely *eros*, the passionate desire of the human soul for God, for the absolute Ideal, the love of the lower being for the higher one; it is, on the contrary, the love of the higher existence for the lower, of God for man.[48]

Through this Christian experience man learns what love really means: To love a person sincerely is not, as Plato thought, to love him for some ideal value which he may represent, but rather to love him for himself, his individual personality. To love the man himself is to love him even when he may appear humiliated or entirely devoid of worth. For in personality lies the highest good and the only truth, compared with which all other goods and ideas are inconsequential. For a Christian, love in this sense becomes the ultimate and exclusive moral precept. 'Love and do as you like,' to Augustine, is the key of all true morality.[49]

Still, the Golden Rule, which says 'do unto others as you would have them do unto you,' has generally been considered the supreme law of rational ethics. It was recognized long before Christ and to this day, indeed, we follow it in all our moral reasoning. But considered as a rational rule it is empty and merely formal, because it does not indicate what we should really strive to do.[50] Christian religion, however, maintains that it is love and nothing but love for which man longs from the bottom of his heart, and that it is love, therefore, which, according to the Golden Rule, I must give to others. This is what St. Paul means by the profound words: 'Owe no man any thing, but to love one another: for he that loveth an-

[48] Cf. A. Nygren, *Agape and Eros;* A Study of the Christian Ideas of Love, London, 1937 ff.; M. Scheler, Vom Umsturz der Werte, 1919, vol. I, pp. 107 ff.; D. Kenmore, *The Philosophy of Love,* London, 1942, pp. 136 ff.; R. Niebuhr, *An Interpretation of Christian Ethics,* New York, 1935.

[49] St. Augustine, *In Epist. Joannis ad Parthos,* Tr. VII, 8: 'Love and do what thou wilt . . . let the root of love be within, of this root can nothing spring what is not good' (transl. by E. Przywara and C. C. Martindale, New York, 1936, p. 341); *Enarr. in Psalms* 32, Sermon 1, 6: 'He who does not love is frigid, is stiff.' Cf. J. Mausbach, *Ethik d. hlg. Augustinus,* 1909, vol. I, pp. 178 ff.

[50] Concerning the rational interpretation of the Golden Rule, cf. P. Weiss's article in *Journal of Philosophy,* 1941, p. 421. The precept, at least in its negative form, is to be found in Judaism (Tobias 4. 16; cf. *Jewish Encyclopedia,* VI, 21 ff.), in Greek philosophy (Aristotle, *Nic. Eth.* IX, 8, p. 1168b ff., and in *Diogenes Laërtius,* v, 21; Epictetus, ed. Schenkl, p. 471), in Chinese literature, in Buddhism, etc.

other hath fulfilled the law.' Love is indeed the solution of all moral problems. So long as we merely abide by the rational law as the ultimate criterion of our moral judgment, we can understand neither man nor God.[51]

In the light of the new experience of love, even rational ethics and moral law itself appear as mere letters whose script becomes understandable through the Spirit alone. Spirit is Love. If the rational philosopher of today objects that man, as we know from experience, is not capable of such a noble idea of morality, nor of its realization in practical life, this is exactly what St. Paul himself maintains. For it is the quintessence of his doctrine that man, as long as his thought is centred in himself, is not capable of this love which consists precisely in overcoming his feeling of self-sufficiency.

In his concept of love, just as in his ideas of freedom, will, and personality, St. Paul gives expression not only to a new interpretation of religion, he also establishes a new view of truth: everything that man can grasp through his own independent thought is merely *letter;* it reveals its spirit only if seen in the light of a more sublime presence.

[51] St. Paul, Romans 13. 8. Then he continues: 'For this, Thou shalt not commit adultery, Thou shalt not kill . . . Thou shalt not covet, and if there be any other commandment it is comprehended in this saying, namely, Thou shalt love thy neighbour as thyself. Love worketh no ill to his neighbour, therefore love is the fulfilling of the law.' Cf. John Chrysostom on this passage (Eng. transl. Oxford, 1841, p. 400): 'He does not seek love merely, but, intense love, for he does not say merely love thy neighbour, but, as thyself. Hence, also Christ said that "the Law and the Prophets hang upon it" [Matthew 22.40].'

CHAPTER 8

Christian Optimism

ÉTIENNE GILSON

The opinion is widespread that Christianity is a radical pessimism, inasmuch as it inculcates despair of the only world of whose existence we are assured, and asks us to pin our hopes to another which may be nothing but a dream after all. Jesus Christ never ceased to preach renunciation of worldly goods. St. Paul condemns the flesh and exalts virginity. The Fathers of the Desert, driven mad by an insensate hatred of nature, embark on a life which is a radical negation of all social or even simply human values. And finally the Middle Ages, codifying so to speak the rules of this *contemptus saeculi,* go on to justify it metaphysically. The world is infected by sin, corrupted in its very roots, essentially evil, a thing to be fled, denied, destroyed. St. Peter Damian and St. Bernard condemn every natural impulse: at their bidding thousands of young men and women betake themselves into solitude, or follow St. Bruno into the desert of the Chartreuse: sometimes fully constituted families are broken up, and their scattered and emancipated members find nothing better to do with their newfound liberty than to mortify the flesh, deaden the senses, and repress the exercise of that very faculty of reason that precisely makes them men. *Ubi solitudinem fecerunt, pacem appellant.* Is not this sense-

"Christian Optimism" is reprinted with the permission of Charles Scribner's Sons from *The Spirit of Mediaeval Philosophy,* Pages 108–127, by Étienne Gilson, translated by A. H. C. Downes.

less aspiration of whole generations towards nothingness the normal fruit of Christian preaching? But then, on the other hand, is not the negation of this negation, the refusal of this refusal, one of the essential affirmations of the modern conscience? Acceptance of nature, confidence in the intrinsic worth of all its manifestations, hope for its indefinite progress, if only we know how to perceive what is good in it and work to make it better—there we have modern optimism, there we have the gage flung down to Christian pessimism. The Renaissance called up the gods of Greece once more from the place where they had laid them, at least it called up the spirit that gave them birth: and to set over against Pascal we have Voltaire, against St. Bernard, Condorcet.

We might have a word or two to say about the perfect serenity of the Greek world were this the place to say it; but that its optimism had it limitations will doubtless best appear on a philosophical plane. It will be pertinent to remark on the other hand that if we wish to determine the true line of Christian thought in this matter we should by no means be content to consult only the heroes of the interior life; rather it would be most dangerous to rely only on these without turning to the background of Christian dogma to which they all appealed, and which alone sets their activities in a comprehensible light. However great was St. Bernard, however indispensable is Pascal, they cannot replace the long tradition of the Fathers of the Church and the thinkers of the Middle Ages. Here, as elsewhere, our best witnesses with be St. Augustine, St. Bonaventure, St. Thomas Aquinas and Duns Scotus, not forgetting, moreover, the Bible whence their inspiration came.

For if we would discover the basic principle on which Christian optimism, as I propose to call it, has always rested, we have only to open the first chapter of Genesis. At once we find ourselves face to face with the capital fact of creation, and the Creator Himself, contemplating His work on the evening of each day, declares not merely that He made it, but that because He made it, it is good: *et vidit Deus quod esset bonum;* and then, on the evening of the sixth day, casting a comprehensive glance over all His work, He gives for the last time a similar testimony, proclaiming His creation very good: *viditque Deus cuncta quae fecerat, et erant valde bona* (Gen. i. 31). There, from the time of Irenaeus, we have the unshakable foundation of Christian optimism. Once more, no metaphysics; good ground, however, for rejecting any number of metaphysical systems until a more satisfactory one shall be forthcoming. All those gnostic sects which would throw responsibility for creation upon some inferior Demiurge in order the better to absolve God from the crime of creating an evil world, are condemned at once as anti-Christian. Since it is the work of a good God, the world is not to be explained as the result of any original error, any kind of fall, lapse, ignorance, or revolt.[1] Irenaeus, moreover, quite understands, and very clearly says, that this Christian optimism is a necessary sequel to the Christian doctrine of creation. A good God, Who makes all things out of nothing, not only gratuitously bringing them into existence, but also establishing their order, allows of no intermediate and hence inferior cause between Himself and His work.[2] As sole Author He takes full responsibility; and He is very well able to do so, for His work is good. What now remains for the philosopher is to show that it is so.

We know how cruelly this problem tormented the thought of the young Augustine. He, too, first fell in with gnosticism under the form of Manichean dualism, and shook it off on the day he left the sect that had held his early allegiance. But although delivered from the gnosticism of Mani, he was not yet clear from all his difficulties, for he still had to explain the presence of evil in a universe created by God. If there is no God, whence comes the good? But if there is a God, whence comes the evil? To this question Plotinus suggested an answer which had deep roots in the Greek tradition, but which doubtless took on consistence in his mind under the influence of that very gnosticism that he so often combated. Why not admit that matter is the principle of evil? Since being is the good, it follows that what is contrary to being is evil. Matter, then, in a sense, is a non-being; in a Platonic sense, however, that is to say not exactly as a non-existence but a non-good. Hence Plotinus is able to maintain simultaneously that matter pertains to non-being, and yet is the real principle of evil.[3] For the young Augustine, so full of

[1] Irenaeus, *Adv. Haereses,* III, 25, 5; V, 18, 2.

[2] *Op. cit.,* I, 22, 1; II, 10, 4; II, 30, 9; II, 26, 3.

[3] Plotinus, *Enneads,* I, 8. On the doctrine of evil in Plotinus, as contrasted with that of St. Augustine, see R. Jolivet, *Essai sur les rapports entre la pensée grecque et la pensée chrétienne,* pp. 102–111.

The only doctrines here considered are those with which Christian thought came into contact during its period of formation. As regards earlier doctrines which may have had an indirect influence, we may say that Plato left us no

admiration for Plotinus, how tempting this doctrine must have been! To reduce evil to matter, adding that matter is next to nothing—in what simpler way could we account for all the necessary imperfections of the world? Why, then, not adopt this very neat solution?

Well, simply because it is no solution. Plotinus' answer to the

systematic solution of the problem of the origin of evil. Aristotle credits him with a frank dualism, that is to say with a recognition of two principles of things, one good and the other bad, and on this point ranges him with Empedocles and Anaxagoras (Aristotle, *Metaphysics*, A, 6, 988 a 7–17). In this view, matter would be the principle of evil in Platonism. It is not easy to find a clear text in Plato to justify the assertion. The *Timaeus* contains nothing precise on matter, which it does not even name. One might, however, be tempted to consider the Chaos that the Demiurge orders as its equivalent, and possibly that is what Aristotle is thinking of. This view is suggested by a text in the *Politics* (273 b), where, without mention of the word, the idea of matter is suggested (*τὸ σωματοειδὲς τῆς συγχράσεως αἴτιον*), with application to something very like the Chaos of the *Timaeus*, and invoked to account for the presence of disorder in nature. We might also cite in support the text of the *Republic* (II, 379 c), where Plato says that the god is the cause of the few goods that happen to us, but that we must seek out another cause for the great number of ills; but he does not say what this cause is, and, since it may be man's own fault, the text is not decisive. Perhaps the *Letter to Dionysius* (II, 313 a), whether authentic or not, strikes the true note when it says that Plato had reflected much on the question of evil in general, but had never resolved it.

Aristotle himself often adopts expressions that resemble those of the Christian thinkers. Evil, he says (*Metaph.*, 9, 1051 a, 17–18), does not exist in nature. Act is being, and being is good. Since, however, he introduces the idea of matter and defines it as potentiality as opposed to act, he finds himself led to connect evil with matter. He does not say that it is bad, but it is the principle of mutability and contingence opposed to form and its necessity. It is on account of the potentiality of matter, that we have corruptions, alterations, monsters, etc., etc. We may say that, without being evil in itself, matter makes disorder possible, and, in a sense, inevitable; it contains, then, a mischievous element (*κακοποιὸν*—in *Phys.*, A, 9, 192 a, 15). But what separates Aristotle and Christianity on this point is, for St. Augustine, the fact that matter is not even the cause of the possibility of evil, nor the reason for its existence; in itself it implies no tendency to disorder. As God created it the material world was excellent: *valde bonum*, and so it would have remained had not a sin that came to birth in the realm of the spirit, and not in that of matter, brought disorder into matter. Thus the eternal and uncreated universe of Aristotle, in which matter opposes an eternal resistance to the perfection of form, is profoundly different from the created universe of the Christian philosophers, in which matter directly participates in the perfection of the divine being, and is, in however humble a way, a participated likeness to God.

question is perfectly consistent with the rest of Plotinus' system, for his God is not a Creator in the Biblical and Christian sense of the term. He is not responsible for the existence of matter, therefore neither is he responsible for its nature, and even if it be evil it does not follow that he is evil as well. But how could Augustine clear a Creator-God from the reproach of having made matter and made it evil, or even of having merely left it evil had He found it so? Reflecting, then, on the philosophical principles of Plotinus in the light of the Biblical revelation, Augustine soon felt their insufficiency.[4] To admit that matter is at once created and evil would be an impossible pessimism, and literally contradictory in any Christian scheme. But what is of chief importance to us here is to see just how this religious optimism became a metaphysical optimism, and all we need do is to inquire the secret of St. Augustine. Now Augustine sends us once more to the text of Exodus.

What he most admirably saw and expressed is this: that matter cannot be considered evil even if we see in it no more than a mere principle of possibility or indetermination. Suppose it reduced to a minimum, entirely uninformed, without any quality, it is still a certain capacity for form, an aptitude to receive it; and if that does not amount to much it is certainly not nothing. But let us go further. To be susceptible of becoming good is doubtless not yet to be very good; nevertheless, it is already to be good, and in any event it is not to be bad. It is better to be wise than merely capable of wisdom, but the mere power of becoming wise is already no

[4] St. Augustine, *Confessions,* VII, 11, 17, to 16, 22. This development is usually interpreted as though Augustine attributed his discovery that all that is good, to his reading of the Platonic books: "Ergo si omni bono privabuntur, omnino nulla erunt. Ergo quamdiu sunt, bona sunt. Ergo quaecumque sunt, bona sunt. Malumque illud, quod quaerebam unde esset, non est substantia, quia, si substantia esset, bonum esset" (*op. cit.,* VII, 12, 18). However, Augustine does not say that he had read in the Platonic books that matter is good, or even that it is not bad; he does not even say that he read the truths there which he then discovered touching the problem of evil. The résumé of what he owes to his reading stops at *Confess.,* VII, 9, 15: "Inveni haec ibi et non manducavi." Then he deals with the conclusions obtained after this reading, but by personal reflection and the help of God: "Et inde ad monitus redire ad memetipsum, intravi in intima mea duce te et potui, quoniam *factus es adjutor meus.*" It is God, therefore, and no longer Plotinus who is his guide here. That is why the problem, otherwise so ingeniously dealt with by M. R. Jolivet, *Essai sur les rapports entre la pensée grecque et la pensée Chrétienne,* p. 113, does not even really arise.

inconsiderable quality. Such dialectical considerations have a certain value of their own, no doubt, but not yet their full weight until they are referred to the basic principle that underlies them, and sets them, moreover, in their true place within the general framework of Christian philosophy. If matter is good we can rest assured that it is the work of God; and here the Manicheans were deceived: but also conversely—if it is the work of God we can be quite sure that it is good; and here Plotinus was deceived. "How gloriously then and divinely did our God say to His servant: *Ego sum qui sum,* and then: *Dices filiis Israel, Qui est misit me ad vos.* For He Himself most truly is because He is altogether immutable. For this in fact is always the result of change: that what once was, is now no more; that, therefore, can truly be said to be which is immutable: but as to other things which have been made by Him, it is from Him that each in its own way has received its being. Since therefore He is being *par excellence* He has no contrary save that which is not, and, consequently, as all that is good exists by Him so everything in nature exists by Him, for everything in nature is good. In one word, every nature is good, now all that is good comes from God, therefore every nature comes from God." [5] Here, then, is the principle on which rests the Christian affirmation of the intrinsic goodness of all that is; and the very same principle will account for the evil that occurs in nature; for Christianity does not deny evil, but it shows its negative and accidental character and so justifies the hope of overcoming it.

It is very certain that all things God has made are good; and no less certain that they are not all equally good. There is the good, and the better; and, if the better, then also the less good; now in a certain sense the less good pertains to evil. The universe, moreover, is the scene of constant generations and corruptions in animate and inanimate nature alike. Now all these relative inferiorities and destructions make up what we may call the mass of physical evil. How are we to explain its presence in the world?

[5] St. Augustine, *De natura boni,* Cap. XIX. In the same treatise, Cap. XXXIV, Augustine appeals to this other Scriptural text: "Omnis creatura Dei bona est," I Tim. iv. 4. It need not be said that this doctrine became the common heritage of all Christian philosophers. See, for example, St. Thomas Aquinas, *De malo,* I, 1, Sed contra: "Praeterea, Joan I, 3, dicitur: *omnia per ipsum facta sunt.* Sed malum non est factum per Verbum, ut Augustinus dicit (Tract. I in Joan., a med.). Ergo malum non est aliquid."

As far as the inequalities observed in creatures are concerned, to call them evil would seem an abuse of terms. If matter itself is good, everything may be properly qualified as good, for it is not only good in itself, but even the fact that it is a lesser good may be necessary perhaps for the greater perfection of the whole. But what we must especially note is that these very limitations and mutabilities for which nature is arraigned, are metaphysically inherent in the very status of a created thing as such. For even supposing that all creatures were equal, and immutable in mode of being, they would, nevertheless, remain limited and radically contingent in their very being itself. Things, in short, are created *ex nihilo,* and because created they are, and are good; but because they are *ex nihilo* they are essentially mutable. If therefore we insist on calling evil the ineluctable law of change in nature, we must recognize that the possibility of change is a necessity from which God Himself could not absolve His creation; for the mere fact of being created is the ultimate root of that possibility. Doubtless the divine omnipotence could annul its effects—God can and does maintain in being all that He has brought to being; and if He wished, He might cause all things to continue indefinitely in one and the same state; but such permanence and immutability would be merely adventitious after all; everything that exists in virtue of the creative action and endures in virtue of continued creation, remains radically contingent in itself and in constant peril of lapsing back into nothingness. Because creatures are apt not to be they tend, so to speak, towards non-being [6] ; all that God makes, taken apart from the act that makes it, tends to unmake itself; and, in a word, the contingence of created things in the order of existence must be regarded as the true root of their mutability.

To accept this consequence, and Christian philosophy cannot refuse it, is by no means to return to the position of Plotinus for whom matter is evil, nor even to that of Aristotle for whom matter brings disorder into the world simultaneously with contingency. From the very outset of Christianity the metaphysic of Exodus was carried down beyond the plane of quality and touched the plane of existence. If there is change it is not on account of any particular class of beings, that is to say material beings, it is simply because there are *beings.* In this sense, the form and act of all that is re-

[6] *Op. cit.,* X; cf. *Enchiridion,* Cap. XI–XII.

mains open to mutability in exactly the same way as matter, and in point of fact, evil, properly so-called, enters the world only at the unhappy instance and initiative of spirit. It was not the body that made the spirit sin, it was the spirit that brought death on the body. The whole problem now stands on a new footing: all that needs to be made in order that it may be, is always tending to unmake itself, so much so that what now permanently threatens the work of creation is literally, and in the full rigour of the term, the possibility of its *defection.* But only a possibility, be it noted, nothing more; a possibility without real danger as far as concerns the physical order which has no control over itself, but a very real and practical danger indeed in the moral order, that is to say when men and angels are concerned; for in associating them with His own divine government, their Creator requires them also to keep watch with Him against their own possible defection.

Thus so clearly to link up the possibility of physical evil with the contingency of created things, constitutes in the first place a remote preparation for one of the most important metaphysical achievements of the Middle Ages. In showing that the composition which most radically differentiates the creature from the Creator is not that of matter and form, but that of essence and existence, St. Thomas merely gives definitive expression to the thought of St. Augustine. But Augustine had already done much, for his metaphysic of evil passed wholly and almost as it stood into Thomism and Scotism. The result, in fact, of his principle is, that if you take physical evil as a positive quality inherent in any being, it is rigorously and by definition excluded from nature. The concept of physical evil is henceforth reduced to the concept of a lesser good, that is to say to that of a good. That a good should be lesser it must still be a good and, consequently, a being, for if the good entirely disappeared the being itself would vanish with it.[7] Let us go further. Even if we define evil as the privation of a due good, a good which should be there, still this privation would be meaningless save in relation to the positive good which thus lacks its proper perfection. It is as if evil were a mere *ens rationis,* a negation without meaning save in relation to positive terms, a fundamental unreality, determined, and so to speak, hemmed in on all sides by the good that limits it. It is therefore true to say that good is the

[7] St. Augustine, *Enchiridion,* Cap. XII, 4.

subject of evil, so that one might almost be tempted to reduce one to the other, as if the non-being of evil had no subsistence and intelligibility save with respect to the being of the good itself.[8] Occasionally Augustine went as far as that, nor would it be possible to go any further in the direction of optimism without emptying the idea of evil of all meaning whatsoever and thus suppressing the problem instead of resolving it. Now the problem is undoubtedly there and has to be faced—especially, we may add, when it presents itself in the moral order.

As applied to beings not endowed with knowledge, the ideas of happiness and unhappiness are obviously void of meaning. It matters very little to them, or rather it matters not at all, that some are more or less perfect than others, or even that the greater part are condemned to corruption to make room for others. It matters even less to the universe as a whole, for as soon as one good is lost another replaces it; indeed, it is highly desirable that this should be so, for the beauty and perfection of the universe are thereby increased rather than diminished. A succession of beings in which the weaker always yields to the stronger issues in a harmony which is not to be disturbed by the death of the individuals, to which indeed this death contributes a good deal. A universe of this type might be likened to an eloquent discourse, where all the beauty arises from the quick succession of sounds and syllables as if it depended altogether on their very birth and death. Thus, as St. Augustine said, all that we call physical evil is reduced to the harmony of a sum of positive goods, or, as St. Thomas Aquinas would say, the presence of corruptible things in the universe, added to the incorruptible, only increases its beauty and perfection.[9] On the other hand, we have to recognize that the problem becomes more complex when we pass from brute matter to reasonable beings; for the latter are aware of their destiny and suffer accordingly: other things merely undergo privation and corruption, but these have to face misery. And then arises the question of moral evil, that is to say of human suffering including the physical conditions on which it depends: pain, sickness, death. What shall we say of these? The principles we have already will be sufficient to pre-

[8] *Op. cit.*, XIV.

[9] St. Augustine, *De natura boni*, Cap. VIII. See the parallel arguments of St. Thomas, *Cont. Gent.*, III, 71: Quod divina providentia non excludit totaliter malum a rebus, and *Sum. theol.*, I, 48, 2: Utrum malum inveniatur in rebus.

pare the way for a solution; but we shall have to make them more precise.

Let us remark in the first place that man, as a reasonable being, is a great good, and that not only in himself but also on account of the whole destiny that awaits him and, above all, of the beatitude of which he is capable. Created in the image of God, he is, in the words of St. Bernard, *celsa creatura in capacitate majestatis.*[10] Now to be capable of entering into society with God requires an intelligence, but to be capable of rejoicing in this society requires a will. To possess a good is to adhere to it, to absorb it by an act of will. Thus, to create a being capable of the highest of goods, that is to say of participation in the divine beatitude, is, *ipso facto,* to create a being endowed with will; and since to will the thing known by intelligence is to be free, we may say that it would be impossible to call man to beatitude without endowing him with liberty at the same time. A magnificent gift assuredly—but a very formidable one too, for to be capable of the greatest of goods is also to be capable of losing it. St. Augustine often dwells on this aspect of human freedom with all the indefinite possibilities of greatness and misery it involves. In a world in which all that is, in so far as it is, is a good, liberty is a great good: there are lesser goods, but still greater are conceivable. The virtues, for instance, are superior to the freedom of the will, for it is quite impossible to misuse temperance and justice, whereas we can very easily misuse our liberty. The truth is, then, that free will is a good, and the necessary condition of the greatest of goods, but not the one all-sufficient condition; everything depends on the use—which in itself is also free—that we make of it.

Now it happens that man, in the first transgression, made an ill use of it. Mutable like all creatures, endowed with a free will, capable, consequently, of rebellion, he did in fact rebel. The fault did not consist in desiring any object evil in itself, for the very notion of such an object is contradictory, but for the sake of a good he turned away from the better: *Iniquitas est desertio meliorum.*[11] Made for God, he nevertheless preferred himself to God, and in so doing brought moral evil into the world—or rather he would have brought it into the world had not the Angel forestalled him. Now this evil has a quite special nature, profoundly different even from

[10] St. Bernard, *In Cant. Canticorum,* sermo 80, art. 5.
[11] St. Augustine, *De natura boni,* Cap. XX, cf. XXXIV.

the moral evil of Greek philosophy. When man subverted order he did a great deal more than merely fall away from the rationality of his nature, diminish his own humanity, which is all that he does in Aristotle's ethics, nor did he merely compromise his destiny by an error, as happens in the Platonic myths; he brought disorder into the divine order, and presents the unhappy spectacle of a being in revolt against Being. That is why the first moral evil has a special name in the Christian system, which extends to all the faults that spring from the first; that is to say the name of sin. By the use of this word the Christian always intends to convey that moral evil, as he understands it, entering a created universe by the act of a free will, directly bears upon the fundamental relation of dependence which unites the creature to God. The prohibition, so light, and, so to speak, so gratuitous, which God had put upon the use, so perfectly valueless to man, of a single one of the good things placed within his reach, was but the sensible sign of this radical dependence of the creature. To respect the prohibition would be to recognize the dependence; to violate it would be to deny the dependence, and to proclaim that what is good for the creature is better than the divine good itself. Every time man sins he renews this act of revolt and prefers himself to God; in thus preferring himself, he separates himself from God; and in separating himself, he deprives himself of the sole end in which he can find beatitude and by that very fact condemns himself to misery. That is why, when there is question of moral evil, we can justly say that all evil is either sin or the consequence of sin.[12] Perverted in soul, subjecting his reason to concupiscence, subordinating the superior to the inferior in the order of spirit, man by the same act, brings disorder on the body animated by the soul. The equilibrium of the constitutive elements of his physical being is upset, just as disorder falls upon a house when it enters the heart of its master. Concupiscence, or rebellion of the flesh against the spirit, infirmity, sickness, death,

[12] St. Augustine, *De genesi ad litt.*, I, 3. See St. Thomas, *Sum. theol.*, I, 48, 5, Resp. But elsewhere St. Thomas adds the important remark that this formula is applicable only to moral evil and its moral or physical consequences. If the mere inequality of physical beings, resulting in no happiness or misery for these beings themselves, is to be called evil, then it is an evil that exists independently of sin. Thus: "Haec divisio non est mali nisi secundum quod in rationali invenitur, ut patet ex auctoritate Augustini inducta." *De malo,* I, 4, Resp.

are all so many ills that have fallen on man as the natural consequence of his sin: *omne quod dicitur malum, aut peccatum est, aut poena peccati;* a phrase of St. Augustine's which is nothing but an extension of St. Paul's: *per unum hominem peccatum in hunc mundum intravit et, per peccatum, mors;* and again, through St. Paul, an echo of the narrative of Genesis. Once more, by revealing to man a fact that he could not naturally know, revelation opens up the way for the work of reason.

And here at last we are at the heart of the question, and if Christian philosophy can justify itself on this point, it will certainly have succeeded in interpreting, in the most optimistic manner possible, a universe in which the reality of evil is in any case an undeniable fact. Attacks on this solution of the problem were not long in coming, and naturally enough they came from the side of Pelagianism; and since they respond to a permanent philosophical difficulty it will be simplest to consider them in their original form. The question in short is whether the Christian position is not itself tainted with Manicheanism. Admit that man is not the work of a Demiurge of more or less limited power, admit that in the beginning he was untainted by any evil principle, but that his sin sprang solely from his free will; then, if he sinned, it was because he willed it, but if he willed it, his will itself must have been bad. And it is useless to object that his will became bad because he willed it so—to do that at all it must have been already bad. We shall not escape by going round and round; a world reduced to universal disorder by the mere presence of a free will can never justly be called good. It would seem that Christian thought, presenting a face of optimism as against Mani, presents a face of pessimism as against Pelagius; or even that some unexorcized shadow of Manicheanism had all unwittingly been left behind by St. Augustine.

To clear up the point, let us for the last time recall the principle that governs the whole problem. The question is not whether God could have made creatures who should not be mutable, the thing would have been just as impossible as making square circles. As we have seen, mutability is as co-essential with the nature of a contingent being, as immutability is in the case of the necessary Being. But now, when the question of moral evil arises, this principle is to be applied to the case of a free being created by God out of nothing. Suppose then that neither angel nor man had ever realized the possibility of defection inherent in their nature, none the less they would have remained radically mutable beings; such virtuality may be unactualized, in a given case it may even be morally unactualizable owing to the effects of divine grace, but nevertheless it is always there, an indelible mark of contingency. Unless, then, we are simply going to deny the possibility of justifying creation altogether, we must accept the possibility of moral evil as its necessary correlative, as soon as we admit the presence, in the bosom of this creation, of a class of free beings. But then, it will be said, why create free beings?

Because they are not only the noblest ornament of creation, but also, after God, its final cause. What God creates, as we have already said, are beings who may be witnesses of His glory, and by that very fact participators in His beatitude. That this beatitude should be really theirs they must will it; but that they may be able to will it, they must also be able to refuse it. The whole physical world is there only to serve as the habitation of spirits created by God in order to participate in His own divine life, and enter into a real society with Him. Subjected to the necessity of sinning, they would be altogether absurd creatures, mere monsters, since their nature would contradict their end; but unable to sin they would be rigorously impossible, since then they would be immutable creatures, that is to say realized metaphysical contradictions. No doubt it is a much greater good to be capable of beatitude without the power of sinning—it is the good proper to God and to His elect whose wills are confirmed in grace—but it is already no small good to be so created that in order to escape misery and achieve beatitude we have nothing to do but to will it. I make no attempt here to compel acceptance of this Christian solution of the problem of evil, for it depends on the acceptance of a certain metaphysic of being, and thereby it stands or falls; but I wish to bring out its fundamentally optimistic character. Now it seems difficult to go further in this direction than St. Augustine went and with him all the other philosophers he inspired. For all evil comes of the will; this will was not created evil, nor even indifferent to good or evil; it was created good, and such that it needed only an effortless continuance in good to attain to perfect beatitude. The only danger threatening such a nature lies therefore in that metaphysical contingence inseparable from the state of a created being, a pure *possibility,* without the least trace of actual existence, a possibility that not only could have remained unactualized but ought to have done so. Thus, without taking into account the divine art which knows so well how to bring good out of evil and to remedy the results of sin by grace, considering this evil strictly in its root, it seems that we may justly claim for Christian thought that it has done everything necessary to reduce it to the status of an avoidable accident, and to banish it to the confines of this fundamentally good universe.

What is true of the problem of the origin of evil, is true also when we come to consider the worth of the world after the introduction of evil by the original transgression. The popular idea of a Christian universe corrupted in its very nature by sin owes much of its favour to the influence of Luther, Calvin and Jansenius; but to look at Christianity through their eyes would be to regard it in a very different light from that of Thomism, or even the authentic Augustinianism. No one, in fact, could be further than St. Augustine from considering the world in the state of fallen nature as worthless. His own metaphysical principles would forbid it, to start with. Since evil is but the corruption of a good and cannot possibly subsist at all save in this good, it follows that inasmuch as there is evil, there is also good. Certainly, we have travelled very far from that degree of order, beauty and measure which God bestowed on the world in creating it, but if sin had abolished all good it would have abolished all being along with the good and the world would no longer exist. In this sense we may say that evil could not eliminate nature without eliminating itself, since it would have no subject left to inhere in, there would be none of which it could be affirmed. It is not in the least surprising therefore to find St. Augustine indulging in genuine eulogies of fallen nature. If he deplores all that we have lost he never dreams of despising what remains; even our present miserable state has not lost all its glory in his eyes. We behold a human race that is still of such fecundity as to spread over the entire earth; man himself, *opus ejus tam magnum et admirabile,* whose intelligence, dormant in the infant, progressively awakens and develops until it produces all these arts lit up with the prodigal splendours of intelligence and invention. How much good must there not remain in such a nature, to enable it to invent so many techniques, of dress, agriculture, industry and navigation; to achieve these noble arts of language, poetry and music, and lastly this very moral science itself which puts it on the road to an eternal destiny! There is nothing even in the very body but Augustine will admiringly detail its beauties, for even these remain radiant, in spite of the Fall. If, then, we misconceive him, it is because we no longer dare to rise to the height of his splendid vision of the world as it was before the Fall, as it will be again in the state of glory. If he qualifies the splendours of this world as "consolations for condemned wretches," it is not because he would belittle them, they are dearer indeed to him than they ever can be now to us.[13] But he believed that the world had known better things, and moreover awaits better things, so that, accepting all that we accept, rejoicing in all that we rejoice in, he hopes for far more. If this hope now fails us, it is not he that should be taxed with pessimism, it is ourselves.

For the technical justification of this Augustinian and Christian feeling we must turn once more to the philosophers of the Middle Ages, and particularly to St. Thomas and Duns Scotus. What was wanting to St. Augustine for the purpose of finding the definitive formula for it, was an exact idea of a nature considered as a stable essence with defined contours. He is quite sure that evil is powerless to destroy nature; what he never succeeded in saying clearly is, that it cannot even alter nature. Nothing on the other hand is clearer in St. Thomas; only one who has never read any one of the articles which he devoted to the question in the *Summa* could possibly understand the expression "corrupted nature" in that *simpliste* sense in which it seems to be so often misunderstood. If, in fact, you take it literally the expression is a contradiction in terms; and it is enough to follow St. Thomas' analyses to see in what an altogether relative sense we should understand it.

When it is asked what effects were produced by original sin on the good of human nature, we must first of all define what we mean by this "good." Three different interpretations are possible. In the first place it may signify human nature itself, as determined by its constitutive principles and defined as "rational living thing." Secondly, it may mean man's natural inclination to good, that natural inclination without which he could not even continue to live since the good in general includes his own proper good. Thirdly, it may mean the gift of original justice bestowed on him by God at the time of his creation and received therefore as a grace. Understood in this last sense, the good of human nature is not a part of that

[13] St. Augustine, *De civitate Dei*, XXII, 24, 3–5.

nature, it is something added, and that is why it was totally destroyed by original sin. Understood in the second sense, the good of nature is a real part of nature, and is not therefore to be suppressed, but simply diminished by sin. Every act initiates a habit, that is to say the first bad act results in a disposition to commit others and thus enfeebles the natural human inclination towards good. But this inclination, nevertheless, remains, and so the way to the acquisition of all the virtues is still open.[14] As for the first and proper sense of the world "nature," that is to say the very essence of man, it can neither be suppressed nor diminished by sin; *primum igitur bonum naturae, nec tollitur, nec diminuitur per peccatum.*[15] To deny this would be to suppose that at one and the same time man could both remain man and cease to be man. Thus sin neither adds to nor takes away from human nature: *ea enim quae sunt naturalia homini, neque subtrahuntur neque dantur homini per peccatum.*[16] Man's metaphysical status is essentially unchangeable and independent of all the accidents that may befall him.

When therefore the Renaissance is held up to our admiration for its discovery of nature and its worth, and opposed to the Middle Ages as the day of its unjust depreciation, we must carefully scrutinize the meaning of this assertion. In so far as it has any it can only be this: that the Renaissance marks the opening of an era in which man will profess to be satisfied with the state of fallen nature. And that, no doubt, happened, although to a much lesser extent than alleged; but it would be altogether unjust to conclude against the Middle Ages that having unfavourably compared the state of fallen nature with another and a better, it had no feeling left for it at all. If anyone showed such lack of feeling, or denied its reality or value, it was certainly neither St. Thomas nor St. Augustine, it was much rather Luther and Calvin. In this sense it is true to say that if the spirit of mediæval philosophy was profoundly accordant with certain positive aspirations of the Renaissance it was precisely because that spirit was Christian.

The tradition goes back to the remotest antiquity. No one did more than Tertullian to defend the unity of the true Church, and yet Tertullian left the Church as soon as he came to the conclusion

[14] It subsists even in the damned, and it is for this reason that they can feel remorse: St. Thomas, *Sum. theol.*, I a, II ae, 85, 2, ad 3.

[15] St. Thomas, *Sum. theol.*, I a, II ae, 85, 1, Resp.

[16] St. Thomas, *Sum. theol.*, I, 98, 2, Resp.

that the human body is bad in itself. St. Augustine was never guilty of this error. He knows very well that since the body was created by God it must be good; he refuses to follow Plato in holding that the soul is imprisoned in the body as the sequel of some metaphysical fall; he will not allow that the duty of the soul is to flee the body, but would rather counsel it to accept the body as a precious charge placed in its care to be brought up in due order, unity and beauty.[17] But just as it is not Christian to run away from the body, so neither is it Christian to despise nature. How can we possibly belittle these heavens and this earth that so wonderfully proclaim the glory of their Creator, so evidently bear on them the marks of His infinite wisdom and goodness? The true Christian feeling for nature is that which finds expression throughout the Psalms, and, above all, in the Canticle of the Three Children in the fiery furnace: *Benedicite opera Domini Domino; laudate et superexultate eum in saecula.* And after many centuries St. Francis of Assisi will echo that song in his Laudes and the Canticle of Brother Sun, wherein not only water, earth, and air, and stars, but the very death of the body itself, will receive their meed of praise and benediction. If anywhere the heart of man entered into fraternal communion with all that lives and breathes and has being, most assuredly it did so there; for this purely Christian soul it was altogether one and the same thing to love the works of God and to love God.

Here perhaps we have arrived at the point where the mistake that obscured the significance of Christian optimism begins to become clear. Not even the Middle Ages knew any ruder asceticism

[17] See St. Augustine's critique of Porphyry's pessimism: "Sed corpus est omne fugiendum. . . . Omne dixit (Porphyrius), quasi omne corpus vinculum aerumnosum sit animae. Et prorsus si corpus qualecumque est fugiendum, non est ut laudes ei corpus, et dicas quomodo Deus docente fides nostra laudat corpus: quia et corpus quod modo habemus, quamvis habeamus hinc poenam de peccato, et corpus, quod corrumpitur, aggravat animam (*Sap.*, IX, 15); tamen habet corpus istud speciem suam, dispositionem membrorum, distinctionem sensuum, erectam staturam, et caetera quae bene considerantes stupent. Verumtamen illud omnino incorruptibile, omnino immortale, omnino ad movendum agile et facile erit. Sed ait Porphyrius: sine causa mihi laudas corpus; qualecumque sit corpus, si vult esse beata anima, corpus est omne fugiendum. Hoc dicunt philosophi; sed errant, sed delirant." St. Augustine, *Sermo.*, 242, VII, 7. There is the authentic Christian spirit: altogether different from the gloomy asceticism to which certain mediæval authors succumbed.

than that of St. Francis—or any more absolute confidence in the goodness of nature. Far from excluding optimism, Christian asceticism is merely the reverse side of its optimism. Certainly there is no true Christianity without the *contemptus saeculi,* but contempt for the world is not the same thing as hatred of being—quite the contrary, it is hatred of non-being. By wrestling with the *flesh,* the mediæval ascetic sought to restore the *body* to its pristine perfection; if he did not rejoice in the world for the world's sake, it was because he knew that the true way to use the world is to restore it to its own integrity by referring it to God; the world that the Christian detests consists of all that mass of disorder, deformity and evil introduced into creation by man's own voluntary defection. He turns away from these, no doubt, but precisely to adhere with all his heart to the order, beauty and good which was willed from the beginning; he works to restore these in himself and others; with an heroic effort he would clear the face of the universe and render it resplendent once more as the face of God. Nothing could be more positive than such an asceticism, nothing could be better grounded in hope and resolute optimism. The disaccord that persists between Christian and non-Christian on this point is of another order therefore than is usually supposed. The question is not whether the world is good or evil, but whether the world is sufficient to itself, and whether it suffices. The testimony, and, we may add, the secular experience of Christendom is, that nature itself is powerless to realize itself, or even fully to survive as nature, when it attempts to do this without the help of grace. If optimism thus consists, not in denying the existence of evil, nor in accepting evil, but in looking it in the face and fighting it, then we may legitimately speak of Christian optimism. The work of creation is shattered, but the fragments remain good, and, with the grace of God, they may be reconstituted and restored.

PART III

Society

CHAPTER 9

Introduction: The Sacral Norm

FRANCIS OAKLEY

> *To establish the connections, in principle and in detail, directly or mediately, between politics and eternity is a project that has never been without its followers. . . . Probably there has been no theory of the nature of the world, of the activity of man, of the destiny of mankind, no theology or cosmology, perhaps even no metaphysics, that has not sought a reflection of itself in the mirror of political philosophy; certainly there has been no fully considered politics that has not looked for its reflection in eternity.*[1]

It was the Greeks of the classical era who first elaborated a "fully-considered politics," and in many phases of our modern political thinking our indebtedness to them is so obvious and so profound that it would be hard to overestimate its importance. Hard, indeed, but not impossible. On this, as on other matters, our very sense of the magnitude of the debt we owe to the Greeks often prevents us from seeing them clearly and disposes us to a persistent anachronism in our understanding of them. Fustel de Coulanges perceived this point over a century ago when he said (of the Romans as well as the Greeks):

[1] Michael Oakeshott, in the introduction to his edition of Thomas Hobbes, *Leviathan* (Oxford: Basil Blackwell, 1946), p. x.

> What we have received from them leads us to believe that we resemble them. We have some difficulty in considering them as foreign nations; it is almost always ourselves that we see in them. Hence spring many errors. We rarely fail to deceive ourselves regarding these ancient nations when we see them through the opinions and facts of our own time.[2]

The mere juxtaposition of a work like Locke's *Second Treatise of Government* with, say, the *Politics* of Aristotle, should serve to illustrate this point. Writers on Western constitutionalism, as Tierney points out below,[3] still sometimes contrive to jump from the ancient world to early modern Europe, and to do so without noticeable strain. But it is clear that the fundamental political vision which informs Aristotle's work is vastly different from that presupposed by Locke's political thinking. Basic to this difference is the fact that Locke's state possesses in its own right no moral or religious dimension. Its very existence and the demands it makes upon the loyalty of its citizens present, for him, a problem. He begins his political thinking, therefore, from the standpoint of the autonomous individual. Only in so far as the state restricts itself to the task of meeting certain limited and specified needs of that individual is the oppressive weight of political authority legitimated.

For Aristotle, on the other hand, this problem of political obligation simply does not arise. For him, Locke's autonomous individual existing in a prepolitical state might be "a god or a beast," perhaps, but certainly not a man. Only by membership in political society can one become truly human. A state as restricted in purpose as that which Locke envisaged would not even, in Aristotelian terms, be a true state at all. For "the end of the state is not mere life," Aristotle asserts, "it is, rather, a good quality of life." [4] And, that is to say, the state exists to make possible not merely man's physical survival but also his moral and spiritual perfection.

The note which Aristotle strikes here was characteristic of classical Greece and it has not been without its harmonics in modern political thinking. But at least on this central point it is Locke rather than Aristotle who informs the common political sense of most

[2] Numa Denis Fustel de Coulanges, *The Ancient City* (New York: Doubleday Anchor, 1955), p. 11.

[3] See below, p. 228.

[4] *Politics,* III, 1280 a; trans. Ernest Barker, *The Politics of Aristotle* (New York: Oxford Univ. Press, 1948), p. 118.

modern thinkers, and it must be insisted that the approach to social and political life explicit in Plato and Aristotle and implicit in the life of the Greek city state presupposed a general view of the world and of the nature and destiny of man which differed radically from that most characteristic of the Western tradition, and one which had its roots in the primitive and antique mythopoeic thought already referred to more than once in the course of this book.[5]

But how did this pattern relate to the nature of human society? On this, the verdict of the anthropologists and of the students of primitive and comparative religion is quite clear. "The mainspring of the acts, thoughts, and feelings of early man was the conviction that the divine was immanent in nature, and nature intimately connected with society."[6] The primitive mentality, we are reminded, was thoroughly *monistic*.[7] The sharp distinctions which we are accustomed to make between nature and supernature, between nature, society, and man, between animate and inanimate—these are almost wholly lacking. Primitive man was encompassed by darkness, mystery, and a natural world that he apprehended almost instinctively, it seems, in terms of his own psyche. "In the significant moments of his life," it has been said, ". . . [he] was confronted not by an inanimate impersonal nature—not by an 'It' but by a 'Thou.'"[8]

Nature was alive; it was "full of gods"; it expressed, both in its benign cyclical rhythms and in its intimidating and catastrophic upheavals, the movements and indwelling of the divine. Hardly surprising, then, that man himself should be conceived less as an individual standing ultimately alone than as an integral part of society, deriving therefrom whatever value he possessed. Hardly surprising, either, that society itself should be conceived as "imbedded in nature," as entangled intimately with the processes of the natural world.[9] Hardly surprising, again, that its primary function should

[5] See above, the general introduction, pp. 1–12, and the introductory essays to Parts I and II.

[6] H. and H. A. Frankfort, John A. Wilson and Thorkild Jacobsen, *Before Philosophy: The Intellectual Adventure of Ancient Man* (Baltimore: Penguin Books, Inc., 1964), p. 237.

[7] Arend Th. van Leeuwen, *Christianity in World History*, tras. H. H. Hoskins (New York: Charles Scribner's Sons, 1965), p. 50.

[8] Frankfort *et al.*, *Before Phiosophy*, p. 238. For what follows I am indebted particularly to Chapters I and VIII of this book.

[9] *Cf.* H. Richard Niebuhr, *Radical Monotheism and Western Culture* (Harper and Brothers, New York, 1960), p. 25, where he describes primitive societies

be something that exceeded the powers of any single man—namely, the preservation of the natural order by a complex system of ritual and tabu, the prevention of natural catastrophe, the "harmonious integration" of man with nature. And, that is to say, nature being but a "manifestation of the divine," that the *primary* function of society (the family, the tribe, and ultimately, what *we* would call "the state"), the first object of its anxious, daily solicitude, should be what *we*, again, would call "the religious."

At the very heart of primitive and antique "politics," then, lay religion—so much so, indeed, that for the greater part of human history it is an egregious anachronism even to make use of those words, the very definitions of which presuppose, of course, our modern Western distinction between the religious and the political, and, therefore, between church and state.

This becomes very clear if one examines ancient conceptions of kingship. "If we refer to kingship as a political institution," Henri Frankfort has said,

> We assume a point of view which would have been incomprehensible to the ancients. We imply that human polity can be considered by itself. The ancients however experienced human life as part of a widely spreading network of connections which reached beyond the local and the national communities into the hidden depths of nature and the powers that rule nature. The purely secular, insofar as it could be granted to exist at all, was the purely trivial. Whatever was significant was embedded in the life of the cosmos, and it was precisely the king's function to maintain the harmony of that integration.[10]

The ancient kings, then, were regarded as sacred figures—always priestly, usually divine—and divine kingship, with all that it involved, has well been described as "the archetypal pattern of the

as "closed societies" (the phrase is Bergson's), and says, "Such a society may number among its members the dead and the yet unborn as well as the living, supernatural as well as natural existences, animals (totem animals, for instance) as well as men, natural phenomena—wind and sky and thunder—as well as animate beings. But every participant in the group derives his value from his position in the enduring life of the community. . . . The community is not so much his great good as the source and value of all that is good, including his own value. But the society is also his cause; its continuation, power, and glory are the unifying ends of all his actions. . . ."

[10] *Kingship and the Gods: A Study of Ancient Near Eastern Religion as the Integration of Society and Nature* (Chicago: University of Chicago Press, 1948), p. 3.

archaic culture which underlies all the most ancient civilizations of the world."[11] Evidence for its existence is broadcast across the globe in regions as far distant from one another as China and West Africa, Scandinavia and Polynesia, India and Peru, Ireland and the Nilotic Sudan,[12] but nowhere more strikingly than in the institutions and practices of ancient Egypt. There the Pharaoh was regarded, quite literally, as a god incarnate, whose task it was to ensure the cyclical rhythm of the seasons, to guarantee the fertility of the land, and to secure the prevention of any disharmony between the supernatural forces and human society. So that it could be said to him:

> If thou thyself shouldst say to this father, the Nile, the father of gods: "Let water flow forth upon the mountains!" he will act according to all that thou hast said.[13]

An extreme case, perhaps, but similar prerogatives were claimed, to a greater or lesser degree by the other sacred monarchs of the ancient Middle East.[14] The belief in the divinity of the ruler was, via the great Hellenistic empire of Alexander the Great and its successor states, to exert a profound influence over the political thinking of the late classical world,[15] and it was able to do so because it came not as an alien heterodoxy, but as the return to an orthodoxy the ideological underpinnings of which had never fully been dismantled. For if the Greeks of the classical era had long since left their own institutions of sacred monarchy behind them, the Greek city-states still remained something more than states in our modern sense of the word.[16] Nor should we allow our Hellenic political

[11] Christopher Dawson, *Religion and Culture* (New York: Meridian Bks., 1960), p. 116.

[12] For valuable summary statements of the recent scholarship on the subject see the articles (English, German, French) collected in *The Sacral Kingship: Contributions to the Central Theme of the VIIIth International Congress for the History of Religions* (Rome, April, 1955), a supplement to the journal *Numen* published as *Studies in the History of Religions*, IV (Leiden: E. J. Brill, 1959).

[13] Frankfort *et al., Before Philosophy*, pp. 89–90.

[14] For the differences between the Egyptian and Mesopotamian attitudes, see Frankfort, *Kingship and the Gods.*

[15] See Calvin W. McEwan, *The Oriental Origin of Hellenistic Kingship*, The Oriental Institute of the University of Chicago Studies in Ancient Oriental Civilization, No. 13 (Chicago, 1934)

[16] Thus the civic cult was maintained under the supervision of a special official who sometimes retained the title of "king"—see Aristotle, *Politics, VI,* 1322b; trans. Barker, p. 277. This was true also at Rome, and Fustel de Coulanges

vocabulary to conceal this fact from us. We ascribe to words like "polity," "politics," "political" and so on, a far narrower meaning than their Greek originals possessed. Classical Greek political theory and political practice acknowledged no real distinction between the political and the religious. Politics *included* religion. The loyalty men owed to their city was equally a loyalty to their city's gods, and (despite the novel and dissenting position occasionally expressed by Plato and Aristotle) that loyalty was in general conceived to be an ultimate loyalty from which there could be no appeal to any higher norm.[17]

The same was true of the Roman state, both Republic and Empire, and in this context it should be noted that the ultimate insistence on the divinity of the emperors and on the obligation to perform public worship to "Rome and Augustus" is not to be dismissed anachronistically as "merely political" and possessed of no truly "religious" significance. Emperor-worship, particularly in the eastern provinces, reflected a genuine piety—though, of course, a piety of the antique civic mode.[18] Its spread throughout the empire owed less to governmental enforcement than to popular sentiment. If it was, indeed, a *political* act, it was political, not in our modern sense of that word, but in the old, broad, inclusive sense that bears the clear imprint of the archaic social vision.

It would be improper, moreover, to give the impression that such ideas were to be found only in the ancient period. The evidence for the existence of divine or sacred monarchy is spread not only across the globe but also across an extraordinary span of time—pointing back to those prehistoric chiefs and medicine men whose power over the phenomena of nature had enlarged their dominion, and reaching forward to the modern sacred monarchs of Polynesia, of Africa, of Central and South America, of Asia. Nowhere, perhaps, has the continuity of this ancient norm been more readily evident than in China. In that country, what van Leeuwen calls "the

comments that even when republican institutions were established, "the name of king, far from becoming a reproach, remained a venerated title"—*The Ancient City*, p. 179.

[17] This point is made with force and clarity by Michael Foster, *Masters of Political Thought: Plato to Machiavelli* (London: Harrap and Co., 1952), pp. 113 ff.; *cf.* his *The Political Philosophies of Plato and Hegel* (New York: Oxford Univ. Press, 1935).

[18] For corroboration of this claim, see H. W. Pleket, "An Aspect of the Emperor Cult: Imperial Mysteries," *Harvard Theological Review*, LVIII (Dec., 1965), 331–47.

ontocratic state"—that is state conceived "as the embodiment of the cosmic totality" with its concomitant notion of kingship as "anchored in the cosmos"—persisted down into the twentieth century, being "accepted unanimously as an axiomatic principle at every level of the population and by the various philosophies and religions, however diverse." [19] Thus, through all changes of dynasty it remained the sacred duty of the Chinese emperor, himself the "Son of Heaven," to harmonize or coordinate the orders of heaven, nature, and society by the scrupulous performance of a cycle of traditional ritual acts. As recently as 1899, an imperial decree appeared in the *Peking Gazette* in which the emperor attributed the current drought to his own sins,[20] and it was only in 1912 that the great Altar of Heaven to the south of Peking ceased to witness the annual sacrifice offered by the Son of Heaven at the winter solstice.[21]

One is tempted, of course, to dismiss phenomena of this type as mere survivals of primitivism, as abnormalities in the life of any truly civilized society. But it would be wholly misleading to do so. In terms of its antiquity, its ubiquity, its extraordinary staying power, the institution of divine or sacred monarchy with all that it entails can lay a strong claim to being the most common form of societal organization known to man. In particular, the blending of the political and religious which it presupposes undoubtedly reflects man's customary mode of apprehending social realities. This being the case, of course, the familiar distinction between religion and politics, the degree of freedom from government control claimed thereby for a whole segment in the life of the individual citizen, the essentially *secular* nature of Western political societies and the complex constitutional devices functioning to prevent them from becoming anything more than secular political entities—all of these characteristics, so much a matter of common sense to us today, stand out instead as novelties, abnormalities, developments peculiar to modern Western civilization and explicable only in terms of the unique history of that civilization.[22] And in that history, it is once

[19] *Christianity in World History*, pp. 166 ff. and 195.

[20] Max Weber, *The Religion of China: Confucianism and Taoism*, Hans H. Gerth, trans. (Glencoe, Ill.: Free Press of Glencoe, 1959), pp. 261–2, note 63.

[21] Van Leeuwen, pp. 170 ff. In Vietnam the old imperial capitol of Hué was the centre of similar rites until 1915—see Nguyen Tran Huan, "Le roi sacré dans l'ancien Vietnam," *The Sacral Kingship*, pp. 164–6.

[22] A fact not irrelevant, perhaps, to the ephemeral life enjoyed by most Western-inspired constitutionalist regimes in the excolonial countries of the non-Western world.

more necessary to insist, the biblical doctrine of creation and the notion of God it presupposes has played a vital and fundamental role.

"There is a divinity that doth hedge a King," Shakespeare said. In terms of the archaic pattern, according to which the divine is apprehended as multiple, as limited in power, as immanent in nature, as trapped by virtue of its tragic multiplicity in the prison of the human body—such a statement is to be taken at its face value. And if this is a pattern of thought which is well-nigh impenetrable to us today, it is so precisely because our very idea of what it is to be divine has been moulded by centuries of Judaeo-Christian thinking with its obdurate insistence on the unity, omnipotence and transcendence of God, centuries during which the meanings ascribed to such words as "god," "divine," "religious," and so on have, by ancient standards, been narrowed down to a degree bordering on the eccentric. For the biblical idea of creation involves not only a dedivinization or de-sacralization of nature and of man,—as we saw in Parts One and Two,—but also (and therefore) a secularization of human society and of the political institutions necessary to the maintenance of that society.[23] In negating the fundamental primitive notion of a divine *continuum* linking man with nature and the state with the cosmos, it undercuts as well the very foundation for the archaic pattern of divine kingship and of the state as "the embodiment of the cosmic totality."

Because of this, and because of the almost universal sway of the "ontocratic" pattern, van Leeuwen has argued that

> the themes of the first eleven chapters of Genesis . . . are universal in character. The major theme running through the Old Testament is that which proclaims the kingship of the Lord and the unremitting struggle against the challenge of the ontocratic state. Fundamentally, the decision which faced the people of Israel was a choice between ontocracy and theocracy.[24]

His discussion of "Kingship in Israel and Babylon," which we include below, will serve, then, to give some inkling of the lineaments of that struggle and of the extent to which the Hebrews did in fact opt for theocracy. In this discussion, it should be noted, and in the complex argument from which it is extracted, van Leeuwen does not

[23] For a very succinct treatment of some of these interrelations, see Harvey Cox, *The Secular City* (New York: The Macmillan Co., 1965), Chap. I.
[24] *Christianity in World History*, p. 173.

overlook the influence exerted on Hebrew thinking by the Babylonian religion, with its "sense of something far more deeply interfused," its conviction of the immanence in the natural world of the divine, and its concomitant espousal of sacral kingship. But he is at pains to identify the degree to which such Babylonian ideas were modified under the pressure of a more exclusive conception of the divine. And for him, as for Frankfort before him,[25] the truly remarkable fact about the Hebrew monarchy is not so much the degree to which it retained a religious aura as the degree to which, in comparision with the other Near Eastern monarchies, it was a *secular* institution.

The judgment, then, is a comparative one. Van Leeuwen is careful not to exaggerate the extent to which the Hebrews themselves were able to break away from the ancient sacral norm. And correctly so. There seems no good reason, for example, to deny that Hebrew kings performed some functions of a priestly nature. Moreover, even if one were willing to be anachronistic one would encounter great difficulty in trying to distinguish church and state as separate corporate entities in any of the successive Hebrew regimes. If the archaic pattern of divine kingship was excluded, we should remember that it was excluded in the name of kingly divinity, and it would be improper to read the modern distinction between the religious and the political into a society in which Yahweh alone was recognized as truly king and in which the governmental ideal remained, therefore, what Josephus later on was to call "theocracy."

The idea of creation, then, and the conception of God it presupposes, however determinative in undermining the ancient sacral norm, does not seem by itself to have been enough to destroy it. On this matter the evidence of the Old Testament is supported by the history of the Islamic world. The monotheism of its orthodox tradition is notably firm; so, too, is its insistence on the transcendence, the creative will and the omnipotence of God. But despite its essential "biblicism" on these critical beliefs, Islam has shown little tendency, even in the modern period, to engineer a clear separation of the religious and the political. The *umma* or community which Muhammed established at Medina was a religious community as well as a political organism and "the concept of the *umma* has remained the one unifying factor amidst the diversity of the Islamic empire." So that

[25] *Kingship and the Gods,* pp. 337–44.

> Islam knows no distinction between a spiritual and temporal realm, between religious and secular activities. Both realms form a unity under the all embracing authority of the *sharī'a* [the law].[26] . . . Politics . . . is the scene of religion as life on this earth as long as the law of the state is the *sharī'a.* This state is the *Khilāfa* or *Imāna*, and if we must operate with our Western terms, it may be defined as a spiritual and temporal unity.[27]

We must look elsewhere, then, for the factor that was to complete the desacralizing process begun with Genesis. The classic statement of Fustel de Coulanges, our second essay, while acknowledging that there were other contributing elements, identifies as this critical factor the coming of Christianity. It was by the teaching of the New Testament, he says, that the polis was reduced, finally, to the status of a merely secular entity. The Kingdom of God (for the Jews an unrealized ideal, no doubt, but nevertheless a "this-worldly" conception) was now declared to be a kingdom "not of this world." [28] As a result, the denial of anything more than a conditional allegiance to the state ceased to be a merely temporary restriction destined for removal in the fullness of time, and became a permanent, universal, and dramatic limitation on the allegiance men can owe to any earthly society.

Even the more affirmative stand of Christian thinking about the state—the strand that drew its inspiration from St. Paul's injunction to obey "the powers that be" because they were "the ministers of God"—never went so far as to endorse the ancient view of the state as existing to make men good. Instead, it conceived its function in a startlingly negative manner as a consequence of the Fall, as a "punishment and remedy for sin." [29] St. Augustine gave this point of view clear and influential expression in his *De civitate dei* when he argued that God "did not intend His rational creature, who was made in His image, should have dominion over anything but the irrational creation—not man over man," that subjection is "a result

[26] For a brief discussion of the *Sharī'a,* see H. A. R. Gibb, *Mohammedanism* (New York: Galaxy Books, 1962), Chap. VI.

[27] Erwin I. J. Rosenthal, *Political Thought in Medieval Islam* (Cambridge: Cambridge Univ. Press, 1958), pp. 8–9, 25–26.

[28] See Frederick C. Grant, "The Idea of the Kingdom of God in the New Testament", in *The Sacral Kingship,* pp. 437–46.

[29] Rom. 13:1–7. For a guide to the relevant texts in the writings of the Church Fathers see the several chapters entitled "Attitude to the State" in C. J. Cadoux, *The Early Church and the World* (Edinburgh: T. and T. Clark, 1955).

of sin," and that "the earthly city . . . seeks an earthly peace, and the end it proposes, in the well-ordered concord of civic obedience and rule, is the combination of men's wills to attain the things which are helpful to this life." [30]

"The victory of Christianity," then, did indeed work "the end of ancient society." But there remains room for disagreement about when exactly that victory occurred. Fustel de Coulanges seems to have assumed that the first three centuries during which Christianity "lived entirely beyond the action of the state" were themselves enough to make the distinction between the religious and the political "a plain and incontestable truth." To realize, however, that this was not the case, one has only to recall the vogue enjoyed by the divine right theory of monarchy in the early modern era, or, indeed, the papalist theocratic claims of the High Middle Ages [31] which seem to have been the original target of that theory. Both of these profoundly conservative developments witness eloquently to the stubborn tenacity of the ancient sacral norm and to the extreme difficulty which even Christians experienced in extricating themselves from that archaic pagan pattern in which the religious and the political interpenetrated.

That pattern took longer to erase than is usually supposed. When the Roman emperors became Christians they did not cease necessarily to be the successors of the emperor-gods of pagan Rome or the priest-kings of antiquity. Nor does the mass of the Christian clergy seem to have demanded that they should. New Testament political teaching concerned, after all, a situation in which Christians confronted pagan rulers, whereas now, by an unexpected dispensation of Providence, they enjoyed the protection and favor of Christian emperors. It is not really too surprising, then, that most of the clergy were willing to accept those emperors' own estimate of the role of the imperial office in the economy of salvation. Nor is it surprising that by the beginning of the fifth century the emperors were well on

[30] *The City of God,* trans. Marcus Dods (New York: The Modern Library, 1950), Bk. XIX, Chaps. 15 and 17, pp. 693 and 695. For a discussion of the ways in which Augustine uses the term "earthly city," see Herbert A. Deane, *The Political and Social Ideas of St. Augustine* (New York: Columbia Univ. Press, 1963), esp. pp. 28–32.

[31] Claims often bolstered by a misinterpretation of Augustine that has not been without its supporters among modern commentators. For the medieval interpretation, see H. X. Arquilliere, *L'Augustinisme politique: Essai sur la formation des théories politiques du Moyen-Age* (Paris: J. Vrin, 1955).

the way to becoming (in fact, if not necessarily in theory) the heads of the Christian church as well as of the Roman empire. Indeed, as the membership of the two societies coalesced, it was becoming increasingly difficult to distinguish the one from the other as discrete corporate entities.

This process of coalescence attained its peak in the Byzantine empire, where the mingling of religious and secular affairs and the extent to which the emperor was supreme in religious matters reached at some periods almost antique pagan dimensions.[32] If this never quite happened in the West, it is essential to realize that it came very close to doing so, despite the fragmenting impact of the barbarian invasions of the fifth and ninth centuries. The notion of kingship which the Germanic invaders brought into Western Europe—like that of the original Celtic inhabitants of that area, like that, again, which lay behind the imperial cult introduced by the Romans—was itself grounded in the ancient and primitive pattern of divine kingship.[33] For centuries even the Christian monarchs of Western Europe regarded themselves, and were in turn regarded by clergy and laity alike, as religious—even priestly—figures, certainly possessed of jurisdictional authority over the church.[34] Not before the late eleventh century, when the Gregorian reform was launched, was the essentially pagan pattern of "pontifical monarchy" decisively challenged. And the Gregorian reform marked merely the beginning of several centuries of intermittent but widespread conflict between the ecclesiastical and temporal authorities in Western Europe. Only after the termination of those conflicts, with the emergence of the "desacralized" state,[35] does it become possible to speak

[32] For a lively evocation of the religious character of the emperor's position, see René Guerdan, *Byzantium: Its Triumphs and Tragedy*, trans. by D. L. B. Hartley (New York: Capricorn Books, 1962), pp. 17 ff.

[33] See Marc Bloch, *Les rois thaumaturges: Étude sur le caractère surnaturel attribué à la puissance royale particulièrement en France et en Angleterre* (Strasbourg and Paris, 1928), esp. Bk. I, Chap. 2.

[34] For a useful discussion of "pontifical kingship" with particular reference to Germany, see the Introduction by Karl F. Morrison to Theodor E. Mommsen and Karl F. Morrison, *Imperial Lives and Letters of the Eleventh Century* (New York: Columbia Univ. Press, 1902), pp. 3–40.

[35] "Desacralized" is perhaps preferable to "secularized" because of the specific connotations of the latter word. On this point, see Larry Shiner, *The Secularization of History: An Introduction to the Theology of Friedrich Gogarten* (New York: Abingdon Press, 1966), pp. 17 ff.

of "the victory of Christianity" at least with respect to the political teaching contained in the New Testament.[36]

The history of these developments in Western Europe is, of course, an exceedingly complex one, and one that defies summary treatment. A few phases in that history can, however, be illuminated, and with that objective in view two further essays have been included. The first of these, by T. M. Parker, seeks to identify some of the factors at work in early medieval Europe to blunt the secularizing thrust of Christian teaching and to prolong the domination of the ancient sacral norm. The second, by Brian Tierney, explores some of the legal, political and constitutional consequences of the ending of that domination. In particular, he stresses the importance of the fact that neither imperial nor papal theocratic ambitions were ever wholly realized and emphasizes the significance of the institutional dualism which for several centuries characterized Western political life.

On this matter of consequences it is necessary to underline only one point, namely: that the "church-state" conflicts inaugurated by the Gregorian reform constituted the birth pangs of something new in the history of mankind, of a society in which the state was stripped finally of its age-old religious aura and its overriding claims on the loyalties of men balanced and curtailed by the claims of a rival authority. And it seems clear that without this dualism, without this tension, without this stubborn insistence that no state could claim a final authority over the conscience of any man, the familiar stress on the ultimate value and autonomy of the individual would not have become so persistently characteristic of modern Western social and political thinking. It was between the hammer and the anvil that Western individualism was shaped.

[36] And even then one may still question whether a complete victory has yet been won. Note Niebuhr's stress on the continued prevalence of what he calls "the henotheistic faith" in *Radical Monotheism and Western Culture*.

CHAPTER 10

Kingship in Israel and in Babylon

AREND TH. VAN LEEUWEN

David's proposal to build a temple for the Lord was closely connected with his own position as king. 'See now, I dwell in a house of cedar, but the ark of God dwells in a tent,' (2 Sam. 7:2). The reaction of the prophet Nathan to David's proposal is to remind him of his own humble past as a shepherd (v. 8). The prophet's deep-rooted objection to the building of a temple should be put alongside Samuel's resistance to the introduction of kingship. Both prophets saw clearly that the longing after a king and after a 'house of cedar' for the Lord which would match with the royal palace sprang from a desire to be 'like all the nations' (I Sam. 8:5). During the period of the Exodus there had been neither king nor temple.

There is a vehement protest against the pattern of kingship shared by the other religions of the ancient Near East in Ezekiel 28, where the prophet denounces the pride of the king of Tyre.[1] This prophetic denunciation is of a piece with the protest against Babylonian mythology which one enounters in the creation and flood narratives and in the saga of the tower of Babel. Here it is focused on the mythology of kingship.

In a rather different form the theme recurs in the 'lamentation

Reprinted with the permission of Charles Scribner's Sons from *Christianity in World History,* pages 82–90, by Arend Th. van Leeuwen, translated by H. H. Hoskins.

[1] Charles Virolleaud, *La légende Phénicienne de Danel* (Paris, 1936), p. 121.

over the king of Tyre' in Ezekiel 28:11–19.[2] The prophet declares that this same king who claims to have his dwelling upon the mountain of the gods is consumed by the fire of those stars amid which he had thought himself able to move. The form and tenor of his protest are not unlike what one finds in the tower of Babel story. They remind one too of the oblique attack on the Eden mythology in the story of Paradise.

Another interesting variation on the theme occurs in Ezekiel 31. The prophecy in this case most likely refers to the mythological notion of the cosmic tree, so closely related to that of the cosmic mountain.[3]

As a final example one might instance Isaiah 14:12–15, a prophecy regarding the destruction of Babel. The assault here is directed against the conception of Babel as the mountain of the gods and against the mythology of kingship linked with it.[4]

These passages make it clear that in the story of the tower of Babel we have a theme which recurs persistently in the prophetic parts of the Old Testament, and more particularly in Ezekiel. The theme is combined—and this is the point of outstanding importance —with a protest against the mythology of kingship. The Old Testament shows itself keenly aware that these two mythological ideas— of the cosmic mountain and of the divine kingship—are interdependent. They are deeply and inextricably embedded in that pattern which constitutes the basis of civilization in the ancient Near East. As H. Frankfort has argued so convincingly in his study of 'kingship and the gods', it was the king's function to preserve a harmonious relationship between society and the universe. Whether he was the very god incarnate—as in Egypt—or the servant of the gods who

[2] The very uncertain text can only be interpreted according to ancient translations. In the Septuagint the construction of the sentences deviates considerably. Cf. T. C. Vriezen, *Onderzoeck naar de paradijsvoorstellingen bij de oude Semietische volken,* (Wageningen, 1937), p. 219. See also Jahn, Gustav, *Das Buch Ezechiel* (Leipzig, 1905), Holscher, G., *Hesekiel* (Giessen, 1924), Herntrich, V., *Ezechielprobleme* (Giessen, 1932), Gressmann, Hugo, *Archiv für Religionswissenschaft* (Leipzig, 1907), p. 365, Eissfeldt, Otto, *Baäl Zaphon* (Halle, 1932), pp. 20 ff., Virolleaud, Charles, 'La Révolte de Košer contre Baäl' (*Syria,* XVI, 1935) pp. 30 ff.

[3] H. Bergema, *De Boom des levens in schrift en historie* (Hilversum, 1938), passim.

[4] Bruno Meissner, *Babylonien und Assyrien* (Heidelberg, 1925), II, p. 17; H. Gunkel, *Genesis* (Göttingen, 3rd. edn., 1910), p. 36.

ruled over the land—as, for example, in Mesopotamia—he was in any event the chief instrument in the integration of society with nature and of concord with the gods.

According to the basic Egyptian conception of kingship the Pharaoh was a god incarnate; and it was he who maintained the cosmic order. His coronation had something of the character of cosmic event, in fact, of the creation of the universe. His throne was a 'copy' of the primeval hill. Since his rule was in itself a reflection of Re, god of the sun, the ideas of creation, sunrise and kingly rule were always being mingled and merged together. At his death the king became one with Osiris, the god of resurrection. The royal tomb was equated with the primeval hill. The king had to die in order to enter the earth and so, as a chthonic god, bring benefits to man. Just as the dead king was identified with Osiris, so Osiris, himself a dead king, represented all kings. In the person of the king—that is to say, in Osiris—there was repeated the ever-recurring mystery of death and resurrection in the cycle of nature.

The mythology of kingship was perhaps less impressive in Mesopotamia than in Egypt. There the king was regarded as a mortal charged with a divine commission; he was the chosen servant of the gods. He maintained the harmony between society and nature simply by watching over the service of the gods and attuning the life of the community to the divine will. Although the king's rôle in the celebration of the New Year festival at Babylon was more modest than that of his Egyptian counterparts, his participation was none the less essential. This was especially the case with the rites of the day of atonement on the fifth day of the festival. The king was then the central figure of a ritual drama in which he was reinvested with the regal insignia in token of the renewed life of nature. On the ninth day of the festival the king guided a triumphal procession to the subterranean temple, *Bit Akitu,* thus representing Marduk's destruction of Tiamat, the power of chaos.

Although Egypt and Mesopotamia held different views as to the nature of the universe and the corresponding function of kingship, fundamentally their conceptions were the same. The royal function was to integrate the powers that govern the universe with the life of society and to maintain that relationship.

We have already shown, with the aid of a number of prophetic texts, that it is precisely this conception against which the Old Testament directly or indirectly takes its stand. Frankfort quite rightly says that as compared with Egyptian and even Mesopotamian kingship, that of Israel lacks sanctity.

> The relation between the Hebrew monarch and his people was as nearly secular as is possible within a society wherein religion is a living force.[5]

Kingship in the Old Testament is caught in a very awkward position between two opposed and apparently irreconcilable points of view. In some of the Psalms the king is treated with very great respect indeed.[6] Other writers, on the other hand, voice the strongest disapprobation. Hosea says point-blank that God will have nothing to do with the kingship: 'They made kings, but not through me. They set up princes, but without my knowledge,' (Hos. 8:4; cf. 7:3, 10:3, 13:10). Between the two extremes of divine approbation and total repudiation the kingship has a fairly stormy passage through the Old Testament.

The Book of Judges already envisages the kingship which was soon to be instituted; and it quite clearly falls into two distinct parts. The first (Chapters 1 to 12) has an unmistakably anti-monarchic bias, whilst the latter part has a frankly pro-monarchic tendency, with its oft-repeated refrain: 'In those days there was no king in Israel; every man did what was right in his own eyes,' (Judg. 17:6; 18:1; 19:1; 21:25). There is then a very evident cleavage running through the Book of Judges. For the tribes of the people of Israel who had come in from the desert it was the time of their first major crisis, when they had their first real encounter with 'the promised land'. The primitive theocracy, run by a rapid succession of military chieftains, largely on the basis of their personal qualities, was simply not suited to cope with the new situation for any length of time; and the demand for a settled, hereditary and central authority grew more and more persistent.

Martin Buber bases his study of 'The Kingship of God'[7] on an examination of the radically theocratic vein running through the

[5] H. Frankfort, *Kingship and the Gods* (Univ. of Chicago Press, 1948), p. 341.
[6] G. Ernest Wright, *The Old Testament against its Environment,* (London, 1950), p. 64, note 36.
[7] Buber, Martin, 'Königtum Göttes' (*Das Kommende* I, Berlin, 2nd edn., 1936). Buber, Martin, 'Biblisches Führertum' in *Kampf um Israel* (Berlin, 1933). Buber, Martin, 'Het geloof van Israël' in *De Godsdiensten der wereld,* ed. G. van der Leeuw (Amsterdam, 1948).

whole of the Old Testament. The watchword of Gideon, 'The Lord shall rule over you!' is echoed with equal forthrightness in a number of 'king-sayings' preserved in the Pentateuch (Deut. 33:2 ff.; Num. 23:21). These sayings are unquestionably old; and they embody the primitive admission of Yahweh's kingship which became a permanent factor in the history of Israel. They take us back to the making of the Covenant on Sinai, according to the oldest tradition of all, preserved in Exodus 24. Every aspect of what is meant by the affirmation that 'Yahweh is king' is present here.

Opposition to the introduction of the kingship did not spring from a desire to cling to the Bedouin way of life—even though small groups, such as the Rechabites, did survive, who were prepared to appeal to ancestral custom. No: the key to prophetic hostility lay in the recognition that Yahweh was king. The great crisis which led to the institution of the kingship was the loss of the Ark to the Philistines. It looked very much as if the office of 'judge' would completely disappear; it no longer meant anything in the military or political spheres, and now even its charismatic aspects were gone. In that political and spiritual vacuum men could think of nothing better to do than to look about them: 'Now appoint for us a king . . . like all the nations (*goyim*),' (1 Sam. 8:5, 20).

Therein lay the sting of that particular remedy. In this longing to order her political and religious life in conformity with the *goyim* Israel was playing fast and loose with her own election. What mattered was not that she wanted to have a human *melekh* (king), but that she wanted to have one after the pattern of her neighbours. If Yahweh is *melekh* in his own unique way, which sets him apart from the pagan gods, so then the people of his Covenant ought to set themselves apart by having a *melekh* who will be the instrument of that Covenant. The people had openly declared, however, that such a *melekh* was not what they desired.

It is only right to pause a little at this juncture, at this moment of profound crisis, and to take the full measure of its significance. Israel's entry into the land of Canaan marks the fulfilment of a journey which had led her out of the land of Egypt, out of the house of bondage. She has reached the promised land, where there is freedom for her to build her own way of life. Now answer must be given to the crucial question whether it lies within her to build in some other way than according to the age-old, well tried pattern of the ancient Near East. Here is Israel, raw and resourceless, with nothing to show but the unbelievable conviction that Yahweh, her God, is alone the true God, set down in surroundings overwhelmingly rich in cultural, social, economic, political and religious traditions. It is therefore not surprising—one would say rather it was inevitable—that what had happened previously to all the tribes and nations who had found their way into that *milieu* of ancient culture should now happen to Israel; after a period of conflict, of clinging to the ancestral customs, of instinctive disliking for whatever was new, she is slowly but surely absorbed, outflanked and intoxicated with the superiority of that civilization the portals of which she had presumed to enter. Israel grows civilized; she casts aside her barbaric past and sets up a state—with a monarchy, like all the *goyim.*

Israel gets her own way; but the manner in which she does so has a disconcerting drawback in the nature of this gift which she has wrested from the Lord. She must bear the responsibility, in fact, for this kingship and for all its consequences; it is her own choice, her own invention. For that very reason it now proves to lack just that essential quality which marks it among the other nations, where its source is in myth, where it is bred and proffered of the gods. That divine kingship of the nations reaches back into the primeval ages and is lost in the obscurity of their mythical atmosphere. Israel's kingship comes by the clear light of day, by an historic act of decision, made at a definite time and in a known place—and it is through and through a decision of men. The Lord has no hand in it. The king is one among the people and of like standing with them (1 Sam. 12:14, 15, 25).

In that radically demythologized form, under that withering condemnation on God's part of the pagan notion of kingship, the king is indeed a divine gift. On that point even those texts which regard the introduction of the human kingship as *ipso facto* a rejection of the kingship of the Lord are perfectly clear. It is the Lord's will, it is his doing, that he is thus rejected. It is he who grants his people a king. Therein lies the paradox: as though through the eye of a needle this novel institution passes into the life of the Israelite nation. Straight is the way that lies before such a king; for he is to walk, not after the way of the kings of all the nations, but after the law of the Lord. At that same moment when Israel, thinking to force the issue and to have her way, seizes the initiative out of God's hands, he is in full control once more, remoulding this act of disobedience and rebellion to serve his own design. The king becomes the anointed of the

Lord, a man chosen by him to be prince over his people Israel (1 Sam. 10:1; cf. 12:3).

In this paradox of the kingship is seen the paradox of Israel's history as the chosen people; and that in its turn bears witness to the paradox of the whole history of man on this earth which the Lord has made. The history of the Israelite kingship is the history of creation, of sin, of destruction, of creation 'anew'.

When the Lord makes a beginning with the history of this kingship, his first act is to expel those mythological powers which are the 'origin of the gods' and of the pagan kingship for which they stand, and then to choose his own king making of him a new creation: he 'gives him another heart', and the spirit of God comes mightily upon him (1 Sam. 10:9 f.). Nevertheless, this first king does not keep the commandment of the Lord; he is overwhelmed beneath the powers of magic and darkness which he has himself invoked (1 Sam. 28: 6 ff.). The kingship, however, is not completely swept away in the flood of this disaster. Just as through Noah a new start was made with the history of mankind, so in David the history of the kingship is re-created and continued; and as mankind after the Flood lives by virtue of God's covenant with Noah and with every living creature, so the kingship in Israel exists after Saul's downfall by virtue of God's covenant with David and with the people of Israel. Just as the rainbow was always to be the sign of God's everlasting favour towards mankind after the Flood, so now the Lord decrees that 'David my servant may always have a lamp before me in Jerusalem, the city where I have chosen to put my name,' (1 Kings 11:34).

There are two specific tokens of God's promise to keep faith with the kingship in Israel: first the Ark of the Covenant and secondly the continuance of David's line. Solomon, like the Ark, is a sign of God's unending faithfulness towards the kingship. The record of his doings is steeped in a sense of the tremendous tension between God's kingship and the efforts of the Israelite king to be 'like all the nations'. Solomon is famed for his wisdom, which enabled him to discern between good and evil. Such wisdom was a gift of the Lord (1 Kings 3; 4:34); and it was by virtue of that gift that Solomon stood out above all who came before and after him and that, more than in any other episode in the history of the Israelite kingship, the history of his reign can be said with justice to resemble the account of Paradise. With him Israel reaches a condition of *shalom,* of peace and prosperity, not altogether unlike the Paradisal state of blessedness. Chapter 11, however, marks a sudden turn, akin to the unexpected change of tone at the beginning of Genesis 3. Right through the record of Solomon's nobility and wisdom there runs something of that vein of irony which appears from the very outset in Genesis 11: 'Now the whole earth had one language . . . Then they said, "Come, let us build ourselves a city, and a tower with its top in the heavens" . . .' Viewed in that light, the description of Solomon's throne acquires a special overtone. The throne of ivory and gold had six steps. The like of it had not been made in any kingdom (1 Kings 10:20). We know that the throne, like the temple tower and the elevated altar, stood for the cosmic mountain. Now we are told that Solomon has out-Babeled Babel itself.

Solomon's empire was brought down by a revolution—and by a revolution of a unique and most peculiar kind, eloquent of the intensity of the struggle which marked Solomon's reign to vie with the splendour and glamour of the Near Eastern absolutist monarchies. In the whole of Egypt's long history, says Frankfort:

> . . . there is no evidence of any popular uprising . . . there could be competing claims among members of the royal house. . . . The people at large could not and did not interfere . . . all power was vested in the king, who alone maintained an order which was thought of as one coherent whole established in all essentials at the time of creation.
>
> The power of the king over his subjects did not cease with death, and . . . was experienced not as a tyranny reluctantly endured but as a relationship which established for each subject his function and place in the world.[8]

In Israel an absolute authority of that kind was unthinkable. Even whilst Solomon was still on the throne, opposition to the heavy yoke which he had laid on the people was brewing. In the end the prophet Ahijah fixes upon Jeroboam to be the chosen instrument of God's judgment on Solomon's idolatrous reign and proclaims him prince over the ten tribes of Israel. In a most profound sense, this is a revolution of the Covenant, directed against pagan absolutism. With this as with all such 'covenant revolutions', the real point at issue is the kingship of Yahweh. Therefore these revolutions share to the full in the Lord's promise regarding his people and regarding the kingship which he has chosen; but equally they fall under the

[8] Frankfort, *Kingship*, etc., pp. 52 f.

full impact of his impending judgment. They are an instrument of his holy will—nothing more nor less; and it is precisely on that score that these revolutions themselves so evidently fail. All that Jeroboam did was to try pitting against the absolutism of the monarchy the absolutism of his revolution. But there is no form of absolutism compatible with the kingship of the Lord. A kingship at the service of his purposes is the only possibility.

The state is in fact an emergency measure,[9] taken by man on his way out of Paradise, the sign of God's manner of election, of choosing, as it were, clean through the facts of human pride and sin. Henceforth David's house and Zion's Temple exist perpetually within the shadow of the northern kingdom of Israel, that sign of humiliation, of schism, of protest and rebellion against tyrants and idolaters. Yet on the other hand Israel cannot dispense with Judah and with Zion; for there it has pleased the Lord to set his name; there rests the Ark of the Covenant; there reigns the house of his chosen servant, David. Though cleft in two, yet still the people of God are one. What does this paradox of mutual dependence in mutual division signify? By it Israel and Judah—that is, the whole people of Israel—are to know that the broken edifice of the kingdom and the state stands on the edge of abysmal ruin and that if it stands, it does so only because God forbears and is patient.

The end of God's forbearance means also the end of the kingship and the state. 'And the Lord said, "I will remove Judah also out of my sight, as I have removed Israel, and I will cast off this city which I have chosen, Jerusalem, and the house of which I said, My name shall be there,"' (2 Kings 23:25 ff.). Such was the end of the road which the people of Israel began to tread when they took to themselves kings 'like all the nations'. The crux of the whole matter is in that phrase: it explains why Israel's political career—the rise, aggrandizement and eventual downfall of the kingship—has a universal and not just a local significance. What befell Israel holds good likewise for 'all the nations' which she so much wanted to be like. The calibre of pagan kingship is here put to the test; the conception of it is weighed in the balance and is found wanting. The Old Testament calls down judgment upon the pagan kingdoms and empires; but God makes an example of his own people. It is upon them that the judgment falls.

[9] Balscheit, Bruno, *Gottesbund und Staat* (Zürich, 1940), pp. 10 ff.

Thus God confounds the pride of pagan kingship; yet in so doing he affirms his own. Just as Israel's political history is an object-lesson to the nations in judgment and destruction, so too does it exemplify God's promise to restore and to renew. The house and kingdom of David are destroyed—but not completely and not for ever. God the Creator sets a limit, in time and space, to the untrammelled power of chaos. 'Be broken, you peoples, . . . speak a word, but it will not stand, for God is with us,' (Is. 8:5 ff.). The tree of David's royal line is felled—root and branch? Not so; for there shall come forth a shoot from the stock of Jesse, and a branch shall grow out of his roots. Then shall the Lord of Israel be king over all nations. For out of Zion shall go forth torah (Mic. 4:1 ff.). State and kingship perish; but the kingship of the Lord remains, because he reigns through the Torah.

CHAPTER 11

Christianity Changes the Conditions of Government

NUMA FUSTEL DE COULANGES

The victory of Christianity marks the end of ancient society. With the new religion this social transformation, which we saw begun six or seven centuries earlier, was completed.

To understand how much the principles and the essential rules of politics were then changed, we need only recollect that ancient society had been established by an old religion whose principal dogma was that every god protected exclusively a single family or a single city, and existed only for that. This was the time of the domestic gods and the city-protecting divinities. This religion had produced laws; the relations among men—property, inheritance, legal proceedings—all were regulated, not by the principles of natural equity, but by the dogmas of this religion, and with a view to the requirements of its worship. It was this religion that had established a government among men; that of the father in the family; that of the king or magistrate in the city. All had come from religion,—that is to say, from the opinion that man had entertained of the divinity. Religion, law, and government were confounded, and had been but a single thing under three different aspects.

We have sought to place in a clear light this social system of the ancients, where religion was absolute master, both in public and

From N. D. Fustel de Coulanges, *The Ancient City*, trans. by Willard Small, 12th ed., Lee & Shepard, Boston, 1901. By permission of the publishers.

private life; where the state was a religious community, the king a pontiff, the magistrate a priest, and the law a sacred formula; where patriotism was piety, and exile excommunication; where individual liberty was unknown; where man was enslaved to the state through his soul, his body, and his property; where the notions of law and of duty, of justice and of affection, were bounded within the limits of the city; where human association was necessarily confined within a certain circumference around a prytaneum; and where men saw no possibility of founding larger societies. Such were the characteristic traits of the Greek and Italian cities during the first period of their history.

But little by little, as we have seen, society became modified. Changes took place in government and in laws at the same time as in religious ideas. Already, in the fifth century which preceded Christianity, the alliance was no longer so close between religion on the one hand and law and politics on the other. The efforts of the oppressed classes, the overthrow of the sacerdotal class, the labors of philosophers, the progress of thought, had unsettled the ancient principles of human association. Men had made incessant efforts to free themselves from the thraldom of this old religion, in which they could no longer believe; law and politics, as well as morals, in the course of time were freed from its fetters.

But this species of divorce came from the disappearance of the ancient religion; if law and politics began to be a little more independent, it was because men ceased to have religious beliefs. If society was no longer governed by religion, it was especially because this religion no longer had any power. But there came a day when the religious sentiment recovered life and vigor, and when, under the Christian form, belief regained its empire over the soul. Were men not then destined to see the reappearance of the ancient confusion of government and the priesthood, of faith and the law?

With Christianity not only was the religious sentiment revived, but it assumed a higher and less material expression. Whilst previously men had made for themselves gods of the human soul, or of the great forces of nature, they now began to look upon God as really foreign by his essence, from human nature on the one hand, and from the world on the other. The divine Being was placed outside and above physical nature. Whilst previously every man had made a god for himself, and there were as many of them as there were families and cities, God now appeared as a unique, immense, universal being, alone animating the worlds, alone able to supply the need of adoration that is in man. Religion, instead of being, as formerly among the nations of Greece and Italy, little more than an assemblage of practices, a series of rites which men repeated without having any idea of them, a succession of formulas which often were no longer understood because the language had grown old, a tradition which had been transmitted from age to age, and which owed its sacred character to its antiquity alone,—was now a collection of doctrines, and a great object proposed to faith. It was no longer exterior; it took up its abode especially in the thoughts of man. It was no longer matter; it became spirit. Christianity changed the nature and the form of adoration. Man no longer offered God food and drink. Prayer was no longer a form of incantation; it was an act of faith and a humble petition. The soul sustained another relation with the divinity; the fear of the gods was replaced by the love of God.

Christianity introduced other new ideas. It was not the domestic religion of any family, the national religion of any city, or of any race. It belonged neither to a caste nor to a corporation. From its first appearance it called to itself the whole human race. Christ said to his disciples, "Go ye into all the world, and preach the gospel to every creature."

This principle was so extraordinary, and so unexpected, that the first disciples hesitated for a moment; we may see in the Acts of the Apostles that several of them refused at first to propagate the new doctrine outside the nation with which it had originated. These disciples thought, like the ancient Jews, that the God of the Jews would not accept adoration from foreigners; like the Romans and the Greeks of ancient times, they believed that every race had its god, that to propagate the name and worship of this god was to give up one's own good and special protector, and that such a work was contrary at the same time to duty and to interest. But Peter replied to these disciples, "God gave the gentiles the like gift as He did unto us." St. Paul loved to repeat this grand principle on all occasions, and in every kind of form. "God had opened the door of faith unto the gentiles." "Is he the God of the Jews, only? Is he not also of the gentiles?" "We are all baptized into one body, whether we be Jews or gentiles."

In all this there was something quite new. For, everywhere, in the first ages of humanity, the divinity had been imagined as attaching himself especially to one race. The Jews had believed in the God of the Jews; the Athenians in the Athenian Pallas; the Romans in Jupiter Capitolinus. The right to practise a worship had been a privilege.

The foreigner had been repulsed from the temple; one not a Jew could not enter the temple of the Jews; the Lacedæmonian had not the right to invoke the Athenian Pallas. It is just to say, that, in the five centuries which preceded Christianity, all who thought were struggling against these narrow rules. Philosophy had often taught, since Anaxagoras, that the god of the universe received the homage of all men, without distinction. The religion of Eleusis had admitted the initiated from all cities. The religion of Cybele, of Serapis, and some others, had accepted, without distinction, worshippers from all nations. The Jews had begun to admit the foreigner to their religion; the Greeks and the Romans had admitted him into their cities. Christianity, coming after all this progress in thought and institutions, presented to the adoration of all men a single God, a universal God, a God who belonged to all, who had no chosen people, and who made no distinction in races, families, or states.

For this God there were no longer strangers. The stranger no longer profaned the temple, no longer tainted the sacrifice by his presence. The temple was open to all who believed in God. The priesthood ceased to be hereditary, because religion was no longer a patrimony. The worship was no longer kept secret; the rites, the prayers, the dogmas were no longer concealed. On the contrary, there was thenceforth religious instruction, which was not only given, but which was offered, which was carried to those who were the farthest away, and which sought out the most indifferent. The spirit of propagandism replaced the law of exclusion.

From this great consequences flowed, as well for the relations between nations as for the government of states.

Between nations religion no longer commanded hatred; it no longer made it the citizen's duty to detest the foreigner; its very essence, on the contrary, was to teach him that towards the stranger, towards the enemy, he owed the duties of justice, and even of benevolence. The barriers between nations or races were thus thrown down; the *pomœrium* disappeared. "Christ," says the apostle, "hath broken down the middle wall of partition between us." "But now are they many members," he also says, "yet but one body." "There is neither Greek nor Jew, circumcision nor uncircumcision, Barbarian, Scythian, bond nor free: but Christ is all, and in all."

The people were also taught that they were all descended from the same common father. With the unity of God, the unity of the human race also appeared to men's minds; and it was thenceforth a religious necessity to forbid men to hate each other.

As to the government of the state, we cannot say that Christianity essentially altered that, precisely because it did not occupy itself with the state. In the ancient ages, religion and the state made but one; every people adored its own god, and every god governed his own people; the same code regulated the relations among men, and their duties towards the gods of the city. Religion then governed the state, and designated its chiefs by the voice of the lot, or by that of the auspices. The state, in its turn, interfered with the domain of the conscience, and punished every infraction of the rites and the worship of the city. Instead of this, Christ teaches that his kingdom is not of this world. He separates religion from government. Religion, being no longer of the earth, now interferes the least possible in terrestrial affairs. Christ adds, "Render to Cæsar the things that are Cæsar's, and to God the things that are God's." It is the first time that God and the state are so clearly distinguished. For Cæsar at that period was still the *pontifex maximus,* the chief and the principal organ of the Roman religion; he was the guardian and the interpreter of beliefs. He held the worship and the dogmas in his hands. Even his person was sacred and divine, for it was a peculiarity of the policy of the emperors that, wishing to recover the attributes of ancient royalty, they were careful not to forget the divine character which antiquity had attached to the king-pontiffs and to the priest-founders. But now Christ breaks the alliance which paganism and the empire wished to renew. He proclaims that religion is no longer the state, and that to obey Cæsar is no longer the same thing as to obey God.

Christianity completes the overthrow of the local worship; it extinguishes the prytanea, and completely destroys the city-protecting divinities. It does more; it refuses to assume the empire which these worships had exercised over civil society. It professes that between the state and itself there is nothing in common. It separates what all antiquity had confounded. We may remark, moreover, that during three centuries the new religion lived entirely beyond the action of the state; it knew how to dispense with state protection, and even to struggle against it. These three centuries established an abyss between the domain of the government and the domain of religion; and, as the recollection of this period could not be effaced, it followed that this distinction became a plain and incontestable truth, which the efforts even of a part of the clergy could not eradicate.

This principle was fertile in great results. On one hand, politics became definitively freed from the strict rules which the ancient religion had traced, and could govern men without having to bend to sacred usages, without consulting the auspices or the oracles, without conforming all acts to the beliefs and requirements of a worship. Political action was freer; no other authority than that of the moral law now impeded it. On the other hand, if the state was more completely master in certain things, its action was also more limited. A complete half of man had been freed from its control. Christianity taught that only a part of man belonged to society; that he was bound to it by his body and by his material interests; that when subject to a tyrant, it was his duty to submit; that as a citizen of a republic, he ought to give his life for it, but that, in what related to his soul, he was free, and was bound only to God.

Stoicism had already marked this separation; it had restored man to himself, and had founded liberty of conscience. But that which was merely the effort of the energy of a courageous sect, Christianity made a universal and unchangeable rule for succeeding generations; what was only the consolation of a few, it made the common good of humanity.

If, now, we recollect what has been said above on the omnipotence of the states among the ancients,—if we bear in mind how far the city, in the name of its sacred character and of religion, which was inherent in it, exercised an absolute empire,—we shall see that this new principle was the source whence individual liberty flowed. The mind once freed, the greatest difficulty was overcome, and liberty was compatible with social order.

Sentiments and manners, as well as politics, were then changed. The idea which men had of the duties of the citizen were modified. The first duty no longer consisted in giving one's time, one's strength, one's life to the state. Politics and war were no longer the whole of man; all the virtues were no longer comprised in patriotism, for the soul no longer had a country. Man felt that he had other obligations besides that of living and dying for the city. Christianity distinguished the private from the public virtues. By giving less honor to the latter, it elevated the former; it placed God, the family, the human individual above country, the neighbor above the city.

Law was also changed in its nature. Among all ancient nations law had been subject to, and had received all its rules from, religion. Among the Persians, the Hindus, the Jews, the Greeks, the Italians, and the Gauls, the law had been contained in the sacred books or in religious traditions, and thus every religion had made laws after its own image. Christianity is the first religion that did not claim to be the source of law. It occupied itself with the duties of men, not with their interests. Men saw it regulate neither the laws of property, nor the order of succession, nor obligations, nor legal proceedings. It placed itself outside the law, and outside all things purely terrestrial. Law was independent; it could draw its rules from nature, from the human conscience, from the powerful idea of the just that is in men's minds. It could develop in complete liberty; could be reformed and improved without obstacle; could follow the progress of morals, and could conform itself to the interests and social needs of every generation.

The happy influence of the new idea is easily seen in the history of Roman law. During several centuries preceding the triumph of Christianity, Roman law had already been striving to disengage itself from religion, and to approach natural equity; but it proceeded only by shifts and devices, which enervated and enfeebled its moral authority. The work of regenerating legislation, announced by the Stoic philosophers, pursued by the noble efforts of Roman jurisconsults, outlined by the artifices and expedients of the pretor, could not completely succeed except by favor of the independence which the new religion allowed to the law. We can see, as Christianity gained ground, that the Roman codes admitted new rules no longer by subterfuges, but openly and without hesitation. The domestic penates having been overthrown, and the sacred fires extinguished, the ancient constitution of the family disappeared forever, and with it the rules that had flowed from this source. The father had lost the absolute authority which his priesthood had formerly given him, and preserved only that which nature itself had conferred upon him for the good of the child. The wife, whom the old religion placed in a position inferior to the husband, became morally his equal. The laws of property were essentially altered; the sacred landmarks disappeared from the fields; the right of property no longer flowed from religion, but from labor; its acquisition became easier, and the formalities of the ancient law were definitively abolished.

Thus, by the single fact that the family no longer had its domestic religion, its constitution and its laws were transformed; so, too, from the single fact that the state no longer had its official religion, the rules for the government of men were forever changed.

Our study must end at this limit, which separates ancient from modern polities. We have written the history of a belief. It was established, and human society was constituted. It was modified, and society underwent a series of revolutions. It disappeared, and society changed its character. Such was the law of ancient times.

CHAPTER 12

The Western Church and the Post-Roman World

T. M. PARKER

The break-up of civilisations is a phenomenon which directly invites the deadliest disease of historiography, undue dramatisation. Apocalyptic is a literary *genre* which has its due and proper place in theology: it is woefully out of place in history, where it produces dangerous misunderstandings of evidence and distortions of sober fact. It is natural that the age of the overrunning of the Western Roman world by barbarians should have suffered more than most from mythologising. Its events, looked at through the foreshortening glass of time, appear intensely dramatic. As a result a whole series of different and highly coloured treatments of the fifth and following centuries have appeared and produced pictures which still colour the thought of those not professionally concerned with exact history.

Gibbon to some extent corrected the old idea of the barbarian invasions as incursions of locust-like beings wiping out civilisation. He wrote: 'Our fancy may create, or adopt, a pleasing romance that the Goths and Vandals sallied from Scandinavia, ardent to avenge the flight of Odin, to break the chains, and to chastise the oppressors, of mankind; that they wished to burn the records of classic literature and to found their national architecture on the broken

From T. M. Parker, *Christianity and the State in the Light of History*, A. & C. Black, London, 1955. Reprinted by permission of the publishers.

members of the Tuscan and Corinthian orders. But, in simple truth, the northern conquerors were neither sufficiently savage nor sufficiently refined to entertain such aspiring ideas of destruction and revenge. The shepherds of Scythia and Germany had been educated in the armies of the empire, whose discipline they acquired, and whose weakness they invaded; with the familiar use of the Latin tongue, they had learned to reverence the name and titles of Rome; and, though incapable of emulating, they were more inclined to admire than to abolish, the arts and studies of a brighter period.'[1]

It would have been well if such a sober estimate of the real state of the case, however in need of correction in detail, could have held the field. But there followed in the nineteenth century (ironically enough partly as a result of the propaganda of the ingenious French aristocrat, the Comte de Gobineau)[2] an opposite myth to that decried by Gibbon, which prospered because it fitted in well with newly discovered German nationalism at a time when the Germans were developing modern historiography. By this the coming of the barbarians was represented as a great cleansing process, replacing the vices of decadent Greco-Roman civilisation by the manly virtues of the Teutonic races. Propagated in England by the doctrinaire ardour which made the learning of E. A. Freeman such a dangerous thing, and popularised by the less documented sentimentalism of Charles Kingsley, this fairy-tale still survives among those whose historical reading is dated. It has indeed behind it the authority of a contemporary witness of the period, Salvian of Marseilles, who, however, even in his own day had difficulty in making such a superb homiletic theme fit the known facts. A reading of Gregory of Tours should be enough to dissipate in any mind the notion of a new and edifying society of simple barbarian saints displacing a corrupt world of refined debauchery. The Merovingians had little to learn from Nero, Commodus or Heliogabalus, not to mention later examples of Roman vice.

It is the social and economic historians who have been foremost in delivering us from romanticism. They have shown us the increasingly precarious economic condition of the later Roman Empire, a society which, from at least the third century onwards, was living beyond its resources. They have insisted, too, upon the increasing

[1] *Decline and Fall,* chap. lxxi, vol. vii, pp. 308–309.

[2] J. A. de Gobineau, *Essai sur l'inégalité des races humaines,* 4 vols. (Paris, 1853–55).

pressure of taxation and compulsory service imposed by the fourth-century emperors upon the ordinary citizen, as a factor both sapping active loyalty to Rome and causing men to try to build for themselves a simpler and more direct economy. Already in Constantine's day we are made aware, from legislative attempts to check it, of the growing independence of the great rural landlords, who were making their domains into strongholds to some degree impervious to the central power. By the fifth century Sidonius Apollinaris complains of men rejecting family traditions of service to the Empire in favour of the life of country squires—an exchange he himself later made.[3] The peasants, too, were revolting against both State and landlords. In general, especially in the West, municipal life, upon which Roman civilisation had chiefly depended, was giving place to a decentralised society based upon the land before ever the barbarian conquests began.

The breakdown of Roman administration in large areas naturally accelerated and confirmed the process, and the new barbarian kingdoms were rural rather than urban in character. The barbarians themselves did not love cities and preferred to settle upon country estates. This suited the situation, for, since land was increasingly recognised as the only sure source of wealth, the warriors of Gothic, Vandal or Frankish armies were rewarded by their leaders with landed estates, because, even had they preferred them, money payments would have been difficult to find. So in the old provinces of the West there sprang up a new, mixed society composed partly of townsfolk and peasants of the old provincial stock, partly of landowners largely of the new conquering races. The new society was organised into independent kingdoms under barbarian kings, who engaged in internecine wars and conquests, the kaleidoscopic results of which were enhanced by the Teutonic tradition of dividing kingdoms among a deceased monarch's sons. Of such a character were the Visigothic kingdom in Southern Gaul and later in Spain; the Ostrogothic régime in Italy; and, destined to become the greatest and most enduring, the Frankish kingdom which at the turn of the fifth and sixth centuries conquered all Gaul and made it France. Such was everywhere the new social and political background against which the Western Church had to live after the Christian Roman Empire had ceased to exist in that half of Europe.

Before judging the effect of this situation upon the relations of

[3] *Epp.* i. 6.

Church and civil power in the West, the structure of the new society must be examined further, for on it many things were to depend. First of all we must realise that the idea of Rome was not lost. The passage from Gibbon quoted earlier [4] expresses rhetorically a profound truth easily substantiated in detail. Many among the new peoples were no strangers to the Empire. Before they attained independent political power they had served Rome, either as individual enlisted men or as *foederati,* mercenary troops fighting under their own native leaders with their own weapons and discipline and settled in time of peace upon lands allotted to them by the Roman authorities. The Goths were admitted within the confines of the Empire on these terms in the fourth century and, despite their many revolts and plunderings, had the service of Rome as a national tradition. Indeed, the great march of the Visigoths under Alaric and later Athaulf from Illyricum to Italy and thence, after the sack of Rome in 410, to Gaul, resembles more a military mutiny for pay and supplies than a barbarian invasion proper. The same cannot be said of the breaking of the Rhine frontier by the Alans, Sueves and Vandals. Yet soldiers of these nations also had for long served in Roman armies. Scarcely one barbarian people which colonised the West was completely new to Roman life and tradition.

So it is not surprising to find among them a real respect for Rome, even a strange reluctance to usurp or to cut free from the Empire. The well-known story, related upon good authority by Orosius, or Athaulf, Alaric's brother and successor, gives articulate expression to thoughts which may well have passed in the minds of other barbarian leaders. Athaulf, so he told a Roman friend, had once wished to destroy the Empire, substituting for the old Romania a new Gothia. But experience had taught him that the Goths were too lawless and barbaric to found a civilisation and he had changed his aim. He wished now to re-establish the Empire by the force of Gothic arms and to be its protector rather than its destroyer.[5] From these, or less well-defined motives, the new kings scrupulously respected the tradition that no barbarian could assume the imperial purple. They regarded themselves, though of regal rank in relation to their own nation-armies, as no more than vicegerents of the Roman Emperor in the provinces in which they settled. They gladly accepted and cherished Roman titles such as *magister militum,*

[4] Above, pp. 208–9.
[5] Crosius, *Historia contra paganos,* vii. 43.

patricius, and the like, and paid at least formal homage to the Augustus. Admittedly their obedience was nominal, and, as time passed, their subjection became more and more unreal. Yet the Empire possessed the force characteristic of all ideas and was sufficiently real to maintain a tradition which did not finally end until the last *soi-disant* Roman Emperor of the West abdicated that title in 1806.

Moreover, the idea was to some extent translated into action. No attempt was made formally to abolish or replace the institutions of the Empire in the barbarian-ruled lands. For the subject provincial populations the authority of Roman law was recognised, even though their barbarian conquerors lived under their own traditional and primitive legal systems. So far as possible the Roman bureaucracy was used by the barbarian kings, until changing times, the decline of education and increasing decentralisation whittled it away. In Gaul even the old system of taxation lingered on.[6] Some more enlightened barbarian kings, such as Theodoric in Italy, tried to patronise learning and urged their own tribesmen to acquire Roman *civilitas.* There was a real, if limited, effort for continuity. The theory held in most of the new kingdoms was that the barbarian armies were occupying Roman land on a system of *hospitalitas,* as allied troops permanently billeted upon the provincials.[7]

How then did the Western Church accommodate itself to these new circumstances, political and social?

It was faced at the outset by one circumstance rarely understood fully at the present day, though in fact it underlies many modern political problems—religious disunion. The barbarians, with the exception of the Franks, were not pagans, for they had been evangelised before entering the Empire. But the missions to them began at a time when the Arian controversy was at its height and the policy of the imperial government inclined towards Arianism. So it was not the Nicene faith, after 381 the assured orthodoxy of the Empire, which they held. They were Arians, and more than nominal

[6] Ferdinand Lot, *L'Impôt foncier et la capitation personnelle sous le Bas-Empire et à l'époque francque* (Bibliothèque de l'École des Hautes Études, fasc. 253, Paris, 1928), pp. 83 *sqq.*

[7] See Ferdinand Lot, 'Du régime de l'hospitalité', in *Revue belge de philologie et d'histoire,* vol. vii (1928), pp. 975–1011. Cf. Marc Bloch, 'Une Mise à point: les invasions', in *Annales d'histoire économique et sociale,* vii. 33–46 and viii. 13–28 (Paris, 1945).

Arians: already that faith had become their national tradition. It may well be that a theology making the Second Person of the Trinity a demigod appealed to those newly converted from a polytheistic belief in Odin and his family. In any case it was not until the eighth century that Germanic Arianism finally disappeared with the conversion of the Lombards to Catholicism. Up to that time some at least of the ruling class in the West were Arians and in the fifth century most of them were so.

We have, no doubt, moved away from the incomprehension of the eighteenth and nineteenth centuries, which, partly because it found the idea irritating, failed to recognise the profound effect of religious dissensions upon history. We have, indeed, come to see the converse of that fact—the equally profound influence of political, social and economic factors upon religious history. But, unlike our grandparents, we realise that theology is not a negligible factor in human development. We can therefore appreciate better than they the very considerable consequences of the historic accident (if it can so be called) of the Western barbarians' Arianism, which were manifested in two ways. First of all there was added to the racial, social and cultural barriers already separating Roman and Teuton a sharp cleavage in religion. So any real assimilation between the subject populations and their overlords was prevented. It may well be that this was the decisive factor preventing the re-establishment of a new Empire in the West of the type hoped for by Athaulf.[8] Already, by the fifth century, Rome had lost much of the assimilative power which had made her what she was. There is apparent, after the death of Theodosius I in 395, a racialist feeling absent in earlier times.[9] Thus, Stilicho was disliked because of his Vandal origin: as Orosius puts it, he was of the 'cowardly, avaricious, treacherous and crafty race of the Vandals'.[10] A similar feeling may have had much to do with the Roman government's failure, at a very critical time, to come to terms with Alaric and his Goths. In any case, therefore, the building of united barbaro-Roman states would have been hindered by the prevailing temper of mind upon

[8] See above, p. 84.

[9] See Santo Mazzarino, *Stilicone: la crisi imperiale dopo Teodosio* (Rome, 1942) and E. Demougeot, *De l'unité à la division de l'empire romain, 395–410* (Paris, 1951) for discussions of this matter.

[10] 'Vandalorum inbellis avarae perfidae et dolosae gentis genere editus' (*Historia contra paganos,* vii. 38).

the Roman side. When to racial and cultural prejudice was added religious abhorrence the thing became virtually impossible.

Except in Vandal North Africa, where they bitterly persecuted Catholics, the barbarian rulers were not greatly to blame for this. Most of them showed real tolerance towards the Catholic Church, and persecution, or even oppression on religious grounds, was the exception rather than the rule. But hatred of Arianism, springing from memories of the fourth century, nursed in their Roman subjects a sullen spirit of non-co-operation which defeated even such promising ventures as Theodoric's attempt to build up a Romano-Gothic state in Italy.

The fact that the first real co-operation between the two elements of the new society took place in Merovingian Gaul illustrates this point. For the Franks were the great exception to the rule that barbarism and Arianism went together. Clovis was converted in 496 direct from paganism to Catholic Christianity. Henceforth he found the Catholic Church throughout Gaul on his side: indeed it proved an active Fifth Column in the Visigothic kingdom when he turned his armies towards the South. Had the other Teutons held the faith of Nicaea the amalgamation of the newcomers and the old populations might have been achieved far more rapidly and successfully than it was. In particular, Teutonic Catholicism would have deprived Justinian's efforts in the sixth century to reconquer the West of much of their justification in the eyes of contemporaries and might even have averted them. And it was his devastating war in Italy which did as much to destroy the weakened remains of Roman civilisation in what had been the nucleus of the Roman West.

Here then is one great factor militating against an adequate *statut* of Church-State relations in the post-Roman West. The Church there was confronted, not by orthodox, but by heretical governments. Another increased the difficulty. Arianism, unlike Catholicism, had no universal organisation. The Arian churches were national and became, as the nations settled, what German historians designate *Landeskirchen.* They had no recognised form of intercommunication, still less the Catholic pattern of patriarchates centering in the Papacy. Less other-worldly than the Catholic Church, the Arian bodies had also a married priesthood and discouraged asceticism. Both characteristics tended to inhibit in the barbarian kingdoms the notion of the Church as a universal supernatural society in competition with the State or of its clergy as raised above worldly concerns. In fact the Arian churches appear, from what is known of them, to have been closely under royal control. This is not surprising, even apart from the facts already mentioned, for, as in the case of all other ancient peoples, German religion in pagan times was linked closely with kingship. And, therefore, as Karl Voigt says: 'One can assume that the part which a German ruler played in pagan times in matters of religion and worship exercised a strong influence in the development of the Germanic State-Church idea.' [11]

If we remember also the fact that before the fifth century the Germanic peoples were migratory nations we can still better understand the situation. To quote Voigt again: 'The development of a Gothic tribal church must evidently have been much helped by the fact that the Goths after the turn of the fourth and fifth centuries entered once again on their wanderings. Whilst they journeyed from country to country without any fixed abodes, close ecclesiastical relations with their bishops, who were ever more closely identified with them alone (especially since those bishops had no definite territorial districts) must have developed.' [12]

We have seen already that the tradition of the Roman Empire implied a close union of Church and State. It is easy to understand how this would be strengthened by inoculation from a parallel tradition of the same kind, a tradition strengthened by the peculiar circumstances of the conversion of the Germanic tribes and given a twist away from the universalist outlook of the Roman Empire and its Church. In short, Arianism gave birth to the idea of national Christianity in something like its modern, particularistic form.

Not surprisingly, then, we find the Western Church tending to develop under barbarian rule into a series of national bodies, each closely linked with the state it served and relatively independent of

[11] 'Und man wird annehmen dürfen, dass die Rolle, die der germanische Herrscher in der heidnischen Zeit in Sachen der Religion und des Kultes gespielt hatte, einen starken Einfluss auf die Ausbildung des germanischen Staatskirchentumes ausgeübt hat' (Karl Voigt, *Staat und Kirche von Konstantin dem Grossen bis zum Ende der Karolingerzeit* (Stuttgart, 1936), p. 118).

[12] 'Die Ausbildung einer gotischen Stammeskirche wurde dann weiter offenbar dadurch sehr gefördert, dass die Goten seit der Wende des 4. und 5. Jahrhunderts wieder Wanderungen antraten. Während sie ohne feste Wohnstätten von Land zu Land zogen, mussten sie mit ihren Bischöfen immer mehr zu einem nur sie umfassenden, zunächst noch mit keinem bestimmten räumlichen Gebiete verknüpften kirchlichen Verbande verwachsen' (Voigt, p. 117).

neighbouring churches. A tendency only, nevertheless. For there were factors working the other way. The Catholic Church in barbarian lands was for long the church of those who did not confess what their kings would no doubt have liked to make the state religion. It was a church of the subject people, not of the *Herrenvolk*. Hence, for support and encouragement it looked outside the frontiers and was not anxious to ally itself too closely with the immediate ruling power. Moreover it had a territorial organisation going back to the days of the undivided Empire. It possessed a provincial system in which the city bishops were subject to the bishop of the provincial capital, the metropolis. This configuration was not at once overthrown by the new territorial groupings. Thus, in Visigothic Southern Gaul, some suffragan sees of the Province of Arles were in Burgundian territory, whilst we find bishops from outside the Visigothic kingdom taking part in the appointment of bishops within it.[13] Later on in the Lombard kingdom of North Italy we find some Lombard bishoprics dependent upon the metropolitan authority of Rome and others under the Archbishop of Ravenna, who was himself a subject of the Roman Emperor in the East.[14]

But these recalcitrant factors in the situation tended to disappear with time: they did not long survive the appearance of the Catholic Franks and the conversion to Catholicism of the Goths in Spain, both events which gave barbarian kings more hold over the Catholic Church in their realms. In France and Spain *Landeskirchen* were formed. The principle of the identity of political and ecclesiastical circumscriptions was from the first adopted in the Frankish realm. In 511, fifteen years only after Clovis's baptism,[15] the first national

[13] See Voigt, p. 117.

[14] Voigt, pp. 217–218. As the author remarks, 'Die katholische Kirche des Langobardenreiches hatte keinen scharf ausgeprägten landeskirchlichen Charakter' (p. 217).

[15] The traditional date of 496 for the baptism of Clovis is adopted here without prejudice to the considerable criticism to which it has been subjected by historians who argue in favour of the date of 506 or later, and, in some cases, for Tours rather than Rheims as the scene of the baptism. For the most recent arguments against the tradition see A. van de Vyver in *Revue belge de philologie et d'histoire,* vol. 15 (1936), pp. 859–914, vol. 16 (1937), pp. 35–94 and vol. 17 (1938), pp. 793–813; the same author in *Le Moyen-Age,* vol. 53 (1947), pp. 177–196; Sir Francis Oppenheimer, *Frankish Themes and Problems* (London, 1952); J. M. Wallace-Hadrill in *Transactions of the Royal Historical Society,* 5th series, vol. i (1951), especially pp. 25–45; Ernest Stein, *Histoire du bas-empire,* vol. ii (Paris-Brussels-Amsterdam, 1949), pp. 147–

council of the Frankish Church met at Orléans.[16] It soon became the recognised rule, to quote Voigt, that 'the boundaries of the ecclesiastical system must coincide with those of the realm' and that 'no part of the realm should be under a bishop who had his see outside the realm'.[17] In consequence, for example, when Theudebert I made conquests, three bishoprics were removed from the ecclesiastical province of Aquileia. When the Lombards ceded Alpine areas to King Guntram, he founded a new bishopric of Maurienne in order to withdraw them from their ancient dependence upon the Bishop of Turin, and Pope Gregory the Great's attempt to get the new arrangement reversed was unsuccessful.[18] The conversion of the Spanish Visigoths to Catholicism in 589 was followed in 610 by the establishment of Toledo, the royal capital, as a metropolitan see in place of Cartagena, then under Byzantine rule. As late as 633 St. Isidore of Seville, and not the Archbishop of the city, presided at Toledo itself over a national council, a fact which shows that the political eminence of Toledo was still not recognised as giving it ecclesiastical primacy in Spain. But later councils met under the presidency of Toledan arch-bishops, whilst in 681 the holders of this see were given the right to install all bishops in Spain, outside their ecclesiastical province as well as within, once they had been nominated by the King and approved by the Archbishop, who thus virtually became Primate of Spain.[19]

148). On the other side see F. Lot in *Revue belge,* vol. 17 (1938), pp. 63–69; J. Calmette in *Académie des inscriptions et belles-lettres: comptes-rendus,* 1946, pp. 193–202, and reviews of Sir Francis Oppenheimer's book by J. M. Wallace-Hadrill in *The English Historical Review,* vol. lxviii (1953), pp. 454–455, and by Margaret Deanesly in *The Journal of Ecclesiastical History,* vol. iv (1953), pp 98–99. Mr. Wallace-Hadrill of Merton College (to whom I am indebted for these references) allows me to say that, whilst not having come to a final conclusion, he is at present inclined to favour the traditional date and place of the baptism.

[16] Voigt, p. 239. Already, in 506, we find the Visigothic monarchy permitting, and perhaps encouraging, the assembling of a council of Catholic bishops of the kingdom at Agde (Voigt, p. 134; Mansi, *Concilia,* viii. 359 *sqq.*).

[17] 'Die katholische Kirche im Frankenreiche war grundsätzlich Landeskirche, die Grenzen der kirchlichen Organisation mussten sich mit denen des Reiches decken, kein Teil des Reiches durfte einem Bischof unterstehen, der seinen Sitz ausserhalb des Reiches hatte' (Voigt, p. 238).

[18] Voigt, *ibid.*

[19] 'Illud quoque collationi mutuae decernendum nobis occurrit, quod in quibusdam civitatibus, decedentibus episcopis propriis, dum differtur diu ordinatio

National churches of this type naturally fell closely under the authority of kings. With variations in detail, it was to the monarchs increasingly that the nomination of archbishops and bishops fell, the old principle of election by the clergy and people of the diocese becoming more and more a dead letter.[20] We find, too, a close relationship between councils of Church and State. National ecclesiastical assemblies meet at the royal summons. Here indeed there was no change from imperial practice: it was the Emperor who summoned oecumenical councils of the Christian Roman Empire. We find also that to have effect conciliar legislation needs royal sanction—another legacy in part of Roman imperial practice.[21] The *agenda* of councils is determined, at least in part, by the king. For example, a feature of the Visigothic national councils at Toledo, from the middle of the seventh century onwards, was the king's *tomus,* laid before the council at its opening, which determined the matters to be discussed and expressed the king's will about the decisions to be reached, sometimes even prescribing the punishments

successoris, non minima creatur et officiorum divinorum offensio, et ecclesiasticarum rerum noscitur perditio. Nam dum longe lateque diffuso tractu terrarum, commeantium impeditur celeritas nunciorum, quo aut non queat regis auditibus decedentis praesulis transitus innotesci, aut de successore morientis episcopi libera principis electio praestolari, nascitur semper, et nostro ordini de relatione talium difficultas, et regiae potestati, dum consultum nostrum pro subrogandis pontificibus sustinet, incuriosa necessitas. Unde placuit omnibus pontificibus Hispaniae, ut salvo privilegio uniuscuiusque provinciae, licitum maneat deinceps Toletano pontifici, quoscumque regalis potestas elegerit, et iam dicti Toletani episcopi iudicio dignos esse probaverit, in quibuslicet provinciis, in praecedentium sedibus praeficere praesules, et decedentibus episcopis eligere successores. . . . Hanc quoque definitionis formulam, sicut de episcopis, ita et de ceteris ecclesiarum rectoribus placuit observandam' (Can. 6, Mansi, xi. 1033–1034). The whole passage throws an interesting light upon Spanish ideas of the respective parts of king and ecclesiastics in Church appointments at this time. Cf. also A. K. Ziegler, *Church and State in Visigothic Spain* (Catholic University of America, Washington D.C., 1930), p. 49.

[20] ¿ Era la confirmación una mera fórmula, o un derecho real y efectivo de los monarcas, que podían suspender y dejar sin efecto lo acordado en los concilios? No occurió en la España visigótica ningun conflicto de esta especie: jamas rey alguno negó su aprobación a los canones de los sínodos nacionales; mas no era tampoco posible que estallaran estas disidencias, porque las asambleas no habían de decretar nada contrario a la volundad del rey, dada la estrecha subordinación del episcopado y del oficio palatino al trono' (E. Pérez Pujol, *Historia de las instituciones sociales de la España goda,* vol. iii (Madrid, 1896), p. 325). Cf. Ziegler, pp. 43–44 and Voigt, pp. 135 *sqq.*

[21] Voigt, p. 138; Ziegler, pp. 42–43.

to be attached to breaches of canons as yet unpromulgated. Sometimes laws already issued by royal authority were adopted by ecclesiastical councils as canons.

Indeed in Western Europe of the Dark Ages it is often difficult to distinguish between civil and ecclesiastical assemblies. To use Visigothic Spain once more as our example, one finds there state officials and the royal court taking part in the councils of the national church, which, as has been said, 'had . . . in a certain degree the character of assemblies of the realm, the functions of which they had taken over'.[22] They handle both properly ecclesiastical matters and what would today be regarded as secular ones, and one finds spiritual penalties, such as excommunication, attached to the violation of political laws and, on the other hand, secular punishments threatened for spiritual offences.[23]

It is a well-known fact that this intermingling of matters civil and ecclesiastical reached its height in the Frankish Kingdom of Carolingian days. The considerable mass of legislation contained in the Capitularies of Charlemagne and his son, Louis the Pious, embodied in a large but still incomplete code by Ansegisus, Abbot of St. Wandrille in 827,[24] deals as much with Church affairs as with those of the State. Most of it emanates ultimately from the will of the monarch, even though promulgated in assemblies of clergy and laity, who, however, seem to have deliberated separately in the first instance.[25] For Charlemagne regarded it as his function to rule the Church, no less than the State. 'Nobis, quibus, in huius saeculi procellosis fluctibus ad regendam commissa est': [26] such is the relationship in which, to quote his own words, he conceives the Frankish Church, indeed the Church of the whole West, to stand to him.

[22] 'Die Konzilien erhielten dadurch in gewissem Masse den Charakter von Reichsversammlungen, deren Funktionen sie auch übernommen haben' (Voigt, pp. 138–139). But it is not clear that the lay members (who were always fewer than the clerics) had decisive votes in other than secular matters. See Pérez Pujol, iii. 297–313.

[23] See Voigt, pp. 140–142.

[24] Text in M.G.H. *Leges,* i. 256–325. See on the code E. Amann, *L'Époque carolingienne* (Histoire de l'Église, edd. A. Fliche and V. Martin, vol. 6 (Paris, 1947), pp. 75–76.

[25] L. Halphen, *Charlemagne et l'empire carolingien* ('L'Évolution de l'humanité', vol. xxxiii, Paris, 1947), pp. 161 *sqq.*

[26] M.G.H. *Concilia,* vol. ii, Suppl. (ed. H. Bastgen, Hanover and Leipzig, 1924), p. 2. Cf. n. 1 *ibid.* for parallel expressions.

Primarily, no doubt, his function appeared to be the defence and extension of Christendom by military force. But equally he believed the reform of the Church to be his duty: he was empowered to watch over and control its day-to-day activities and to force all his subjects to accept its faith and observe its discipline, as he understood them.

For Charlemagne's interest in and control of ecclesiastical affairs did not stop short at administrative matters of moral discipline—the natural first concern of a ruler. He took a most active part in doctrinal controversy, following in this the example of the Roman Emperors whose successor he was proclaimed to be before the end of his life. In 794 the Council of Frankfort was summoned by his orders, and, with the Pope's legates on either side of him, he presided over it. The parallel with Constantine at Nicaea is complete. Two main matters were dealt with, the Adoptianist heresy in Spain and the Iconoclast controversy, now raging in the East. In the first, Charlemagne did little more than lend his support to a condemnation already effected by the Pope. The Spanish bishops who supported Felix of Urgel, the protagonist of the heresy, had appealed to Charlemagne from this, but, since they were not his subjects (being under Moslem rule), their appeal was not respectfully couched. The monarch, as his opening speech made clear, had no desire to listen to defences of Adoptianism. He left the decision to the bishops present, and, when they had condemned the teaching, contented himself with exhorting the Spanish episcopate to fall into line if they wished for his help against the Moors.[27]

The other controversy shows him in a very different light. The question at issue was the endorsement of the work of the Second Council of Nicaea in 787, which, with the Pope's approval, had condemned Iconoclasm and defended the veneration of images. One must admit that the information about it was very faulty. Its acts had been translated into Latin by one of those ill-equipped translators who in all ages rush in to do work at which angels might tremble. (Anastasius the Librarian later described him as one who

[27] Text in M.G.H. *Concilia*, vol. ii (Hanover and Leipzig, 1906), pp. 157–164. 'Ecce ego [*sc.* Carolus Magnus] vestris petitionibus satisfaciens congregationi sacerdotum auditor et arbiter adsedi. Discernimus et Deo donante decrevimus quid esset de hac inquisitione firmiter tenendum' (p. 161). See also Amann, p. 145.

knew neither Greek nor Latin adequately.)[28] Though we do not possess his translation in full, sufficient fragments remain to make clear that at important points he seriously misrepresented the teaching of the Council. Certainly, to the Frankish mind his work suggested that it had approved idolatry. That must have shocked Charlemagne, under whose name appeared the famous *Capitulare de Imaginibus* (better known as the *Libri Carolini*). Like many royal treatises on theology it cannot be regarded as all his own work. Charlemagne's always limited scholarship—he was indeed technically illiterate[29]—could never have produced it, and Alcuin, his English friend and theological adviser, has been suggested as the most likely author.[30] What is of interest, however, is the attitude taken up by Charles, who fathered it. He rejects both the Iconoclastic council of 753 and the assembly 787 and subjects the acts of the latter to a detailed scrutiny, denying the relevance and force of the Biblical and patristic passages they cite and at the same time attacking the council's claim to oecumenicity. Instead he sets forth a doctrine of his own. Images are lawful and right, but are merely the books of the illiterate and therefore not to be worshipped. This definition he caused to be endorsed by the Council of Frankfort.[31]

The outcome was embarrassing to the unfortunate Pope, Hadrian I, who had already approved the Second Council of Nicaea unofficially in his negotiations with the East, though he had not yet pronounced formally for it. He was now faced by a declaration in the opposite sense made by a council which represented virtually the whole West, a council at which his own legates had been present. He temporised with Charlemagne. He explained that the Eastern theologians had not really intended to set the worship of images

[28] 'Non quod ante nos minime fuerit interpretata, sed quod interpres pene per singula relicto utriusque linguae idiomate, adeo fuerit verbum e verbo secutus, ut quid in eadem editione intelligatur, aut vix aut nunquam possit adverti, in fastidium versa legentium, pene ab omnibus hac pro causa contemnatur' (*Praef. Anastasii in Septimam Synodum ad Joannem VIII*, P.L. cxxix. 195).

[29] 'Temptabat et scribere tabulasque et codicillos ad hoc in lecto sub cervicalibus circumferre solebat, ut, cum vacuum tempus esset, manum litteris effigiendis adsuesceret, sed parum successit labor praeposterus ac sero inchoatus' (Einhard, *Vita Caroli*, 25).

[30] Amann, p. 125 and n. 2.

[31] M.G.H. *Concilia*, vol. ii, *Capitulare Francofurtense*, 2, p. 165. For the varying orders of events suggested by different historians, see Amann, p. 157, n. 2.

upon a level with the adoration of God, as the Franks imagined, and refused to reject their work in so many words. But at the same time he suggested the unworthy expedient, if the Frankish king should insist upon some reprobation of the East, of being ready to declare the Eastern Emperor a heretic on another ground, namely that of refusing to return to Roman jurisdiction territories filched from the authority of the Holy See in South Italy during the Iconoclastic quarrel.[32] Eventually the matter became merged in another quarrel between Frankish theologians and Constantinople over the Double Procession of the Holy Spirit and in the complicated diplomatic difficulties with Byzantium resulting from Charlemagne's coronation as Roman Emperor in 800. But in effect it caused a doctrinal tension between the Franks and the Papacy which lasted during the remainder of Charlemagne's reign.

The interest of this curious affair, as already indicated, lies for us in the light it throws upon Charlemagne's idea of his function in the Church. On the one hand the King of the Franks complained bitterly that the very important section of the Church over which he presided as temporal ruler had never been consulted about what claimed to be an oecumenical decision.[33] He was protesting against the Byzantine policy which virtually identified the universal Church with that of the East—for Rome, which had been consulted, was viewed at Constantinople, as part of the Eastern Empire.[34] On the other hand, however, Charlemagne was claiming, at least in Western Christendom, the historic rights of the Emperor in doctrinal disputes, namely to cause their settlement by means of imperially

[32] M.G.H. *Epist.* vol. v (Berlin, 1899), pp. 6–57.
[33] M.G.H. *Conc.* ii, Suppl. '. . . dumque suorum gestorum ordinem volunt mandare memoriae posteritatis, discindant vinculum ecclesiasticae unitatis' (p. 3).

'Nam si novas constitutiones ecclesiae ingerere iactantia est, scisma est, quod tamen in ecclesia fieri non debet. Quod si scisma est, macula est, quae in sponsa esse negatur. Si igitur novas constitutiones ecclesiae ingerere iactantia est, macula procul dubio est, quae in sponsa esse negatur' (p. 4).

'Contra cuius errores ideo scribere compulsi sumus, ut sicubi forte aut manus tenentium aut aures audientium inquinare temptaverit, nostri stili divinarum Scripturarum auctoritate armati invectione pellatur et inertem vel potius inermen orientali de parte venientem hostem occidua in parte per nos favente Deo adlata sanctorum patrum sententia feriat. Quod opus adgressi sumus cum conhibentia sacerdotum in regno a Deo nobis concesso catholicis gregibus praelatorum, non arrogantiae supercilio, sed zelo Dei et veritatis studio' (p. 5).
[34] Amann, p. 124.

summoned councils whose decisions would be imperially enforced. 'It is not certain,' says M. Amann of the Frankish Church, 'that its temporal head was already thinking of taking the imperial title which would make him the equal of the Greek *Basileus.* But quite certainly—and the prologue to the *Caroline Books* can leave no doubt upon the subject—he thought of himself as possessed in ecclesiastical matters of the same rights as the sovereign of New Rome.'[35]

The remark raises an important question with the discussion of which this lecture may well close. It seems to me that underlying all the complications of this confused period of transition from classical to medieval society there is one fundamental point which we have already encountered in casting our eyes upon Byzantium. We saw there that the peculiar and almost indefinable relationship between Church and State is best understood by realising that in distinguishing the two we are making use of a category of thought alien to contemporary minds. To the Byzantines both were but aspects of one Christian society, inseparable as two facets of a jewel. In the light of what we have just considered, we have to ask ourselves whether such a distinction would not have been in the Dark Ages as meaningless in the West as in the East. It is easy to exaggerate the effects of the political division caused by the barbarian conquests and to assume that because of them the West must necessarily have viewed Church-State relations in a wholly different way from Byzantium. Is that assumption correct? On the one hand, as we have seen, the idea of the Empire was never lost in the West and could easily be revived by Charlemagne. (Indeed it received an important revival in the sixth century, when Justinian reconquered much of the barbarian-held territory.) On the other hand, every Western State, be it as barbarised as one pleases to think—and none was wholly barbarian—thought of itself as in a sense a microcosm of the old Empire. We have seen that the powers claimed by barbarian kings over the Church were largely revivals of imperial custom, and

[35] 'Que son chef temporel songeât des lors à prendre le titre impérial, qui ferait de lui l'égal du basileus grec, ce n'est pas certain. Mais, à coup sûr,—et le prologue des *Livres carolins* ne peut laisser à ce sujet aucun doute—il se considérait comme investi, en matière ecclésiastique, des mêmes droits que le souverain de la Nouvelle Rome. Comment dès lors aurait-il pu admettre que des questions doctrinales fussent décidées par la seule initiative de l'Église d'Orient?' (Amann, p. 125).

with Charlemagne we witness a startling resurrection of what may be called the Constantinian view of Christian imperialism. We must, then, not be too hypnotised by what might seem to be the novel phenomenon of the *Landeskirche.* Teutonic it may have been in its actual historical emergence. Coloured it probably was by a background of Teutonic paganism and early Teutonic Arian Christianity. But, given the ineluctable fact of the breakdown of unified administration in the Western world, it was only in the form of the *Landeskirche* that the old constitution of the Christian Roman Empire could now be continued and express itself. The Roman subjects of the barbarian kings may well have seen no revolutionary difference between the relation of Church and State in the new kingdoms from that which folk memory recalled of the old system as it had existed from Constantine to Honorius. The idea of an almost absolute identity between Church and Christian State did not need to be created by the Teutons: it was there already in the soil they conquered. However much we take for granted today a distinction between the spiritual and the secular community, we must not antedate its emergence. As I have tried to show, that distinction is the very antithesis of the habitual thinking of almost all early societies and in particular of the Greco-Roman world. Like Charles II, the notion of an identity of Church and State took an unconscionable time dying.[36]

[36] 'We would say that in the early Middle Ages, that is to say, up to the Investiture struggle—and perhaps inclusive of it—the conflict is habitually considered as between the Sacerdotium and Regnum or Imperium, and, in nine cases out of ten at least, as taking place in the Ecclesia, rather than in the Respublica. Only in the later Middle Ages are Respublica and Ecclesia used as convertible terms for Regnum and Imperium and Sacerdotium respectively: and the conclusion we would draw is that, when this happens, the conception of the single society is breaking up' (C. N. S. Woolf, *Bartolus of Sassoferrato: His Position in the History of Medieval Political Thought* (Cambridge, 1913), p. 104).

CHAPTER 13

Medieval Canon Law and Western Constitutionalism

BRIAN TIERNEY

During the past twenty years an extensive literature has grown up concerning the ecclesiology and political theories of the Decretists and Decretalists.[1] We are beginning, not only to understand the general outlines of their thought, but to appreciate the individual characteristics of many particular teachers, of men like Huguccio, Alanus, Laurentius, Hostiensis, great masters in their own day, whose names are just beginning to creep into the textbooks on medieval history. My own intention is not to present yet another technical paper on some detailed point of canonical scholarship but rather to attempt a broad survey of the significance of all this recent work for a central problem of Western history—the emergence of the constitutional state in the Middle Ages.[2] I should be especially happy if I could succeed in conveying to you that the objective of

From *Catholic Historical Review*, Vol. LII, November 1, 1966. Reprinted by permission of the publishers.

[1] The literature for the period 1945–1955 was discussed in my article, "Some Recent Works on the Political Theories of the Medieval Canonists," *Traditio*, X (1954), 594–625. For the years since 1955 a convenient guide is provided by the bibliographies of the Institute of Medieval Canon Law published annually in *Traditio*.

[2] My debt to two recent works will be especially apparent. They are Ernst H. Kantorowicz, *The King's Two Bodies* (Princeton, 1957), and Gaines Post, *Studies in Medieval Legal Thought* (Princeton, 1964).

modern canonistic studies is not simply to add a few additional esoteric footnotes to the standard works on constitutional history, but rather to find fresh answers for the new problems concerning the nature and origins of constitutionalism that are posed inescapably by the circumstances of our own age.

I am using the word "constitutionalism" to signify simply the most basic, taken-for-granted ideas that are implied by the most familiar platitudes of our political discourse, by phrases like "government under law" or "government by consent." We mean, I take it, a system in which the citizen is guaranteed due process of law and in which law itself is not merely the arbitrary will of a despot but rather reflects the moral outlook of the whole society, at least in its broad principles. And "government by consent," of course, means to us not just that the majority imposes its will on the minority but that machinery exists for eliciting a consensus of opinion, for formulating courses of action that all the citizens are prepared to accept, even though with differing degrees of enthusiasm. The characteristic institutional machinery for eliciting a consensus in modern constitutional states is the elected representative assembly with effective rights of consent to legislation and taxation.

The point which must strike a contemporary historian most forcefully at the outset is the extreme improbability of this kind of system ever emerging anywhere or persisting if by chance it has emerged. During my own lifetime ancient European peoples that might have known better have willingly handed themselves over to the most revolting forms of despotism and new nations that, a few years ago, were everywhere embarking on brave adventures in constitutional government have usually abandoned the system after a brief period of unsuccessful experimentation. Adlai Stevenson once observed that, "The natural government of man is servitude. Tyranny is the normal pattern of human government." And the historian cannot fail to discern that the normal story of human government is indeed one of alternation between different forms of tyranny with occasional interludes of anarchy. All this is not to say that our political system must necessarily be dismissed as a mere freakish aberration in the general history of mankind. Perhaps things will be different in the future. Constitutionalism is the distinctive contribution of Western civilization to the art of government, and, in India, the leaders of half a billion people are still striving—not unsuccessfully so far, though the outcome is unpredictable—to adapt our Western institutions to the needs of an Asiatic society. Constitutionalism may after all represent the main axis of development in the growth of human government for the next thousand years. Or it may not. The historical problem of how constitutional structures of government could first grow into existence is a fascinating one for the scholar precisely because the practical issue of whether such structures can survive and expand is poised so delicately in the modern world.

Now nations first began to organize themselves into constitutional states during the Middle Ages. We can indeed trace an interesting and most important chapter in the pre-history of constitutionalism in the life of certain classical city-states; but the problems of government by consent become so much more complex when one moves from the intimate society of a single little city to an area the size of a nation or a whole continent that they become essentially different in kind and necessitate for their solution a different kind of institutional machinery from any that existed in the ancient world. Individual city-states lacked the principle of representation in anything like its modern form. The occasional leagues of city-states that arose lacked the principle of sovereignty in anything like its modern form.

In a quite different sphere the anthropologists could point out to us dozens of primitive societies that experience limited government in the sense that they have tribal councils and customary laws. Such institutions are in no way peculiar to the Teutonic peoples of northern Europe. One can find them among West Africans or Red Indians, almost anywhere indeed where the appropriate research has been conducted; and this is the most obvious reason why the mere exploration of primeval Teutonic folkways—a once popular pursuit among medievalists—can provide no adequate explanation for the rise of medieval constitutionalism. Primitive societies provide no real analogue for the constitutional state because they lack most of the essential attributes of the state itself—ordered departments of government, written records, the idea of legislation as a deliberate product of reason and will; and when primitive peoples have outgrown their tribal customs to develop a civilization and a state it has normally taken the form of a despotism, most commonly a theocracy. Many examples were classified in Wittfogel's book, *Oriental Despotism.*

In Western Europe, from the twelfth century onward, events took a different turn. A great revival of classical Roman law re-introduced into the feudal world of the West with its countless petty jurisdictions the idea of strong central government exercising broad powers of legislation and taxation for the public welfare. Moreover, the example of the Roman *Corpus Iuris* stimulated the monk Gratian to undertake a major systematization of the law of the Church and, about 1140, he completed his Decretum, an immensely influential work that created an ordered synthesis for the first time out of the chaos of conflicting canons, decretals, and patristic texts that had been accumulating in the Church for a thousand years. The next two centuries saw a great growth of governmental activity, first in the ecclesiastical sphere, then in the secular. Kingdoms built up more sophisticated bureaucracies. There was increased taxation, judicial centralization and, by 1300, a great upsurge of legislative activity. But this growth of centralized government coincided precisely with a growth of constitutional theories and practices. Administrative structures were emerging that we can reasonably call states but for the first time they were constitutional states. It was a major turning point in the history of human government.

Not everyone, to be sure, agrees with this way of looking at the Middle Ages. One can still encounter books on the origins of Western constitutionalism that dwell lovingly on the Athenian democracy and the Roman republic—and then leap over the intervening centuries to take up the story again with Hobbes and Locke and the Glorious Revolution. Indeed some scholars seem disposed to turn the study of medieval institutions into a mere recondite branch of anthropology by arguing that medieval men, like other primitive peoples, lacked any sophisticated conception of sovereignty and the state. The most common error in this approach is for an author to start out from a nineteenth-century theory of sovereignty, usually Augustinian or Hegelian, and then demonstrate that there was no state in the Middle Ages (which can accordingly be shrugged aside as irrelevant to his subject) because the organization of medieval political life did not conform to the chosen stereotype. It is true enough of course. The point is that these nineteenth-century theories are just as inapplicable to contemporary constitutional states as to medieval ones. The study of such doctrines can perhaps help us to understand some modern forms of absolutist government, but that is precisely because they are aberrations from the central tradition of Western constitutionalism. They have little relevance for the historian who seeks to explore either the origins of that tradition or its modern manifestations.

The discussion of these problems can become extremely complex, but the immediate point that I am concerned to make is not oversubtle. A modern institution of representative government like the American senate has no meaningful connection whatsoever with the ancient Roman senate. On the other hand its whole nature and mode of functioning is rooted in an antecedent tradition of parliamentary government—and parliament did not come into existence in ancient Greece or ancient Roman but in medieval England. The fact of the matter is that in 1200 there were no national representative assemblies anywhere and there never had been any, while by 1400 the whole Western Church was engaged in trying to replace papal monarchy with conciliar government, and almost every country from Scandinavia to Spain and from England to Hungary had produced constitutional documents stating that the ruler was under the law and had experimented with representative assemblies seeking to give effect to that principle. This is the phenomenon of medieval constitutionalism. It is, as I have emphasized, a rare, perhaps a unique phenomenon. There is no general work of synthesis that would explain the whole phenomenon satisfactorily. It is surely interesting enough to deserve an explanation.

Medievalists have always been aware of the importance of constitutional history. It has always been a central theme of our discipline. But they have not always approached it from the point of view that I have been suggesting. On the contrary, when the subject first began to be studied scientifically in the nineteenth century, there was a widespread assumption that a constitutional, representative system was a kind of natural norm of human government, which the English had come to exemplify first because of their innate Anglo-Saxon virtue, but toward which all societies could be expected to progress in due course given a little goodwill and a modicum of elementary education. With that preconception the whole task of explaining the origins of constitutionalism became one of merely documenting the stages by which medieval men pursued this normal and natural course of development from Teutonic tribesmen to members of the House of Commons. This in itself presented some problems, and it is widely held nowadays that William Stubbs, the greatest of the early constitutional historians, presented the stages of development wrongly. Around 1900 revisionists like Maitland and McIlwain began to criticize him. The argument proliferated, and it is still going on. We now have a fantastically elaborate bibliography of hundreds of books and articles devoted to this one question and all the fascinating subsidiary issues that arise out of it—whether the English Parliament was already some kind of representative legislature in 1297 or whether we are so radically to modify our whole view of human progress as to suppose that this felicitous state of affairs did not begin to come about until, say, 1327. The material that has been unearthed in the course of the controversy is invaluable. If there is ever to be a satisfactory account of medieval constitutionalism as a whole the interpretation of English parliamentary records will play a major part in it. But this can hardly come about so long as parliamentary studies are conducted in an insular spirit and are dominated to such an extraordinary degree by the discussion of technical problems arising out of an academic dispute of sixty years ago. They need to be set in a broader perspective.

The study of the law of the universal Church can provide such a perspective. If we set out from the terms of reference that impose themselves in the 1960's, from the surely self-evident premise that constitutionalism is not a normal stage in the evolution of societies but extremely abnormal—its emergence improbable, its extension most difficult, its survival always precarious—then we must ask a new kind of question of the age that first produced it. The obvious question is this. What was abnormal about the Middle Ages? What elements of social organization or economic life were common to all the countries of Western Europe between 1200 and 1400 but peculiar to that medieval civilization as a whole compared to the others that we know of? This kind of question leads straight to the topics for which medieval canonists provide the primary source material. For there is nothing very out of the way about the medieval economy—a primitive agrarian basis diversified by a little commerce. Nor is the technology especially striking—more advanced than we used to think but not really remarkable. Nor is the basic social structure, with prestige accorded to a military aristocracy, highly unusual. It is only when we turn to the ecclesiastical aspects of medieval culture that we encounter situations that are indeed extremely abnormal by the standards of most other civilizations.

When students first come to consider the conflicts of popes and kings in the Middle Ages they are sometimes surprised at the pretensions of both sides. They find it remarkable that popes should claim to depose kings or kings to appoint bishops; but there is really nothing unusual in one ruler aspiring to exercise supreme spiritual and temporal power. That again is a normal pattern of human government. Innumerable societies have been ruled by a god-emperor, a divine king or a chieftain of magical potency. The unusual thing in the Middle Ages was not that certain emperors and popes aspired to a theocratic role but that such ambitions were never wholly fulfilled. There remained always two structures of government, ecclesiastical and secular, intricately interlinked but dedicated ultimately to different ends, often in conflict with one another, each constantly limiting the other's power. Evidently the very existence of such a situation would enhance the possibilities for a growth of human freedom by preventing medieval society from congealing into a rigid despotism, and Lord Acton pointed this out long ago. "To that conflict of four hundred years," he wrote, "we owe the rise of civil liberty."

But, although important, this is only part of the story. We have to deal with two societies that were not only frequently in conflict with each other but that were also in a state of constant interaction. Throughout the Middle Ages there was a very frequent interchange of personnel and also of ideas and institutional techniques between the spheres of ecclesiastical and secular government. Kings were anointed like bishops and bishops became feudal lords like kings. Secular laws relating to the ancient Senate were used to define the status of cardinals in the Roman church, and canonical rules regarding the choice of bishops were used to regulate the elections of emperors. The pope assumed the imperial tiara, and the emperor the episcopal mitre. One could multiply such examples endlessly.

To understand the distinctive characteristics of medieval government, therefore, we have to consider two sets of problems—problems of conflict and problems of interaction between Church and State. On the whole the problems of interaction are more complex and more important, and these are the ones that I want particularly to consider. It is quite easy to see in the abstract that a very duality of Church and State in any society would produce a situation of exceptional flexibility. It is very difficult to explain in the concrete how that particular ecclesiastical organization interacted with that particular system of secular government to produce the new forms of constitutional organization whose origins we are trying to explore. Merely to mix ecclesiastical autocracy with feudal anarchy does not sound very promising, and it was widely assumed until recently that all canonical theories of papal authority were indeed starkly autocratic. But a major conclusion arising out of all the recent research is that medieval canon law was not merely, as it was once called, "a marvellous jurisprudence of spiritual despotism." On detailed investigation we find that the great canonistic glosses and *summae* of the age of Innocent III contain, not only the familiar and expected passages exalting papal authority, but also other sections that are filled with constitutional concepts, with sophisticated discussions on representation and consent and on the due limits to lawfully constituted authority, even papal authority.

Before we turn to this structure of ideas we ought to consider a preliminary question that inevitably presents itself. How could medieval canon lawyers, of all people, have been led to pioneer in the development of constitutional principles, of all things? To understand this we must consider one more way in which Western history has pursued an unusual course—I mean in the extraordinary convolutions of its chronological structure. Perhaps no other civilization, through the centuries of its existence, has enjoyed so many and such varied love affairs with its own past as those of the Western world, ranging as they do from the most prolific unions to the merest illicit flirtations. From the twelfth century onward there were all those Renaissances of ancient culture that historians delight in multiplying until, the wheel coming full circle, the Middle Ages themselves became an object of flirtatious advances from the Romantics of the nineteenth century. To the historian, for whom time is the very raw material of his craft, the situation is one of intriguing complexity. For us the essential point is that, in the first great encounter of Western man with his past, the "Renaissance of the twelfth century," a revival of classical Roman law coincided precisely with a new systematic study of all the ancient Christian sources assembled in Gratian's Decretum. Roman law re-introduced the ideas of sovereignty and the state into the Western world but the canonical texts had a distinctive contribution to make too. Early Christianity was not just a belief, but a body of believers, a communion, a community. The earliest references to Christian life are full of community meetings, community sharings, community participation in decisions, community election of officers. Something of this had persisted down to the twelfth century in that the Church was still a structure of elective offices, and the early tradition was reflected very strongly in many of the texts assembled by Gratian.

It would be tempting to assert simply that the first formulation of the basic concepts of Western constitutionalism was stimulated by an encounter between the Roman law idea of a sovereign state and the patristic ideal of a corporate Christian community in the works of the medieval canonists. But this would not be quite the whole truth. After all there was classical law and Christian doctrine in the ancient world and they led on only to Byzantine absolutism. We have to deal with ancient law and early Christian institutions as they were perceived by the eyes of medieval men. The canonists had grown up in a world soaked in the preconceptions of feudalism and of Teutonic customary law, preconceptions that inevitably helped to shape their own personalities and temperaments. Moreover, men of the twelfth and thirteenth centuries did not have the advantage of knowing that they were living in the Middle Ages. They thought they were living in the latest age of the Roman Empire. They were hardly conscious of the great gulf between their own culture and that of the ancient world. This led them to assimilate classical ideas the more readily but almost inevitably to read into them new interpretations of their own. One finds the same pattern in many activities of medieval men. They read Vitruvius—and built Gothic cathedrals. They read Ovid—and wrote about courtly love. They read Justinian—and founded the constitutional state.

One of the most familiar platitudes of our textbooks is the assertion that Western culture was formed from a fusion of classical and Christian elements. It is true of course like most platitudes. But the textbooks do not always emphasize sufficiently that often the fusion took place in the Middle Ages, and still less that in the fields of law and government the works of the medieval canonists played a crucially important role in the whole process. Yet it could hardly have been otherwise. The canonists were the only group of intellectuals in Western history who were professionally concerned with classical law and with Christian doctrine to an equal degree. They delighted in applying to the papal office all the exalted language which Roman law used in describing the majesty of the emperor. They called the pope a supreme legislator whose very will was law, a supreme judge from whom there could be no appeal, a "lord of the world," "loosed from the laws." But these same canonists never forgot St. Paul's reminder that in the Church all power is given "for edification, not for destruction." Moreover, although they lacked the critical insights of a modern historian, there was a profoundly historical dimension to their thought. Gratian's Decretum depicted for the canonists all the ages of the Church's past—and depicted them "warts and all." The misdeeds of several popes who had sinned and erred in former times were recounted in the Decretum and such examples apparently had a sobering effect on the canonists. One of Gratian's texts (Dist. 40 c.1) suggested that all popes were to be considered holy. The Ordinary Gloss, written about 1215, commented somewhat drily, "It does not say that they are holy but that they are to be presumed holy—until the contrary becomes apparent." The Decretists were fascinated by the potentialities for reform of a papacy wielding vast power but at the same time appalled by the dangers for the Church if all that power should fall into evil hands. They were up against the very nub of the problem of sovereignty. It is easy enough to avoid a despotism if one is content to tolerate an anarchy. The difficult task is to concede to a ruler all the very great powers needed for effective government while guarding against the dangers of arbitrary tyranny.[3]

The canonists' approach to this problem was to seek in the consensus of the whole Christian community, in the indefectible Church guided by the Holy Spirit, norms of faith and order which could define the limits within which the pope's supreme legislative and judicial powers were to be exercised. (The English parliamentary leaders of a later age would set themselves an analogous task in relation to the political community and the limitations of secular kingship.) A juridical basis for the canonists was provided by a text of Pope Gregory the Great, incorporated in the Decretum at Dist. 15 c.2, which declared that the canons of the first four General Councils were always to be preserved inviolate because they were established "by universal consent" or "by a universal consensus" (*universali consensu*). The canonists gave a more precise meaning to Gregory's vague dictum by interpreting it in terms of their own categories of corporation law. They glossed it with phrases like these. "No man can withdraw from the common consent of his community," or "What touches all should be approved by all"—this latter text being used to defend the right of lay repre-

[3] The following discussion of Decretist theories on church government is based on my *Foundations of the Conciliar Theory* (Cambridge, 1955) and "Pope and Council: Some New Decretist Texts," *Medieval Studies,* XIX (1957), 197–218.

sentatives to attend General Councils when matters of faith were to be discussed. In the years around 1200 it was commonly maintained that even the pope was bound by the canons of General Councils, representing the whole Church, "in matters pertaining to the faith and the general state of the Church." Such a doctrine could be developed without any attack on the ancient principle of papal primacy because of course the pope himself was normally the presiding head of a General Council. Its canons could be regarded as manifestations of the papal will expressed in its highest, most sovereign form and so as binding on the pope himself considered as an isolated individual. The English canonist who, toward 1200, declared that "the authority of a pope with a council is greater than that of a pope without one" was expressing the same idea that King Henry VIII of England would apply to the secular sphere some three centuries later when he said, "We be informed by our judges that we at no time stand so highly in our estate royal as in time of Parliament wherein we as head and you as members are conjoined and knit together in one body politic."

There remained the possibility of an irreconcilable conflict between the pope and the representatives of the Christian community assembled in a General Council. The canonists of the early thirteenth century were deeply divided over this question but the more radical of them taught that a pope could be corrected and even deposed by a council if his conduct endangered the "state of the church." Fifty years later we find the barons of England claiming the right to oppose their king in defense of the "state of the realm." Long ago historians came to realize that the canonists influenced the history of Western political thought in that their theories of papal sovereignty provided an archetype for later theories of divine right monarchy. We are just beginning to understand the importance of their work for theories of representative government also.

It is a complicated task to reconstruct all the constitutionalist elements in the canonists' thought from their voluminous but scattered glosses, and still more complicated to explain in detail how their ideas influenced the growth of secular government. Basically there were two processes at work. Most obviously the canonists offered reflections on the constitutional law of the Church which could and did influence subsequent speculations on the right ordering of the State. But they also formulated a series of doctrines in the sphere of private law which eventually proved of the utmost importance in the growth of representative government although, at first, they had nothing to do with high matters of state. These private-law doctrines again reflected the collegial structure of the medieval Church. Much of the canonists' day-to-day business dealt with the affairs of ecclesiastical communities. They were therefore led to develop an elaborate jurisprudence concerning the representation of corporate groups, the prerogatives of the head of a juridical society in relation to its members, and the rights of individual members in relation to the whole community before such matters began to be discussed as overt issues of political theory.

Just as in some primitive economies there is a shortage of good currency, so too in the medieval polity there was a shortage of good law, especially of constitutional law. When the need for more sophisticated structures of public law came to be urgently felt men naturally turned to the legal rules that were already available in the province of private law—especially in the well-developed canonical law of corporations—and applied them in the constitutional sphere also. A typical line of development was the assimilation of technical rules of Roman private law into canon law, the subsequent inflation of such rules into general principles of church government by the canonists, and the eventual transfer of those principles to the public law of the growing states by the usual medieval process of osmosis. For instance the already mentioned phrase, *Quod omnes tangit ab omnibus approbetur* (What touches all is to be approved by all), was developed from a mere technicality of the Roman law of cotutorship into a juristic theory about the right relationship between popes and General Councils in the works of the canonists who were writing around 1200. Then, moving from legal theory to real life, we find it in official documents convoking church councils and, finally, by the end of the thirteenth century, it occurs in writs of summons to secular representative assemblies.

This is not the occasion for a detailed exploration of all the maze of arguments that has grown up around the phrase *Quod ommes tangit* and around other terms that underwent a similar development—*plena potestas, status, necessitas.* Let me rather try to summarize the over-all effect of the quite exceptional interplay between all the diverse influences that were at work in thirteenth-century legal thought. The most striking result of their interaction was to produce a peculiar ambivalence in all the concepts commonly used in medieval political discourse. The ruler's power was conceived of as flowing from both God *and* the people. It was held to be in some ways above the law and in some ways below it. The medieval term *status,* the origin of our "state," was used to extend the authority of rulers by justifying extraordinary or extra-legal actions undertaken by them for the defense of the community, but it also served to define a condition of public welfare that the ruler himself was not permitted to disrupt. Representation could mean either the symbolizing of a community in its head, with absolutist implications, or a delegation of authority from the subjects, with constitutionalist implications. The doctrine of natural law provided both a stimulus to new legislation and a criterion for judging its value. It is not that we find popes and princes, intent on building up centralized power, using one set of concepts, and subjects, intent on limiting that power, using another. The very concepts that all had in common were ambivalent; every building block of sovereignty had a constitutional face; Western political thought was already beginning to revolve around the central problem, or paradox, that has fascinated its greatest exponents ever since, the problem of reconciling the idea of sovereignty with the ideal of limited government, of government "under the law."

Some scholars will think that ideas and ideals have little enough to do with the growth of governmental institutions. One young expert has recently observed that, "It did not matter too much what one or another theorist said. . . ." And, certainly, we could all agree that, when medieval kings summoned representative assemblies, they were not normally inspired to do so by protracted meditations on the subtleties of canonical jurisprudence. Kings needed help or counsel or money. They wanted assent to their policies and political support for them. These obvious facts should indeed receive due emphasis in any institutional history of the Middle Ages, but it is a delusion to suppose that, by merely calling attention to them, we are providing a sufficient explanation for the rise of medieval constitutionalism. The problem of maximizing assent to governmental policies arises for all rulers in all societies. It is not normally solved by the development of representative assemblies. Our argument is not that hard-headed medieval statesmen behaved in such-and-such a way because some theorist in a university had invented a theory saying that they ought to do so. The argument is rather that all men behave in certain ways in part at least because they adhere to certain ways of thinking. No doubt the ideas that are most influential in shaping actions are ones that the agent is hardly conscious of at all—he takes them so much for granted. But the historian has to make himself conscious of those ideas if he is to understand the men of a past age and the institutions that they created. The works of the medieval canonists provide invaluable source material for the constitutional historian precisely because they can help him to become aware of the implicit presuppositions about man and society that lay below the surface of medieval political thought and political action.

Epilogue

In the General Introduction we were at some pains to indicate what it was that we were attempting to say in this book. Perhaps it will not be altogether redundant to return to that matter now, and, in the process, to make clear as well what we were not attempting to say. With that objective in view we include, by way of epilogue, a recent article by Hans Jonas. Its focus is both broader and narrower than that of this book. Broader, in that it is in part concerned with the impact upon Western philosophies of some motifs of purely Christian provenance. Narrower, in that its discussion of the influence exerted by the doctrine of creation is confined to theories of nature and of man; it does not reach out to comprehend theories of society. But these differences apart, its central theme is the central theme of this book. The context it assumes is the context in which the book must be read if it is to be properly understood. The conviction it expresses is the conviction in terms of which the book was framed. The context: that of Western cultural peculiarity. The conviction: that of the uniqueness of the West in precisely those characteristics that have enabled it to dominate and reshape so much of modern world history.

Unique of course is a much abused word. But we use it advisedly. Uniqueness does not admit of degree. The unique is unmatched, unequalled, the only one of its kind, and what we are suggesting is that our Western civilization is not simply one among many but a civilization different qualitatively, and in some very critical respects, from those which preceded it and from those which today continue to bend beneath its impact.

Historians have not always been conscious of this fact and many today would not choose to stress it. It is a fact easy to miss if one's main concern is with the internal histories of Europe and North America, or even with the intellectual development of the Western world as a whole. Indeed, it is still possible to miss it if one's interests broaden out to include the non-Western world, for so much of non-Western history in the modern era has been, in effect, a history of westernization. But it is a fact vitally important for us to grasp today, living as we do in a wholly unprecedented era in which for the first time in history the world has become one, and in which Western and non-Western cultures are in daily and increasingly intimate contact. And the extent to which our era is an unprecedented one can be comprehended only in the degree to which we realize the truly extraordinary nature of the forces which have shaped it.

On this matter Max Weber was notably clear. Our characteristically Western modes of life and thought, he insisted, do not represent any *natural* or inevitable culmination towards which all other civilizations strive or have striven. They represent, instead, only one very particular line of development, one possibility out of several radically different ones.

> A product of modern European civilization, studying any problem of universal history, is bound to ask himself to what combination of circumstances the fact should be attributed that in Western civilization, and in Western civilization alone, cultural phenomena have appeared which (as we like to think) lie in a line of development having universal significance.[1]

Among these "combinations of circumstances" the historic encounter of the biblical doctrine of creation with archaic and Hellenic modes of thought, and the complex and novel synthesis that emerged therefrom, are absolutely fundamental. That is all we were attempting to say. But that, it may well be, is quite enough.

[1] Max Weber, *The Protestant Ethic and the Spirit of Capitalism,* trans. Talcott Parsons (New York, 1930), p. 13.

Jewish and Christian Elements in the Western Philosophical Tradition

HANS JONAS

If one wishes to assess the respective roles of Jewish and Christian elements in the Western philosophical tradition, one is immediately confronted by two questions. First of all, in what, if any, sense can these elements be separated in such a context? Judaism and Christianity in themselves are distinctly separate entities, to be sure; but when considering their influence on Western thought, we must bear in mind that Christianity alone, or almost alone, transmitted the Jewish share, simply by what it contained of it in its own, original constitution. Thus if Jewish elements are to be found in the history of Western thought, they are Christian elements there, and our theme which calls for a confrontation of them in this medium seems to collapse at the outset. It seems to collapse into the well-worked theme of the Judaeo-Christian component of Western thought, with the hyphen denoting an indissoluble connection—as indissoluble, indeed, as the connection between the Old and New Testaments in Christianity itself.

Even if it should prove possible to separate, for our purposes, the elements of this hyphenated whole, one would still have to face another question: in what sense can these elements—Jewish, Christian, or Judaeo-Christian—be considered a part of the *philosophical* tradition? They are, according to their own testimony, based on revelation, while philosophy is based on reason. This being the case, can religion enter philosophy without either disrupting it or forsaking itself? If the answer to this question were to be No, the history of Jewish and Christian influence on philosophy could be

Originally appeared in *Commentary* (Nov., 1967); this somewhat altered form reprinted by permission,

nothing but a history of trespass and mutual adulteration. Such elements of religion as actually found their way into philosophy would then be there not by right but by encroachment; they would be non-philosophical elements within philosophy, and the study of them would constitute a merely historical rather than a genuinely philosophical investigation. In short, it would seem that one ought to speak not of elements within philosophy, but of interference with philosophy.

Yet to philosophy even the experience of encroachment, including the eventual overcoming of it, would itself be a philosophical experience. Unlike the interference of ordinary interest, power, or prejudice, which touches philosophy only at its outskirts and becomes at most a matter for philosophical tactics, the claim of revelation to the highest truth touches philosophy at its core and must affect its whole strategy. Thus the totality of the claim made by revealed religion imposed *questions* and perspectives on philosophy which it would otherwise not have faced, and which were destined to outlive the answers that philosophy at first obediently accepted from revelation. And even if "Christian philosophy," or "Jewish philosophy," is finally recognized to be a contradiction in terms, the very recognition and assimilation of *this* truth would be a philosophical feat, and one that leaves philosophy different and more self-knowing than it was before. Philosophy's reflection, e.g., on the scope and limits of rational knowledge, was infinitely radicalized through the confrontation with revealed truth. This and similar radicalizations, forced on philosophy by the exacting coexistence with religion, changed the whole climate of philosophizing. Philosophy could not but try to match the unconditional spirit of its rival. That is one reason why later philosophy lacks the composure, the spirit of moderation, so characteristic of ancient philosophy.

But in the course of the religious-philosophical dialectic, something more occurs than an imposition on philosophy of alien themes and the subsequent self-assertion and radicalization of philosophy. Since philosophy is the work of living men, the philosopher's participation in the common heritage of faith asserts itself in his philosophizing. As a result, certain ideas, motifs, and choices of revealed religion pass over, open or concealed, into the patrimony of philosophy itself and—eventually dissociated from their origin in revelation and its authority—become genuine parts of the modified philosophical landscape.

This is not merely a matter of the insinuation of extraneous ideas into philosophy through the all-too-human psychology of the philosopher. Rather, it is a matter of the legitimate continuation, in the medium of philosophy, of existential insights and emphases whose original locus is the world of faith, but whose validity and vitality extend beyond the reaches of faith. A basic concept of man and the world speaks through the Word of God and hence informs the understanding of man as a general premise that will underlie even his worldly philosophizing. And it will be at home there, by rights and not by stealth; it may even come fully into its own there. In this sense of an assimilation which may be transforming enough to make us speak of a secularization of originally religious thought, one can meaningfully look for Jewish or Christian elements in a philosophy that need not therefore be a Jewish or a Christian philosophy, or indeed a religious philosophy at all.

But this conclusion leaves unanswered the prior question: can Jewish and Christian elements be separated in the Western philosophical tradition? Strictly speaking, they cannot. When the Western world constituted itself a Christian world, Christianity gained something of a monopoly in mediating the Jewish heritage, and once this situation prevailed authentic Judaism had little opportunity to exert its influence independently and directly. This being the case, we must accept the Jewish theme mainly in the form in which Christianity transmitted it. As it was through the Church that Jewish teaching, however partially, was impressed on the West, so it was mainly in the Christian embrace that it also entered the orbit of Western philosophy. If, then, we reclaim it there for the Jewish side, we must realize that we are somehow splitting the phenomenon of Christianity down the middle. We do violence to the consciousness of a past age when we divide what was indivisible to it: the one sacred truth of the Christian creed.

One justification for such a procedure lies in the fact that in their *philosophical* reception, with which we have to do, the fortunes of the two halves of the Christian whole were indeed markedly different. This becomes apparent if we understand by the "Jewish half" whatever Christianity still has in common with Judaism, and as specifically Christian whatever goes beyond that. For the sake of brevity we can identify the former by the concept of Creation, the latter by the concept of Incarnation. Having made this distinction, we can see at once the different philosophical fortunes of the two halves. The doctrine of creation, with all that flows from it concerning the concepts of nature and man, was thematically close enough to the terms of natural theology to fall, as an issue, within the philosophical domain and thus *had* to be taken up by philosophy, whether affirmatively or negatively. On the other hand, the doctrine of the trinity and of incarnation was more alien to the established themes of philosophy; it seemed to defy philosophical assimilation and compel recognition as a supra-rational mystery. In short, the *rational* status of the two components of the Christian complex, and therefore their suitability for philosophical assimilation, were *intrinsically unequal.* We shall therefore not be surprised by the seemingly paradoxical finding that in a Christian intellectual universe it was the Jewish component which had the major philosophical impact. In fact, as far as I can see, it was not before Hegel's theory of the absolute Spirit, its alienation and self-consummation through human history, that the theme of incarnation found major expression in philosophy—and then only by the boldest transmutation.

II

Let us turn first to the cardinal and most obviously Jewish theme thrust on Western philosophy by Christian faith, the theme of creation, and to that aspect of it on which so much philosophical controversy centered: the teaching that the world had a beginning in time. The controversy arose because classical philosophy—Neoplatonic as well as Aristotelian—had taught that the world was eternal. At first glance, the difference between the two views seems to be about the past only and to have no bearing on the conception of the existing nature of things. But in truth it profoundly affects the latter. The encounter with the biblical doctrine of creation brought to light what the philosophical doctrine of the eternity of the world really meant. Making it antithetically a doctrine of the noncreatedness of the world, it changed it from being *the* philosophical view into being a particular philosophical view of the world. In turn, the encounter with the original philosophical view elicited from the biblical doctrine its latent implications concerning the whole nature of reality and made these at home in philosophy as an alternative, no less philosophical, theory of the world. Seen from the long perspective of modernity, it can be said that the challenger, in a purely secular garb, eventually prevailed over the classical view, philosophy's native child.

What was the philosophical meaning of the classical view that the world is eternal? We may summarize it in the following eight points:

(1) The sensible world is in some sense (variously specified in various systems) an extension of the divine nature. That is to say, it is itself a mode of divine being, even if a derivative and diminished mode.

(2) The nexus of derivation is one of necessity. That is to say, the world is a necessary consequence of the divine nature, and this in the double sense that it exists because the divine exists, and it exists as it is because the divine nature is what it is. In short, the existence as well as the essence of the world are necessitated by the existence and the essence of God.

(3) The necessity of the world's *existence* entails co-eternity with God. Given the eternity of divine being, the world as its accompaniment or expression cannot at any time not be; thus it cannot have a beginning or an end (though the things in the world can either be or not be and thus have a beginning and an end).

(4) The necessity of the world's *essence* means that its *order,* deriving from the divine nature, is as eternal as its existence, deriving from the divine reality. The fullness of the proposition that the world cannot not be, is that it cannot be *other* than it is.

(5) That the world cannot be other than it is, holds only insofar as God Himself cannot be other than He is. The necessity of the world's essence is predicated on the necessity of God's essence—the eternity of the former on the immutability of the latter. Thus God has an essence or nature if the world has one, and a nature of the kind which intrinsically excludes mutability.

(6) The intrinsic impossibility of "being otherwise" pertains to logical or rational necessity. Thus if God is the primary locus of necessity, He must be pure reason or intellect. This, indeed, is the divine nature.

(7) Accordingly, the "essential" necessity of the world is equivalent to its rationality, i.e., to what it possesses of rationality and is thus open to knowledge. The rational necessity of the world is a qualified one, while the divine rationality is unqualified. The qual-

ified rationality of the physical order, the degree of its intrinsic intelligibility, is the measure of its divinity—and indeed the inductive path to the conception of pure divinity.

By now it is clear that the thesis of the eternity of the world involves a whole ontology. In other words, this thesis is intimately connected with the theses that God has a nature; that this nature consists of pure intellect and thus enjoys the immutability of intrinsic necessity; and that the world's lesser nature has the relation of analogy, similitude, or image to the divine original, a relation which is attested by the world's degree of intelligibility.

(8) This brings us to the final point. Terms like "similitude" and "degree" suggest that God and world are members of a continuum in which God is the summit of a scale that comprises degrees of approximation to His absolute norm. The system of being, to which God Himself belongs, is thus a hierarchy with intermediate levels between the minimum and the maximum, between grossest matter and purest form. Thus a pervading homogeneity of being unites man, nature, and God.

All this is involved in the doctrine of the eternity of the world. Upon this integrated scheme of theory burst the biblical doctrine of creation, which posited a temporal beginning of the world. What conceptual adjustments did its acceptance enforce on the philosophical stage? To put it as briefly as possible, the biblical doctrine pitted contingency against necessity, particularity against universality, will against intellect. It secured a place for the "contingent" within philosophy, against the latter's original bias. If we add to this the divorce of mind and nature which followed from the Jewish-Christian separation of God and world and eventually led to the specifically modern division of philosophy into human and natural philosophy, we need not fear that we are exaggerating when we speak of the immense consequences of the encounter between the biblical and the classical views.

When that encounter had to all intents and purposes run its course, and philosophy was just turning to new tasks, Francis Bacon pointed out that it was "heathen opinion" (i.e., ancient philosophy) which had supposed the world to be the image of God, while "sacred truth" (i.e., Scripture) had denied this honor to the world and reserved it to man, declaring the world to be God's handiwork only, and not His image. I leave it an open question whether the spokesman of the new philosophy, which aimed at the subjection of nature to man, was sincere or rhetorical in this appeal to "sacred truth." But I do maintain that it was the long impact of "sacred truth" on philosophical thought which in the end made the new direction of philosophy possible—and therewith, for better or for worse, the modern mind. Clearly, in contrast to pagan nature worship, the very idea of Jewish monotheism implied a certain demotion of the world, and much of prophetic energy was expended in hammering home the truth that no part of the world was divine and that all its parts, with the sole exception of man, were equally different from their Maker. This essential equality of createdness implicitly did away with any natural gradations toward God and thus with the idea of a cosmic hierarchy.

The full consequences of the biblical doctrine were received into philosophy only at the end of a long process of erosion of classical metaphysics. The first polemical stress was on the idea of contingency. In its earliest and most extreme form, that of the Islamic Kalam, it went somewhat as follows: If, as the philosophers claim, the world came forth with necessity from the divine essence, then it must, in plan and in detail, be deducible from first intellectual principles. But it cannot be so deduced. Its constitution cannot be demonstrated *a priori.* There is a refractory, irreducible factuality about the structure and concrete manifoldness of the world. Everything, from the color of a blossom to the order of the stars, could as well—that is to say, without contradiction—be other than it actually is. The nature it actually has represents a choice from among all the possible alternatives; strictly speaking, from an infinite range of possibilities. But choice is a matter of the will. Thus the logical evidence of the world is more in accord with its having been called forth by the free spontaneity of divine will than with its having emanated or otherwise derived from the divine essence. God could have willed the world otherwise than it is, or not have willed it at all. And the world itself proclaims its createdness by its intrinsic contingency.

In this argument of the Kalam, an immanent character of worldly being is made to yield testimony for the transcendent fact of creation. To this extent, it is a philosophical argument; but it is destructive of knowledge and thus of philosophy itself, for it makes each particular at each moment the creature of a divine will that is bound by no general law. It deprives the created things of any nature and force of their own and thus of all explanatory connection among them. Only God's arbitrary pleasure saves each thing from instant relapse into nothingness.

The skeptical import of this extreme view can be seen clearly in al-Ghazali's critique of causal knowledge, by which he buttresses the theological attribution of causality to God alone. In a remarkable anticipation of Malebranche and Hume, al-Ghazali argues that the connection of so-called cause and effect, that is of one thing following upon another, is not a necessary, i.e., intelligible, connection. No one thing really entails another. The sequence of things is all that is known, and since its grounding is not to be found in any antecedent thing, nor within the physical series at all, it must be sought in the sole power of God. In that case, however, there is no possibility of a science of nature, which must be a science of causes.

This "Humean" skepticism was to find its "Kantian" answer. It was Maimonides who lifted the consideration of contingency onto a higher plane, which combined contingency of the whole with necessity among its parts. To Maimonides, an Aristotelian and a creationist at the same time, the world is a coherent whole governed by laws—the laws of Aristotelian physics—which concretely determine what is necessary and possible within it. Thus there *can* be a science of nature, and the mere abstract possibility of logical alternatives does not lessen the cogency of that science.

According to Maimonides, however, the governing laws themselves, from which everything else follows in intelligible order, are not logically deducible in turn, nor are they rationally self-evident. These laws, the ultimate conditions of the given cosmic reality, must be accepted as pure fact, as must the particular layout of the macrocosmic framework in which they operate. In other words, contingency is shifted from the single existences to their principles, from the conclusions to the premises of the cosmic syllogism, with that syllogism retaining its internal necessity once its terms have been granted. Not each single item is contingent, as the Kalam maintained: it is their total set that represents an arbitrary choice and is in that sense contingent. As Thomas Aquinas later put it, God freely selected for realization *this* world from all the possible worlds. But a world, of course, is a determinate order.

This Maimonidean synthesis saved both the Aristotelian rationality of the universe and the biblical non-rationality of its origin. However, since Maimonides recognized the validity of Aristotelian physics, he was compelled to face the Aristotelian proofs for the eternity of the world, derived from that physics.

It is at this point that Maimonides evolved his profound doctrine of the relative scope of all reasoning that makes use of the laws of nature. Holding it to be true, as Aristotle had taught, that every motion within the universe involved a preceding motion, and so forth *ad infinitum;* and that all becoming presupposes matter, so that a coming-to-be of matter itself would presuppose another matter, and so forth again *ad infinitum*—he, against Aristotle, held it not to be true that these laws, valid for things within the world, can be extended to apply beyond the world, for instance, to the relationship of the world as a whole to God. The laws in question do indeed specify the internal conditions of the system we call the world, but they have nothing to say about the coming-to-be of that system itself.

This is the first enunciation of a principle concerning the area of pertinence of natural categories and the limits of their speculative use, which was to find its final formulation in the philosophy of Kant. Thus was the long self-examination of speculative reason brought under way. Nothing short of the encounter with creationist faith and its transcendent demands on speculation could have compelled reason to such a relentless probing of itself and its possible range.

Kant still used the question of a temporal beginning or non-beginning of the world as one of the instances by which he demonstrated that the perennial issues of metaphysics are beyond the competence of reason to resolve. It is to be noted, however, that in Kant "contingency" is relocated once more: this time it is shifted from the principles of nature to the principles of knowledge. To put it differently: the rational limitation imposed by createdness now resides in the finite nature of the knowing subject rather than in the nature of finite things. The tradition had seen in man's theoretical faculty his eminent title to being "in the image of God," for notwithstanding all the difference between the created and the uncreated, the finite and the infinite, man's intellect was considered to be of a kind with absolute intellect. According to Kant, however, it is precisely the *theoretical* intellect which bears the main burden of createdness by being unaccountably cast in a particular mold. If man is "in the image of God" it is because of his *practical* reason, that is, his *will,* in which his potential of moral perfection resides: the self-determination of the will is his only remaining point of contact with the absolute. As we shall presently see, this line of reasoning puts Kant closer to the "voluntarist" line of medieval thought that culminated in Duns Scotus, than to the "intellectualist" line represented by Maimonides and Aquinas.

To come back to Maimonides, his strictures on the scope of natural reason fall on friend and foe alike: he acknowledges that the disproof of Aristotelian arguments for the eternity of the world does not prove the alternative of "creation from nothing," but merely gives it logical eligibility. In regard to the truths of revelation, reason can generally demonstrate no more than that they are not repugnant to reason, and perhaps that they have an edge when it comes to probability or plausibility. In this form, with some variation as to the exact drawing of the line, the idea of a demarcation of the domains of faith and reason was taken over by the Christian West.

Here a word about Thomas Aquinas is in order. In the matter of creation Aquinas went beyond Maimonides' critical caution. By distinguishing between *ex nihilo* and *post nihil* he separated the question of creation as such from that of a temporal beginning (a separation which Maimonides had considered but rejected): the latter Aquinas too held to be beyond rational decision; but *creatio ex nihilo,* regardless of time, he included among the demonstrable truths, on a par with those concerning God's existence and attributes. Thus he widened the scope of natural theology. Createdness to him is a demonstrable property of the world. At the same time, the realm of the non-demonstrable was swelled by those Christian mysteries—trinity, original sin, incarnation, purgatory, etc.—about which Jewish and Islamic thought did not have to concern themselves. Thus the extension of the rational domain did not entail a contraction of the suprarational one, or a lessening of the chasm between the two. On the contrary, the mysterious character of the peculiarly Christian doctrines led to a greater tension between reason and faith than the "Jewish part" of revelation had required. Indeed, when Thomas says that "through natural reason we can know that about God which pertains to the unity of His essence, but not that which pertains to the distinction of His persons," he is, in effect, spelling out the different rational status of the "Jewish" and the "Christian" elements of the Christian faith. The former are at most beyond rational proof (as they are for Maimonides); the latter are "supra-rational" in a sense that bears a suspicion of their being contrary to reason. Consequently, there is merit in the faith that holds on to them in the teeth of such rational strain; and a priority (*principalitas*) is assigned to the will, which moves the intellect to assent to these propositions. In spite of Aquinas's own unifying spirit, then, the Christian universe of discourse inevitably shows a sharpening of the dialectics between reason and faith.

III

Let us return once more to the subject of creation. It will have been noted that the argument from contingency places the sign of "createdness" on a negative rather than a positive feature of the world: on the absence of that rational necessity which, according to classical doctrine, the world should have. The negative aspect becomes even more manifest in the insistence on creation "from nothing," whose philosophical significance we must now probe, especially since it was not really demanded by the biblical text. In general, of course, the doctrine falls into the observed pattern of "putting the world in its place." That which is called into being from sheer nothingness is totally dependent on its transcendent cause not only for its origin but also for its continued existence. By reason of its "natural priority" (*secundum ordinem naturae*), the "nothing" looms in the very heart of things, ready to reclaim them at every moment, were it not for their continuous re-creation by God. This is the extreme of negativity with which the doctrine of creation imbues mundane being. But in true dialectical fashion, this very extreme brings to light the positive aspect of the reappraisal of being which the idea of creation caused in philosophy. We can discover that positive aspect by turning to that ingredient in the doctrine of "creation from nothing" which directly relates it to the philosophical tradition, namely the negation of pre-existent matter. Why is this negation important, apart from the motive of homage to divine omnipotence? One answer to this question can be given in terms of the traditional philosophical doctrine of matter and form. If matter were pre-existent, creation would consist of imparting form to it and in that case God would be the principle of form, which means intellect; but form is universal, as is intellectual knowledge. Thus God, being the author of the universal only and not of the particular, would not know the particulars; and thus there would be no individual providence. If there is to be individual providence, and its condition, divine knowledge of particulars, then matter, the principle of individuation, must be divinely created too, or it must be as directly an object of the divine will as are the forms. Thus for the sake of particular providence, so vital to both Judaism and Christianity, *creatio ex nihilo* had to replace or to recast the "essentialist" form-matter ontology of the past.

The philosophical effect of this line of thought is to change the whole ontological status of individual existence. And here we can see how utter negativity in one respect turns into utter positivity in another. Against the background of nothingness from which it is called forth, individual being assumes a rank of primacy which all ancient philosophy had denied it. To be called forth from nothing and to exist only by virtue of a constant renewal of this act, assures each individual being of the immediate interest of the creative cause and so makes it interesting in itself. The divine attention required individually for their mere existing gives the single entities their own truth and a corresponding claim on the attention of knowledge. This changed approach benefits both the knower and the known, the human subject and the things of the world as his potential objects: both, in their ultimate particularity as willed by God, have gained a status in the conceptual scheme of things which they had not enjoyed before. As Maimonides put it: all parts of creation are with equal authenticity intended by the divine will; all therefore are ends in themselves. When, in the later Middle Ages, this train of reasoning was joined by the mighty tide of nominalism, which itself was actuated by a similar concern with individuality, Petrus Aureoli (in the 14th century) could say that "it is nobler to know the thing individuated . . . than to know it through the abstract and universal mode."

IV

In our discussion, we have repeatedly come upon the concept of the "will." This concept is, indeed, the common denominator in which the different aspects of the idea of creation meet and in which they fully reveal their positive—and explosive—side. Will is equally the principle of the contingent and of the particular. It chooses for being what could also not be; it chooses this thing rather than another; and it chooses, in the first place, that there be anything at all. While its choice may be guided by essence, will is directed toward existence, and its results share in the uniqueness of its own decisions: they are "this," and "this once," and unexchangeably themselves. Pure intellect, the principle of the necessary and the universal, cannot determine the transition from essence to existence, from universal to particular, from the eternal to the temporal. This is why creationist theology always interposed divine will and its freedom between divine wisdom and divine power, and increasingly emphasized will among the attributes of God. And this emphasis on the divine will was soon reflected in the emphasis on man's will—first as the respondent of God's will, which in His commandments addresses itself to will more than to anything else in man; then increasingly as the dominant attribute of man himself. The theological doctrine of God's attributes engendered, or at least encouraged, a philosophical doctrine of man's attributes.

It is beyond the scope of this essay to trace the rise of the Western metaphysics of the will, a metaphysics whose roots were Jewish-Christian, and the anti-Christian culmination of which we behold in Nietzsche and in modern existentialism. But it is worth pointing out that the vigor of its growth is a fruit of the encounter between the Jewish-Christian and the Greek standpoints: without the dialectical stress against the essentialist-intellectualist bias of traditional philosophy, there would hardly have arisen a theory of the primacy of the will—with all the consequences that such a theory entails.

Though no account can be attempted here, we may at least point out some aspects of the development of this Western voluntarism. It had, in fact, two distinct points of departure: on the one hand, Augustine's stress on the will in *man,* as the ultimate locus of the drama of sin and salvation; on the other hand, the Jewish-Islamic stress on the will in *God,* as the first principle of creation and individual existence. It was the fusion, in later medieval thought, of these two strains, the theological and the anthropological, or the metaphysical and the psychological, or the objective and the subjective, which terminated in the powerful ascendancy of voluntarism in the West. In terms of the attribution of lineage adopted for our purposes, the one strain represents the more Jewish, the other the more Christian, contribution to what finally emerged. The Jewish factor can be identified as such by its connection with the idea of creation, as well as by its prior appearance in the Arabic-Jewish orbit; we have dealt with it as much as space permits. The Christian or Augustinian factor, bound up with the mysteries of original sin, faith, and grace, was in itself less directly "philosophical" in import, but the enormous stress it laid on the subjective life interpreted in volitional terms could not fail to shape the general self-consciousness of man, and through it also the philosophical interpretation of man. Jewish thinkers were content to stress the freedom of man's will as the counterpart of divine justice: but freedom of the will need not mean its primacy; and on Jewish premises there is no reason for "radical" voluntarism, that is to say for focusing the total essence of man in the unfathomable doings and events of his will. Nor, in Jewish thought, is the eternal salvation of the individual soul the total object of divine concern; nor, for that matter, did the moderate Jewish suspicion of nature ever reach anything like the radical distrust of nature that went with the dualistic mood of Christianity. We may note here that Judaism, radical as it could be on occasion, is not intrinsically wedded to extremism. But the "Cross" is an extreme conception to begin with; and in the Pauline version adopted by Augustine, it centers all of eschatology in the personal reenactment by each individual will of this extremity of divine death and resurrection. This was one existential meaning that could be given to the doctrine of incarnation. To summarize: although both voluntarism and individualism were native to the Jewish position in its confrontation with the Hellenic one, we find both—and the issues they posed—immeasurably sharpened in the Christian ambient.

As to individualism, its battle was fought and won in the struggle between nominalism and realism, that long medieval conflict over the status of universals which is very much part of our story but which can only be alluded to here. Voluntarism independently found its most powerful statement in Duns Scotus, the greatest of the Augustinians who countered Thomas's Aristotelian synthesis.

Duns Scotus claims the primacy of the will on both the human and the divine plane. On the human plane, this means that will exercises dominion over the intellect (*voluntas imperans intellectui*). Will determines the otherwise neutral thought to the contemplation of this or that object; and when thought in turn determines volition by its insights, it does so in the service of the overarching will that activates it from the first. Will, in other words, sets intellect its task, causes it to act, and employs it for its end. It is thus first in the order of causes and of actuality. Instead of the "active intellect" of Aristotelianism, we have here the "active will" as the principle which moves the passive intellect. And willing in turn has no other cause but itself; it is free in radical indeterminacy.

Together with this elevation in rank goes a vast extension of the area in which the will must make its decisions, unaided by the intellect. Scotus's list of what is rationally undemonstrable engulfs most of the propositions of natural theology, which together with the specifically Christian mysteries are now relegated to faith—a mode of the will. Indeed, beatitude itself is placed in the volitional sphere and not, as by Thomas, in the intellect. This shift breaks with a millennial tradition that had understood consummate bliss to consist of a state of knowledge.

Even more pregnant with philosophical consequences is Scotus's doctrine of the primacy of will in God. It is absolutely sovereign, the sole cause of His willing, and bound by no rules other than those of logic. Accordingly, the laws of nature and of morality are as they are by mere decree of the divine will, and could as well be otherwise: "His will is the supreme rule."

Let us consider what this doctrine implies as to the nature of the moral law. Almost at the beginning of the philosophical tradition, Socrates (in Plato's *Euthyphro*) raises the question of whether "the holy" is holy because it is pleasing to the gods, or whether it is pleasing to the gods because it is holy. The question addresses itself to the intrinsic nature of "holiness" and the like, and more basically still to the problem of whether or not there is such a "nature" independent of anyone's pleasure and choice. In Socrates's case the answer could not be in doubt. Given the many gods, and the frequent disagreements among them, the knowledge of what is holy and unholy, honorable and dishonorable, right and wrong, cannot be derived from the accidents of such pleasure and displeasure, even though they be divine; on the contrary, divine pleasure and displeasure must be based on, and if need be judged by, the knowledge of what is right and wrong in itself. The implication is that there are essences of these things, binding in their validity even on the gods; or, that there is a realm of truth entirely beyond the realm of power. The Socratic answer stood up for over a thousand years of "essentialist" tradition in Western philosophy.

Monotheism, however, somewhat altered the conditions of the question. With the many gods gone, the question affected the conception of the omnipotence of the one God, which would be less than absolute if limited by the laws of eternal reason. And so Duns Scotus, having reversed the classical order by which the will in God was subordinated to His intellect, and therefore determined by its immutable verities, concluded that the biblical commandments were morally valid because He willed them, not that He willed them because they were morally valid. The goodness of anything apart from God consists in its being willed by Him. And by virtue of God's absolute power, another moral order would also be possible.

What is of importance for the subsequent evolution of thought is the connection here established between value, will, and power. The will to set values and the power to make them law are jointly at the bottom of all operative norms. When linked to divine wisdom, this source of moral law is still in safe hands which man can trust. Nevertheless, the meaning of law as such has changed, and God's purely positive will and power becomes its sole available ground, God's wisdom being inscrutable. But when that ground vanishes, as it does with the vanishing of faith, there is only *man's* will and power to ground any norm or law. In the Socratic answer, the commandments would stand even without God, based as they are on intelligible essences; in the Scotist answer, radicalized by the subsequent victory of nominalism, they collapse without God unless another will steps in and takes over their guardianship. Man inherits the role of creator and guardian of values, with no light to guide his choice, since he is not wise and has no vision of eternal wisdom on which to draw. This is a profoundly paradoxical outcome of what had begun as a pious self-abnegation and a giving of all honor to God. First the ancient distinction between laws valid "by nature" (therefore immutable) and laws "instituted" (therefore mutable) was obliterated by the creationist-voluntarist creed for which everything was "instituted" and the distinction became that between divine and human institution. Then this distinction in turn, when its creedal support was withdrawn and its divine term vanished, collapsed into the remaining, human term, and man's lawgiving alone, immersed in the flux of his being, was left in possession of the field. This was the potential dynamite in the Scotistic-plus-nominalistic turn with which the Middle Ages passed over into the Modern Age.

Many obvious, and not so obvious, lines extend from these considerations to salient phenomena of later philosophy, down to our own, post-Christian era. One has only to recall the Baconian nexus of knowledge, power, and the kingdom of man; the Cartesian ego and the suspicion of the deceiving demon; Nietzsche's will to power; and the philosophy of Heidegger. But in this connection one must also remember Kant's majestic effort to synthesize voluntarism and rationalism. That effort culminated in his categorical imperative (surely of Hebrew vintage), grounded in the autonomy of the moral will (a transformed Christian doctrine), but objectively valid because this will is itself reason and thus universal—a classical conception.

The case of Kant shows, what the examination of other thinkers would show as well, that the original, classical-intellectualist source of the philosophical tradition never ceased to flow and to provide the mainstream into which the Jewish-Christian catalysts injected themselves. The last great reassertion of that tradition was at the same time the grandest bid at reconciliation with the other side: Hegel's dialectical system, which at the very moment when the Christian source began to dry up, at last gave philosophical room to the one distinctly Christian teaching which philosophy had never ventured to assimilate before: the doctrine of the incarnated God. It is true that this doctrine is not easily recognized in the eschatological philosophies of history into which Hegel and his successors transformed it. But this aftermath—the ultimate in the secularization of a theology—would require a separate discussion. Here I can only indicate my unargued opinion that, all Jewish messianism notwithstanding, the idea of history as a self-operative vehicle of redemption is much more of Christian than Jewish provenance. One may see in it the transmuted form of the Holy Ghost doing his work through man in the interval between the incarnation and the second coming.

If, in looking back over the road we have taken, we find that our attempted differentiation between "Jewish" and "Christian" elements did not always succeed, this is only what was to be expected in the nature of the case. But whatever may be the verdict on the particular attributions proposed, one truth should have impressed itself on us: that the shadow which these past things cast is long indeed and still lies upon our present scene. And perhaps our discussion has enabled us to see better how it is due to a unique historical configuration, the meeting of Athens and Jerusalem, each itself a unique fact, that Western mankind has taken a road so different from that of any other civilization. To the accident of this meeting (though not to it alone) we can trace the unique combination of rationalism and voluntarism, individualism and activism, of which we have yet to decide whether it is a blessing or a curse, but through which, to the vexation of ourselves and the world, we have become what we are.

An Introductory Bibliography

General———A few of the most useful books for the beginning student

Armstrong, A. H. and Markus, R. A., *Christian Faith and Greek Philosophy* (New York: Sheed and Ward, 1960). Brief very readable accounts of some of the main themes in this book.

Boman, Thorleif, *Hebrew Thought Compared with Greek* (Philadelphia: Westminster Press, 1960). Views Christianity as continuous with Hebrew thought, thus providing a useful background for the present book.

Bultmann, Rudolf, *Primitive Christianity in its Contemporary Setting* (New York: Meridian, 1956). Brief sketches of Hebrew and Hellenic intellectual background and Christian beginnings.

Chadwick, Henry, *Early Christian Thought and the Classical Tradition: Studies in Justin, Clement and Origen* (New York: Oxford Univ. Press, 1966). Considers each of these Fathers against the Greek background.

Cochrane, C. N., *Christianity and Classical Culture: A Study of Thought and Action from Augustus to Augustine* (London: Oxford Univ. Press, 1940). See, in particular, Chapters XI–XII.

Frankfort, Henri and Others, *Before Philosophy: The Intellectual Adventure of Ancient Man* (Baltimore: Penguin Books, 1949). Essays on the speculative thought of the pre-Hellenic Western world.

Gilson, Étienne, *The Spirit of Medieval Philosophy* (New York: Scribner's Sons, 1936). The classic text on the great themes of Christian intellectual history. *A History of Christian Philosophy in the Middle Ages* (New York: Random House, 1955). The definitive history, this is the place to start for any of the historical figures in the Patristic and Medieval periods.

Jaeger, Werner, *Early Christianity and Greek Paideia* (Cambridge: Harvard Univ. Press, 1961). An historical essay concerning the reception of Greek *paideia* in the early Christian world.

Kroner, Richard, *Speculation and Pre-Christian Philosophy* (Philadlephia: Westminster Press, 1956) and *Speculation and Revelation in the Age of Christian Philosophy* (Philadelphia: Westminster Press, 1959). These two volumes constitute a "history of philosophy from the Christian point of view," *i.e.*, a selection of problems and themes meant to explore the tension between speculation and revelation.

van Leeuwen, Arend Th., *Christianity in World History: The Meeting of the Faiths of East and West,* trans. by H. H. Hoskins (New York: Charles Scribner's Sons, 1965). Operating skillfully on the broadest level of comparative history, the author throws into sharp relief the distinctive character of Judaeo-Christian religion.

Tresmontant, Claude, *La Metaphysique du Christianisme et la Naissance de la Philosophie Chretienne* (Paris: Editions du Seuil, 1961). A rich source of texts, both Greek and Christian, on the themes treated in the present book. For those who do not read French, some idea of this author's thesis may be found in *The Origins of Christian Philosophy* (New York: Hawthorne Books, 1963) and *Christian Metaphysics* (New York: Sheed and Ward, 1965).

For Part I———(See also the books mentioned in the introductory essay)

Duhem, Pierre, *Le Systeme du Monde; Histoire des doctrines cosmologiques de Platon à Copernic* (Paris: Hermann, 1913–1959), 10 volumes. This pioneering work is still the most important study of the variety of cosmological schemes and their systematic relations to philosophies of nature and empirical sciences.

Foster, Michael, "Christian Theology and Modern Science of Nature," a two-part essay in *Mind,* 1935 and 1936. This essay develops in detail and in masterly fashion the thesis formulated by his contribution to Part I.

White, Lynn, *Medieval Technology and Social Change* (Oxford: Clarendon Press 1962). The definitive work on this subject.

Whitehead, Alfred North, *Science and the Modern World* (New York: Macmillan Co., 1925). See in particular Chapter One for a brief statement of the role played by Christian theology in the making of empirical science.

Cambridge Medieval History, Vol. IV, *The Byzantine Empire,* Part II, *Government, Church and Civilisation* (Cambridge, 1967). See Chapter XXVIII for the latest findings on Byzantine science and for extensive bibliographies.

For Part II———(See also the books mentioned in the introductory essay)

Cullmann, Oscar, *Christ and Time, The Primitive Christian Conception of Time and History* (Philadelphia: Westminster Press, 1950). The whole book is worth reading but Part I is the most important of our theme.

Eliade, Mircea, *Cosmos and History, The Myth of the Eternal Return*

(New York: Harper Bros., 1959). A general treatment of the representation of time in archaic and in modern societies.

Frank, Erich, *Philosophical Understanding and Religious Truth* (London: Oxford Univ. Press, 1949). See in particular Chapter III "Creation and Time" and Chapter V "History and Destiny."

Frank, Erich, *Knowledge, Will and Belief, Collected Essays,* Ed. by L. Edelstein (Chicago: Regnery, 1955). See in particular the following important essays: "St. Augustine and Greek Thought," "Faith and Reason," "Time and Eternity," "Nature and History," all of which tend to bring out the novelty of Christian thought.

Henry, Paul, *St. Augustine on Personality* (New York: Macmillan Co., 1960). A persuasive argument for the thesis that Augustine was the first to work out a satisfactory philosophical concept of personality.

An excellent way to pursue the themes of Part II is to study them in the writings of the Fathers and particularly of St. Augustine. A good guide to the latter is Portalie, *Guide to the Thought of St. Augustine* (Chicago: Henry Regnery Co., 1960). For the Fathers see Gilson's *History* and individual volumes of the series: *Ancient Christian Writers* (Westminster: Newman), and the older but still useful *Ante-Nicene Christian Library* (Edinburgh: T. and T. Clark). The books listed above under the heading *general* should also be consulted, in particular those by Armstrong, Gilson, and Tresmontant.

For Part III———(See also the books mentioned in the introductory essay)

Cadoux, C. J., *The Early Church and the World* (Edinburgh: T. and T. Clark, 1955). An excellent guide to the social teachings of the Christian apologists and Church Fathers. A rich source of relevant texts.

Coulanges, Numa Fustel de, *The Ancient City* (New York: Doubleday Anchor, 1955). The whole book is a powerful, sustained and coherent argument for the centrality of religion in the political and social life of the classical world.

Cox, Harvey, *The Secular City* (New York: Macmillan Co., 1965). In the Introduction and Chapter I, Cox analyzes succinctly the secularizing impact of the Biblical message.

Frankfort, Henri, *Kingship and the Gods: A Study of Near Eastern Religion as the Integration of Society and Nature* (Chicago: University of Chicago Press, 1948). Treats Egyptian and Mesopotamian Kingship in depth and in an Epilogue contrasts the Hebrew monarchy with both.

Parker, T. M., *Christianity and the State in the Light of History* (New York: Harper and Bros., 1955). Clear and uncluttered. The whole book is worth reading.

Tierney, Brian, *The Crisis of Church and State:* 1050–1300 (Englewood Cliffs, N.J.: Prentice-Hall Spectrum, 1964). Designed for classroom use. Consists of a series of sophisticated essays illustrated by an unusually rich selection of documents. An excellent sequel to the article of Tierney's included in the present book.